THE HOLISTIC WAY TO
HEALTH & HAPPINESS

A NEW APPROACH TO COMPLETE LIFETIME WELLNESS

Harold H. Bloomfield, M.D. • Robert B. Kory

Simon and Schuster • New York

Copyright © 1978 by Harold H. Bloomfield, M.D., and Robert B. Kory
All rights reserved
including the right of reproduction
in whole or in part in any form
Published by Simon and Schuster
A Division of Gulf & Western Corporation
Simon & Schuster Building
Rockefeller Center
1230 Avenue of the Americas
New York, New York 10020

Designed by Irving Perkins
Manufactured in the United States of America
1   2   3   4   5   6   7   8   9   10

Library of Congress Cataloging in Publication Data

Bloomfield, Harold H., date.
The holistic way to health & happiness.

Bibliography: p.
Includes index.
1. Health. 2. Mind and body. I. Kory, Robert B.,
joint author. II. Title [DNLM: 1. Hygiene—
Popular works. 2. Mental health—Popular works.
WM75.3 B655h]
RA776.5.B56   613   78-5683

ISBN 0-671-22812-9

To Robin
To Clifford and Carol
and all who wish
to take charge of their
health, happiness, and fulfillment

Contents

Part V • Spirit: The Forgotten Dimension of Health

Appendices

Bibliographic Note

General bibliographic references are indicated by superior numbers. Specific quotes are identified within parentheses by the bibliographic reference and its page number.

PART I

How Much Health Would You Like to Enjoy?

Health is a precious thing . . . the only thing indeed that deserves to be pursued at the expense not only of time, sweat, labor, worldly goods, but of life itself; since without health life becomes a burden and an affliction.

—MONTAIGNE

1. Your Full Capacity for Health

The subject of this book is your full capacity for health, and our purpose is to help you achieve the robust state of health that you deserve. If we can convince you to re-evaluate your capacity for health and to take some simple steps toward realizing that capacity, you stand to make gains that you will cherish for the rest of your life.

You will learn how to achieve a state of fitness and well-being that will afford improved resistance to disease and provide a physical-emotional springboard for greater enjoyment of living. You will learn how to slow the aging process. You will learn to look better and feel better, and with each succeeding year look forward to further rewards from living, not to illness, incapacity, or isolation. Finally, you will learn to forestall unnecessary illness that can cripple or kill.

The first and most important step in achieving your full measure of health, vitality, and emotional well-being is to recognize your own natural healing abilities. Most health books, programs, and educators reinforce the antiquated idea that achieving robust health is an arduous task that requires considerable time, self-denial, and sometimes even pain. We do not subscribe to this philosophy, nor do we believe it effective.

How many times have you tried to force yourself to lose weight, give up smoking, start exercising regularly, cut down your drinking, or take more time for relaxation? And how many times have you found that the system you tried didn't work or helped only for a short while? How many programs or pills have failed to relieve your headaches, insomnia, indigestion, neck or back pain, or constipation? Most conventional remedies are based on the assumption that the human body is a machine that can be forced to work by hammering, twisting, oiling, and kicking. But the body is not a machine; it is an enormously complex living system that depends upon balance, harmony, and kind attention for the full expression of its potential.

This criticism of the conventional programs for improving health does not mean that all are without value. In fact, some have been useful for our patients. But we have also found through work with hundreds of patients that improvement is increased manifold when individuals are concomitantly drawing upon their inner capacity for health. This principle applies whether a person is trying to lose weight, improve physical fitness, give up smoking, improve emotional well-being, or recover from serious illness, such as pneumonia, kidney disease, physical injury, heart attack, or cancer.

Rather than exhort you to follow punishing regimens of diet, exercise, or abstinence, we will show you how to tap your deepest capacities for health. Attaining your full measure of health and vitality need not be difficult and can in fact be quite a simple matter. But first you must overcome the greatest obstacle to robust health, that is, lack of knowledge about health.

What is health? Most people (including doctors) would answer that health is the absence of any signs of illness. If you feel "OK," "not bad," or "all right," and your doctor can diagnose no specific illness, then you are "healthy"—even if you feel low-grade fatigue, get headaches, worry, suffer from mild indigestion, drive after drinking, or feel frustrated at work. But what about zest for living? What about the ability to wake up refreshed and eager to begin the day? What about sustaining full vigor and vitality long into your retirement years? What about natural well-being without chronic reliance on cigarettes, alcohol, and stimulants? What about a loving and harmonious family life? What about a sense of meaning and purpose that provides a profound experience of inner satisfaction? Our modern understanding of health fails to acknowledge these questions as important issues. Worse, there is substantial evidence that the modern concept of health is so inadequate that reliance on it may cost you your life.[39,96]

The modern understanding of health as the absence of symptoms has become imprinted on the public mind through the ritual of the annual physical. The doctor begins by asking you how you are feeling. He or she explores your general response (whether it be an enthusiastic "Fine!" or a less enthusiastic "OK") to determine whether you are suffering from any overt symptoms. You then undress so that the doctor can perform a physical exam, again to determine whether obvious signs of disease are present. A series of basic tests of blood and urine will probably be ordered. Finally, the doctor may ask you about your emotional life to detect any serious emotional distress. If you are not suffering from any signs of obvious discomfort (fever, cough, severe or chronic pain), show no abnormal test results (elevated white count, hypertension, sugar in your urine), and do not complain of any serious emotional or family problems, you will receive a "clean bill of health." But this "clean bill of health" means only that the physical examination and diagnostic tests have uncovered no signs of illness. It does not necessarily mean that you are healthy. This assertion may seem startling because it challenges one of the bases of modern diagnostic medicine. But we cannot emphasize strongly enough that there is a critically important difference between the mere absence of recognizable or measurable abnormalities and the state of robust health.

Despite the widespread prevalence of disease during our frontier days, health was then considered a positive condition. It was understood to be a state of well-being and internal harmony, a vigorous state in which individuals felt fully alive and were able to engage in their daily routines with energy and satisfaction. Robust health was thought to be well within the average person's capability and could be attained through sound living habits. Perhaps the threat of serious illness in the past was a primary reason why people aspired to the state of robust health. They knew it provided the best protection against disease and allowed maximum enjoyment of their lives. In an age when smallpox, tuberculosis, pneumonia, and many other infectious diseases killed or crippled millions, people could not afford to take their health for granted.

With the development of sophisticated medical technology and the decline of infectious disease, the ancient concept of health began to lose its importance. Old-fashioned ideas about health were deprecated. Simple qualities such as vigor, zest, ruddy cheeks, alertness, and optimism seemed far too subjective for a scientific evaluation of a person's health. It became quite evident that levels of energy, emotional tone, and general fitness varied widely in a group of individuals, all of whom showed normal values on a battery of basic diagnostic tests. As a result, those characteristics once thought to be the most important signs of health began to be disregarded by medical professionals and the public they serve.

The result is the current inadequate understanding of health as the absence of symptoms and the nearly total dependency of the lay public on their doctors for information and guidance about health. But research conducted over the last decade has shown that this view of health has caused serious shortcomings in modern health care. For none are these shortcomings more important than for you, the average person who trusts your health, and thereby your life, to your doctor.

Dangers of the "Clean Bill of Health"

If you think about it for a moment, the shortcomings of the modern definition of health are obvious. Many of today's most serious diseases—cancer, heart disease, emphysema, to name a few—begin years, even decades, before they are detectable, and when symptoms finally do appear, it is often too late to avert the crippling or mortal effects of the illness. The classic case is the forty-four-year-old man who appears to be in good health, gets a clean bill of health from his doctor, but suddenly falls prey to a terminal heart attack. Second, and equally important, the patient may experience a variety of vague and troubling symptoms such as chronic fatigue, bodily aches and pains, frequent indigestion or constipation, inability to lose or gain weight, sexual problems, tension at work or at home, or just plain feeling "blah," but the doctor may find no evidence of underlying disease. Thus, whether the doctor and patient are led into a false confidence about the patient's health or whether the doctor can find no organic cause for the patient's symptoms, the consequences for you the patient are serious. You must put up with bothersome though vague symptoms that restrict your ability to perform at your best and fully enjoy your life, or you may suffer the crippling effects of serious disease just as you reach the height of your career.

The current, limited theory of health provides few clues about how you can tap your inherent mental and physical potential for achievement and enjoyment of life. It fails to give you any insight into your ability to resist disease or how to improve that ability beyond getting the half-dozen or so useful vaccinations. Finally, it offers little understanding or practical insight into how you can maintain maximum vigor and vitality not only during middle age but long into your retirement years.

On the basis of extensive research conducted over the last ten years on several thousand exceptionally healthy and long-lived individuals, we and a growing number of medical professionals believe that the health of the so-called healthy (in the sense of having a clean bill of health) individual can be vastly improved.[49,60,130] It appears that only a small fraction of the population currently enjoys anywhere near its full capacity for health. Furthermore, this failure of people to make use of this capacity seems to be the single most important cause of much of today's illness.[241] To put it plainly, research is showing that by not achieving your full, natural measure of vigor and vitality, you invite not only unnecessary minor illness and unnecessarily rapid aging, but also heart attack, lung disease, and cancer, the most serious diseases of our era.[174] One in five men will have a heart attack before age sixty; half of all smokers will have serious lung disease by that age; the incidence of cancer of all types is rapidly rising to epidemic proportions. These alarming facts underline the importance of reconsidering your full capacity for health and taking steps to begin making use of it.

Illness vs. Wellness

The first step in tapping your full inner capacity for health is to understand health as a positive state of well-being rather than the mere absence of symptoms. The old-fashioned concept of robust health must be made meaningful in modern terms to you and your doctor. Dr. Lester Breslow, noted public health researcher and dean of the UCLA School of Public Health, has pointed out that the dominant public concept of health "forms the basis of understanding the phenomenon of health and disease and . . . *it profoundly influences what people do individually and socially to advance health.*" (31, p. 349) In other words, how you understand health significantly influences what you do to make yourself healthy or ill.

Scientific interest in a new concept of health began nearly three decades ago when the founders of the World Health Organization proposed that health be defined as "a state of complete physical, mental, and social well-being, and not merely the absence of disease or infirmity." These visionaries saw that health care was on the verge of a new era in which the most significant approach to world health would be improving individual well-being rather than treating disease. Farsighted physicians and medical researchers were aware that with the conquest of the infectious diseases, the medical profession faced a new onslaught of disease traceable not to a particular virus or bacillus, but to faulty living habits and failure of individuals to make use of their full capacity for health.

When WHO first proposed its definition, many physicians and researchers believed it was too vague and unscientific to be of any real use. There was a strong cry to maintain the traditional medical approach to improving health through the almost exclusive concentration on the study of ill health, i.e., specific diseases. Since then, however, research and a crisis in health care have confirmed the beliefs of the WHO founders.

Medical investigators such as Dr. Breslow have evolved a new concept of health to replace the antiquated "clean bill of health." This new concept is called *positive wellness*. It does not denote a state of exceptional physical health or ability such as that attained by a champion athlete; rather it refers to a level of physical fitness and physical-emotional harmony that affords maximum resistance to disease and supports a sustained joy of living. The words *"positive"* and *"wellness"* make clear that this state is more than the mere absence of illness, although lack of symptoms or abnormal test results is one of its primary characteristics. In addition, however, people enjoying positive wellness are:

—trim and physically fit
—full of energy, vigorous, rarely tired
—free from minor complaints (e.g., indigestion, constipation, headaches, insomnia)
—alert, able to concentrate, clearheaded
—radiant, with clear skin, glossy hair, and sparkling eyes
—active and creative
—able to relax easily, free from worry and anxiety
—self-assured, confident, optimistic
—satisfied with work and the direction of their lives

—able to assert themselves, stand up for their rights
—satisfied with their sexual relationships
—free from destructive health habits, particularly smoking, overeating, and excessive drinking
—fulfilled and at peace with themselves

In this state of highly developed well-being, all your body's mechanisms for preventing disease, repairing damage, and fighting infection remain poised to work at their best when and if needed. As a
result, positive wellness provides the most effective protection
against disease by enabling you to draw upon your inner healing
abilities. For this reason alone, aside from its value in slowing the
aging process and enhancing your enjoyment of life, we believe that
this state is worth striving for. In order to begin making progress
toward positive wellness, however, you must first be convinced that
it is possible for you to attain this state. Too few people outside the
medical profession are aware of all the evidence indicating that positive wellness is well within the reach of the average person. The
number of backup systems that operate in the body to prevent or to
fight disease puts to shame all the safety systems built into our most
advanced technological systems such as the manned space capsule.[76]
When studying the body's disease prevention mechanisms—from the
cough reflex, to the liver's detoxification system, to the immune system, and even to the molecular activity within the cell and the cell
membranes—first-year medical students often wonder how people
ever become ill. With the conquest of infectious disease and the
availability of adequate nutrition, positive wellness is a practical possibility for the vast majority of people in America.

Unfortunately, however, positive wellness is rare. Health surveys
indicate that fewer than 6 percent of Americans enjoy this level of
optimum health.[13,49] Moreover, mounting costs of the degenerative
diseases, both in dollars and human suffering, have become a subject
of major national concern. The unprecedented dimensions of this
health care crisis illustrate clearly the need for you and your doctor
to reassess the basis of your health and well-being.

2. The Health Care Crisis and You

It may be convincingly argued that modern medicine has achieved unprecedented success in treating disease but has proved virtually incapable of promoting health.[96] On the one hand, vaccines, intensive care units, and open-heart surgery are prolonging the lives of millions. On the other hand, approximately 60 to 70 percent of the American public takes a prescribed medication every twenty-four to thirty-six hours. This amounts to more than forty billion doses of medication annually. Add to this the tens of billions of nonprescription pain relievers, cold and sinus tablets, sleeping pills, and antacids sold over the counter, and the picture of health in America seems bleak despite pharmacological miracles (e.g., insulin, antihypertensive drugs, antipsychotic tranquilizers) that help people ameliorate and cope with serious illness.

Behind this enormous consumption of medication lie some alarming statistics that suggest the severity of what is now known as the health care crisis.[39] For example, high blood pressure continues to jeopardize the lives of more than twenty-four million Americans, including one out of three adult males. Another twelve million people endure the chronic pain and crippling effects of arthritis. Between twenty and twenty-two million Americans need some kind of mental health care at any one time in addition to the six million known to be retarded. When statistics on cardiovascular disease (angina, myocardial infarction, cardiac arrhythmias, stroke), pulmonary disease (emphysema, bronchitis, asthma), and cancer (all types) are added to these figures, it becomes evident that more than one-third of all Americans suffer from a chronic ailment or disability. In addition to these serious illnesses, there is a virtual epidemic of minor complaints. It is estimated that headache, lower back pain, gastrointestinal distress, anxiety, chronic fatigue, and other stress-related symptoms account for 80 percent of all visits to family doctors. The amount of radio and television time devoted to advertising nonprescription pain relievers, decongestants, antacids, laxatives, and soporifics is an obvious indication of how widespread the epidemic of stress-related complaints has become.

Several public health researchers have determined the incidence of illness in America through large-scale health surveys of typical cross sections of the public. At the Human Population Laboratory in Berkeley, California, Dr. Nedra Belloc and his co-workers conducted one of the largest and most well regarded of these surveys.[13,14] They distributed a twenty-three-page health inventory to more than seven thousand people living in Alameda County, California, and received 6,928 completed questionnaires (86 percent of the original sample). Dr. Belloc and his colleagues identified seven principal levels of health and the percentage of respondents in each category. By reading the following summary, you can estimate how healthy you are compared with the rest of the American population.*

LEVEL I: Severely disabled (7 percent of population).
- Do you have trouble feeding yourself?
- Dressing yourself?
- Climbing stairs?
- Getting outdoors?
- Have you been unable to work for six months or more?
- Did you report any of the above? If yes, you are in this category. If no, continue.

LEVEL II: Mildly disabled (8 percent of population).
- Have you cut down on your hours of work due to illness or disability?
- Have you changed your work due to illness or disability?
- Have you had to cut down on nonwork activities for six months or longer?
- Did you report any of the above? If yes, you are in this category. If no, continue.

* This summary is adapted principally from the work of Drs. Nedra Belloc and Lester Breslow; we have modified it to include findings of other epidemiologists who have pursued similar lines of research.

LEVEL III: Chronically ill—severe (9 percent of population).
- Has your doctor told you at any time in the past year that you have any of the following?

—arthritis (rheumatism)
—asthma
—cancer
—chronic bronchitis
—chronic gall bladder trouble
—chronic kidney disease
—chronic liver trouble
—diabetes
—duodenal ulcer
—emphysema
—epilepsy
—heart trouble
—high blood pressure
—stomach ulcer
—stroke
—tuberculosis
—ulcerative colitis

- Do you have a missing hand, arm, foot, leg?
- Do you have trouble seeing even with glasses?
- Do you have trouble hearing even with a hearing aid?
- Did you report any *two* of the above? If yes, you are in this category. If no, continue.

LEVEL IV: Chronically ill—moderate (19 percent of population).
- Do you have any *one* of the conditions listed under Level III? If yes, you are in this category. If no, continue.

LEVEL V: Symptomatic but not diagnosed (28 percent of population).
- Have you ever experienced any of the following during the last twelve months?
  —frequent coughing or wheezing
  —frequent cramps in legs
  —frequent headaches
  —heavy chest colds (more than two per year)
  —pain in back or spine
  —pain in heart or chest
  —paralysis or poor coordination of any kind
  —repeated pain in stomach or rectum
  —stiffness, swelling, or aching in any joint or muscle
  —swollen ankles
  —tightness or heaviness in chest
  —tire easily, often low in energy
  —trouble breathing, shortness of breath
  —chronic sadness or depression, major sleep difficulty
  —frequent anxiety or worry

—sexual problems

—major difficulties at work, school, or home

- Did you report any of the above? If yes, you are in this category. If no, continue.

LEVEL VI: Without complaints, but low to moderate energy level (23 percent of population).

- Do you have about the same or perhaps less energy than people your age?
- Do you sometimes or frequently have trouble falling asleep or staying asleep through the night?
- When you have only four or five hours' sleep, are you worn out the next day?
- Are you sometimes or often worn out at the end of the day?
- Did you answer yes to any *two* of the above? If yes, you are in this category. If no, continue.

LEVEL VII: Without complaints, high energy, robust health (6 percent of population).

- Would you say that you have more energy than others your age?
- Do you only rarely have trouble falling asleep or sleeping throughout the night?
- When you get only four or five hours' sleep, do you feel only somewhat tired the next day?
- Do you only rarely feel completely worn out at the end of the day?
- If you answer yes to *three* of the above four questions, you are in this group.

If you answered these questions honestly, you should have a rough idea of how much room for improvement there is in your health. Your responses can help you determine whether you want (or need) to begin a program to achieve positive wellness.

This survey contains some surprising results. Perhaps the most important is how few people actually enjoy robust health and feel great most of the time. Many people have come to accept their symptoms of stress and strain as a normal part of living. At first glance this survey might seem to justify the common rationale, "I'm not feeling so great, but who does?" It is somehow easier to accept the fact that you feel lousy if you believe that everyone else does also. A closer look shows, however, that 6 percent of Americans don't suffer what have become known as everyday complaints, and, in fact, feel great, look great, and have lots of energy. No, these people are not all athletes or "health nuts." The survey indicates that individuals enjoying this level of positive wellness can come from all ages, income levels, occupations, and educational backgrounds. The study of these individuals—their health habits, how they handle stress, their attitudes toward work and recreation, and so on—has provided a wealth of insights into the basics of achieving positive wellness. These insights form the basis of the program outlined in this book and can help you enhance your wellness, no matter what your current level of health.

It should be made clear that this brief inventory is not a diagnostic tool, and we have not included it to help you determine whether or not you have any of the illnesses mentioned. That kind of determination requires a careful assessment of your health by your doctor. In fact, if you are at Level I, II, III, or IV, you should be under a doctor's care. If you are at Level V and have not had a physical exam recently, you should do so in the near future because your symptoms may indicate an underlying illness, possibly serious, that can be treated. This recommendation does not invalidate our earlier criticism of the annual physical. We do not question your doctor's skill in detecting and treating serious illness once symptoms appear; but we do believe that modern medicine fails in helping you achieve a level of health that will protect you from serious illness, and we will outline basic steps you can take on your own to begin achieving that level of health.

Who Is to Blame for the Health Care Crisis?

Although most doctors are trained to treat illness but not to promote health, we do not believe that the medical profession is solely responsible for the current health care crisis or the poor health of so many Americans. Doctors are too often easy targets for complaint, especially when the patient has symptoms but the doctor can find no evidence of disease. To find the cause or causes of the health care crisis, we must look to the social and cultural attitudes that have largely determined the direction of modern medical practice.

One of the most significant of those attitudes has been the modern passion to deny death. Though cultural attitudes about death are changing, particularly through the work of Drs. Elisabeth Kübler-Ross and Raymond Moody, the abhorrence of death and the worship of youth still abound. As a result, prestige and income in the medical profession are directly related to how closely the doctor works with death. For example, heart surgeons command enormous incomes and may even become folk heroes because they often retrieve patients from the brink of death. In contrast, there are no TV shows about pediatricians; yet it may be argued that pediatricians do as much or more to launch people on the road to positive wellness than do heart surgeons.

The medical profession and the general public alike have become enamored with the sophisticated technology of modern medicine only to discover that treating illness and prolonging life are not equivalent to achieving optimum health. The verb *to heal* stems from an Old English root meaning *to make whole*. To experience the full vitality and natural joys of good health, you must attain more than freedom from symptoms; you must reach a level of wholeness and integration wherein you enjoy a high degree of internal harmony and an equally high level of natural attunement. And make no mistake about it, you can achieve this high level of wellness if you want to.

Another social attitude underlying the health care crisis is most people's abdication of responsibility for their health to their doctors. Too many people seem to believe that they can treat their bodies however they please because a doctor will always be available when illness strikes. Warnings about cigarette smoking, overweight, high-fat diets, excessive drinking, and overwork go unheeded because people believe either that "it can't happen to me" or that "the doctor will somehow save me if I go too far." Paradoxically, doctors often adopt these attitudes. This mystification of the doctor's power over illness and death results in the image of the doctor as folk hero. The problem is that doctors are omnipotent only on television.

There is one factor that is rapidly making the need for a new direction in health care evident to all—escalating costs. Over the past five years, Americans spent more than $500 billion on health care. Despite this vast expenditure the major causes of morbidity and mortality—the degenerative diseases such as heart disease, cerebrovascular disease, and atherosclerosis—increased significantly.[39] Average life expectancy did not change. A fifty-year-old American man still has a life expectancy of about twenty more years; a man of the same age in Sweden or Ireland, however, can expect to live another twenty-nine years, or almost 50 percent longer than his American counterpart. Other statistics indicate that the number of Americans who stayed home from work, went to their doctors, or spent time in the hospital rose each year. The incidence of cancer increased steadily. Mental health statistics were equally disappointing. Sharply rising numbers of people sought professional help for their emotional distress, marital problems, tensions at work, or other problems of living. According to the National Institute of Mental Health, the number of people suffering from a medically significant depression reached fifteen million in 1975. Some evidence indicated a decline in certain forms of drug abuse, but alcohol abuse continued to increase and now affects one in every ten American families. These statistics are but a few of those forcing medical professionals, legislators, and public health officials to ask what our society is getting in return for its vast expenditures on health care. We are clearly not achieving better health and increased resistance to disease.

You, the consumer, must ultimately bear the economic strain of wildly escalating health care costs, just as you must bear the physical and emotional burden of illness. More than four hundred years ago, Montaigne wrote, "Without health, pleasures, wisdom, knowledge, lose their color and fade away." Today, if you become ill, you must bear not only this physical-emotional burden but also an economic one. In the last twenty-five years the cost of medical care rose 330 percent while the cost of living rose only 74 percent.[129] To keep pace with these rising health care costs, health insurance premiums must also rise, so much so that an annual increase of 15 to 30 percent in health insurance premiums is not unusual.[156] Though inflation, sophisticated new diagnostic tests, and advances in lifesaving technology may account for spiraling medical costs, the question remains whether more money, more medication, and more medical technology are actually leading to better health.

These statistics on rising health care expenditures and the deteriorating level of the average person's health show that something is wrong. Disagreement abounds about what the real causes of the health care crisis are and what should be done.

What You Can Do

Some health care planners assert that a general improvement in public health will never be achieved without a re-evaluation of public priorities.[241] In 1977 Americans spent more than $30 billion on tobacco and alcohol, but only $4 billion on medical research, disease prevention, and health education. How can health improve, some physicians ask, as long as Americans spend more than seven times as much on agents known to cause illness than on efforts to prevent illness?

Rather than bemoan the irrational priorities of society as a whole, another group of health care planners suggests a readjustment of priorities within the medical profession itself.[115] More than 95 percent of health care resources is used for the treatment of diseases. Less than 2.5 percent goes for research and prevention, and only .5 percent is spent on health education. More than 50 percent of all health care resources is spent on the treatment of the final stages of illness such as cancer, stroke, and heart disease. Because the medical profession is still a long way from learning how to prevent or cure these illnesses, current treatment is very expensive and often produces short-lived results. To cite one example, coronary care units cost hundreds of dollars per day for each coronary patient, but two recent studies indicate that some coronary patients over sixty-five may have a slightly better chance of survival when treated properly at home than when treated in a coronary care unit.[32]

Until the medical profession conquers a serious disease, treatment is invariably inadequate and almost always expensive, because the treatment involves "halfway" technologies. For example, the iron lung and leg braces, the principal halfway technologies in the long struggle against polio, were the best aides available prior to the polio vaccine. Similarly, a long stay in a sanatorium was the best treatment for a tubercular patient before the discovery of streptomycin. In this light, some health planners have argued that more money be spent on health education as well as cancer and coronary research and less on halfway technologies such as intensive care units that will one day be obsolete. This argument becomes especially cogent when bolstered by statistics indicating that escalating medical expenditures could well result in the bankruptcy of hospitals and the Medicaid-Medicare system, if not the average taxpayer. On the other hand, for those who have a loved one in need of intensive care or kidney dialysis, the argument is not cogent, but cruel.

Can the medical establishment prevent heart disease, cancer, emotional illness, or the other serious diseases of today? Can your doctor not only relieve but prevent headaches, insomnia, gastrointestinal distress, anxiety, or depression? The answer to both these questions is still no. Great medical discoveries have made it possible to prevent smallpox, yellow fever, polio, and many other dread diseases, but these achievements required decades of painstaking experiments. Researchers investigating cancer, coronary disease, and stroke are just beginning to understand the disease mechanisms involved. Research on everyday complaints such as headache, insomnia, and anxiety is barely in its infancy.

Despite these observations, we are not pessimistic about your possibility for achieving your full measure of vigor and health. Recent research suggests that *you* can substantially improve your health by taking full advantage of your inner healing capacities and following a simple program for better living. Contrary to popular belief, the average person need not remain at the mercy of many of today's most ravaging illnesses. Disease is not just a matter of chance, destiny, or fate. An overwhelming body of scientific evidence indicates that most of today's illnesses, whether major or minor, have their roots in lack of vigor, poor health habits, and failure to take advantage of the full inner capacity for health. In short, you and not your doctor are ultimately responsible for your health. You and not your doctor determine whether you will achieve positive wellness or whether you will meet premature death (or, perhaps worse, whether you will spend the last dozen years of your life suffering the slow suffocation of emphysema, the debilitating paralysis of stroke, or the crippling effects of accidental injury). You and not your doctor determine whether you will face high medical bills or whether you will qualify for low medical insurance rates.

Your health is your own responsibility. You can and should take your health into your own hands. This book will help you begin to do so through the following basic steps:

STEP 1. Develop a new goal of physical-emotional-spiritual well-being, *positive wellness*.

STEP 2. Reassess the basis of your health and your innate capacity for healing.

STEP 3. Identify effective techniques and strategies for developing your full capacity for health.

STEP 4. Resolve specific health problems through a balanced, comfortable, and integrated program.

At each succeeding step, you should be enjoying increasing ease and well-being. Of course at times there will be some rough spots, but spartan self-denial is not the way to improvement. Your goal will be to make long-term permanent improvements in your health. We believe that these changes cannot occur in a climate of struggle and frustration. If followed carefully, our program should unfold so naturally that it may not seem difficult at all. We cannot promise magic or instant results, but we can promise a high probability of success.

Fundamental to the success of the entire program will be your adopting a technique to begin drawing upon your inner capacity for healing, a dimension of your life that we call the "healing silence." The healing silence will help you cope with stress, increase your energy level, and improve your emotional well-being. Once you begin increasing your overall well-being directly from within, you will have a physical-emotional foundation for making efforts to improve specific aspects of your health and change your health habits.

3. This Book Is for You

Nothing can undermine a health improvement program more than false expectations. For example, you may follow the latest diet exactly, but your scales may not show the promised loss of two or three pounds a week. If you are like most people, you will soon feel discouraged and go back to your old eating habits. Ironically, your problem may have been not that the diet was not working, but that because of your physiology, the diet was working more slowly for you. Had you started the diet with more reasonable expectations, you might have achieved your goal.

To establish realistic expectations for our program, it is helpful to distinguish long-term from short-term goals. The principal long-term goal is indeed an ambitious one: to help you live a long and illness-free life. On the basis of ample scientific evidence, we are sure that this goal can be achieved if you accept responsibility for your health, set positive wellness as your personal health standard, and follow the simple steps necessary to make use of your inner capacity for health. We will not emphasize speed of results. Few people are aware of their physiological uniqueness. No two people will respond in the same way to a diet, fitness plan, or any other health improvement program. And each person reading this book has a different level of health. Therefore, our emphasis will not be on achieving wellness within so many weeks or months, but rather on establishing a better style of living that will eventually result in positive wellness.

If your long-term goal is positive wellness, your short-term goal is the elimination of the habits that undermine your health. Scientific data show indisputably that the vast majority of Americans systematically undermine their health through faulty living habits.[28,130,241] The Nobel laureate Albert Szent-Györgyi summed up this evidence in saying, "Very few people know what real health is because most are occupied with killing themselves slowly." [208] Our program will reverse this process of self-destruction. It should be obvious that this program may touch many parts of your life. Because people are different, all our recommendations may not be relevant to you. Only the first steps establishing positive wellness as your health standard and starting to draw upon your inner capacity for health will be common to all. Once you have taken these steps, you will be able to design a health improvement program that fits your personal needs.

Keep in mind that the longer you have undermined your health through chronic stress, emotional tension, and poor health habits, the longer it will take you to notice significant progress toward positive wellness. If you have been smoking two packs of cigarettes a day for twenty years and now go through a coughing ritual every morning, your progress will be slower than that of the person who has smoked for only ten years and does not cough as much. Similarly, if you have been carrying forty extra pounds for the past five years, you must expect to spend more time reaching your optimum weight and achieving a permanent solution to your weight problem than the person who is only twenty pounds overweight.

But even if you have a long way to go to positive wellness, you should not be discouraged. Each step along the way will result in increased well-being, and we will not ask you to set unreasonable goals that will thwart your best intentions from the outset by causing frustration and anxiety. If you have been smoking, drinking, or eating too much for a long time, then you should recognize that you are at a critical crossroads. If you are a man, your coronary arteries are already significantly occluded with fatty plaques. If you are a smoker, the lining of your bronchial tubes may already be speckled with precancerous lesions. If you are at least 30 percent overweight, your blood pressure is probably too high and creeping steadily upward every year. Though you may have the precursors of heart disease, cancer, diabetes, kidney disease, stroke, or other serious illness, fully developed symptoms may still be ten, twenty, or thirty years away. By taking steps now to reverse the gradual deterioration of your health, you can both avert serious illness and improve your day-to-day level of physical-emotional well-being.

While you can significantly improve your health by following our program, this book is not a replacement for orthodox medical care.

Most importantly, it is not directed to the problems of the acutely ill. If a person has smoked two packs a day for thirty years and now has advanced lung cancer, or has been a chronic alcoholic and is now dying of liver disease, we have little to offer. Some of the suggestions in this book, especially those concerning the healing silence, may provide some comfort, but we offer no magic.

True, one of our purposes is to help you take your health into your own hands and reduce your need for your doctor's care. This will occur automatically as your health improves. When you begin approaching positive wellness, you will probably have no need for your doctor other than for an annual checkup (after age thirty) or for a medical emergency. A thorough physical exam including breast palpation and rectal exam can detect the early stages of such serious illness as breast and rectal cancer, hypertension, heart failure, and liver disease. In all these cases, early detection increases the likelihood of successful treatment. If you have a serious condition, conventional medical care is essential. Accordingly we may suggest, sometimes emphatically, that you consult your doctor. For example, if you have high blood pressure, are severely overweight (30 percent or more), or frequently suffer deep depressions, we will strongly urge you to take advantage of your doctor's ability to treat your disorder. If you are acutely ill or suffer from a chronic condition such as diabetes, your need for orthodox medical care should be obvious to you. Whenever we suggest a medical examination, we will state in simple language the reasons for our recommendation.

Health Problems You Can Solve

At some point during almost every medical examination, the patient will ask, "Doctor, can you help me?" You may now be posing a variation of this classic question: "Can the programs in this book help me overcome problems such as overweight, insomnia, chronic fatigue, and smoking?" One way for us to answer this question is to describe the initial health status of several real individuals who solved their health problems through the basic steps we outline. (Because the individuals in our case histories are still active members of their communities, we have disguised their identities.)

CASE 1. Jack is a forty-two-year-old manager in an electronics firm where he began as a salesman seventeen years ago. He has been married for eleven years and has two sons and a daughter. A soccer player in high school and college, Jack has always prided himself on his physical condition. He rarely gets colds and will tell you without much prodding how little he thinks of the medical profession and how he hates to take pills. Despite Jack's self-assurance about his health, his most recent physical exam (he had managed to avoid one for more than three years) revealed that he is a prime candidate for coronary disease.

Jack is a highly aggressive man who spends a tremendous amount of energy trying to accelerate everything he does. He hurries his thinking, his speech, his movements. His subordinates at work know that when he wants a job done, he wants it done fast. Even when he is not under pressure at work, he pushes himself. Waiting in line at the bank, at the theater, or to tee off at the golf course is anathema to him. Driven to get more done in less time, he has cultivated the ability to do two things at once—dictating while driving, reading his mail while talking on the telephone, even thinking about a business problem while "listening" to his wife or children ("Hmm, is that so?" and "Hmm, really" are his usual conversational devices).

Jack's blood pressure and weight are both up. Carrying 192 pounds on his 5' 11" medium frame, he is about 25 pounds overweight. Three years ago, his cholesterol reading was high and his doctor suggested a low-cholesterol diet. Jack gave up butter but could not give up his steaks and chops every night. In fact, food caused so much tension at home that his wife, Sandra, finally gave up trying to prepare low-cholesterol meals. His cholesterol level today is very high.

With increasing pressures at work, Jack has less and less time for his wife and children. He feels they do not appreciate his efforts to provide them a high standard of living. He believes his tension headaches are due to what he calls the inordinate demands placed on him at home. Jack has great difficulty in relaxing, but finds that a martini or two after work often helps. He smokes at least a pack per day. He wants to quit but has not yet succeeded.

Though Jack says he feels fine, his health is dangerously below positive wellness. If he does not make some significant changes in his life, he has little better than a 20 percent chance of avoiding coronary disease by age fifty, and no better than a 10 percent chance of escaping his first heart attack before age sixty.

CASE 2. Marianna is thirty-seven years old, married, and the mother of two children, aged seven and ten. Until the birth of her first child, Marianna worked as an airline stewardess. Her job demanded tremendous energy, endurance, and good spirits under sometimes trying circumstances. She performed her work well and still misses the excitement of travel. She and her husband, Stan, have talked about traveling and spending more time together when he receives a long-expected promotion. But Marianna's health has become a serious and perplexing problem. Her principal complaint is the "blues," which come often enough to disturb the family and to cause her considerable worry. She periodically becomes so low that she can't get out of bed in the morning or she wakes up at four A.M. and is unable to get back to sleep, even though she feels exhausted. When she hits one of these low periods, she says she "feels her age" and complains of aches and pains in her lower back, neck, wrists, and knees.

Aside from her somatic symptoms and sleeping difficulties, what worries Marianna most is her inability to enjoy life as she used to. She feels left out of her husband's work and tied down to taking care of the children at home. When her frustration builds, she gets angry with the children, only to feel guilty later for being "an unloving mother." Going out to dinner or to the movies or staying home to read—activities she used to enjoy—do little to help her break through one of these "blue periods." While six to eight cups of coffee help her get through the day, the coffee adds to her irritability and makes her very difficult to be around. In her words, she "gets upset with Stan, the children, friends, even the dishwasher repairman, about nothing, just nothing at all."

When Marianna went to her family doctor, he found no evidence of an underlying illness or abnormality. His advice that she get out of the house more often or go on a vacation with Stan only added to her feelings of frustration. Her problem is her inability to get out of the house. In cases like this, a conventional medical exam sometimes fails to reveal the underlying problem because the symptoms are too vague. In fact, Marianna is suffering from bouts of moderate depression, a very real and extremely common condition that can be effectively treated.

CASE 3. Laura, a buyer for a large department store, is thirty-two years old and single. Over the past four years, she has advanced rapidly and has a bright future with her firm. Laura is pleased with herself, her financial independence, and her prospects for the future, but she is beginning to suffer from the stress that is a routine part of her work.

Laura is aging more rapidly than she would like. When she looks in a mirror, she is surprised almost to the point of worry. Nearly every day she needs make-up under her eyes to hide the dark circles that don't go away even after she sleeps late on weekends. (This darkening under the eyes results from an accumulation of pigmentation, a telltale sign of chronic stress.) Laura's complexion is pretty pasty, a far cry from the naturally rosy cheeks she had in college. And she has developed more fine wrinkles around her eyes and mouth during the past year than in her previous thirty-one years.

Two or three times per week, she feels completely worn out at the end of the day. She believes this didn't happen two years ago. She now has sleeping medications in her medicine cabinet and keeps a small bottle of aspirin in her purse. She rarely needed aspirin and never sleeping pills when she was younger, but tension headaches and occasional insomnia have become a regular part of her life. Laura also reports that her smoking has increased to one pack per day, even though she dislikes the smell of smoke on her clothes and would like to quit.

Laura is thin, never has more than a cup of coffee for breakfast, and frequently eats only yogurt for lunch. She takes vitamins because she has read that they help combat stress and fatigue, but she has not noticed that they have helped her.

As yet there has been little research on the effects of chronic stress on women; therefore Laura's future health cannot be predicted. She may be subject to premature coronary disease or high blood pressure like her male counterparts. At the very least, unrelieved stress will cause Laura to age prematurely and to continue to suffer from insomnia, headaches, and fatigue.

CASE 4. Ralph and Susan are a middle-aged couple with three children. Both work—he as a computer programmer and she as a secretary—but neither gets enough exercise, in part because their jobs are sedentary. They are overweight, one of the most common health problems in America. Ralph carries 205 pounds on his 6′ medium frame, and Susan, 172 pounds on her 5′ 8″ small frame. Both are about 40 pounds overweight. They have tried to diet many times and

have a shelf full of diet books, but they have yet to achieve a permanent weight loss.

Ralph and Susan want to lose weight not so much because of their
health but because they feel they would enjoy themselves more if
they achieved a normal weight. In Susan's words, "Fat is unattractive," and in Ralph's, "Carrying forty extra pounds has got to be sap-
ping my energy." Both are right. Although Ralph and Susan do not
smoke or drink and control their cholesterol intake, their overweight
alone is a serious health risk. They already have slightly elevated
blood pressure, and their overweight increases their risk of diabetes.
Should diabetes appear or their blood pressure shoot upward, their
chances of becoming seriously ill would increase dramatically. Their
life expectancy is four to five years less than the same aged individual of normal weight. Continued overweight will rob them not only
of those years but also, and perhaps more importantly, of their full
vigor and vitality for the rest of their lives.

CASE 5. A thirty-five-year-old lawyer, Paul is married and the father of one. He has just become a partner in a large firm and works
hard, perhaps too hard considering how he takes care of himself. His
wife is also a highly active person who works for several volunteer
organizations and paints in her spare time, and she is very understanding when Paul comes home late or works on weekends. But
Paul brings home a full briefcase so often that he is never free from
the worries of his work. Paul can't say no to a request from a colleague or a client if he feels that a yes would further his career.
Though he used to read and collect stamps, he no longer has time for
hobbies. Exercise has also fallen by the wayside. Because he has not
adjusted his caloric intake to account for his increasingly sedentary
life, he is about twelve pounds overweight and well on the road to
obesity. Paul has a cocktail almost every day at lunch and a martini
or two every evening to relax. He takes sleeping pills several nights
a month, and his doctor has recently prescribed a mild tranquilizer
for him. And he is a big consumer of laxatives and antacids. Though
he has not yet developed his first ulcer, colitis, or diverticulitis, he is
a prime candidate for gastrointestinal disease.

Paul frequently suffers from constipation and indigestion. Unless
Paul takes significant steps to improve his level of wellness, he has a
very significant chance of getting an ulcer before age forty-five and is
almost guaranteed gastrointestinal problems (which may at some

point require surgery) for the rest of his life. In one sense, Paul may be lucky that his weak point is his stomach rather than his arteries, because ulcers, unlike heart attacks, are rarely fatal. On the other hand, gastrointestinal problems take much of the joy out of living.

CASE 6. Carol is a twenty-nine-year-old chemical engineer who has recently married. She has just begun to face the fact that she has a problem with alcohol. Though her husband was aware of her excesses at parties long before their marriage, he only recently learned that she sometimes drinks alone.

When she was in graduate school, Carol started drinking to control anxiety. This worked well at first, and Carol grew to rely on alcohol as a crutch. But her tolerance to alcohol steadily increased while the underlying causes of her anxiety remained. Only when her husband pointed out how much and how frequently she was drinking did she begin to realize what was happening to her. Carol is not yet an alcoholic, but unless she learns to control her drinking, alcoholism with all its serious physical and emotional consequences is a near certainty.

CASE 7. Henry is a forty-seven-year-old manager in an auto-manufacturing plant. He has two teen-age sons who live with his first wife. He remarried after the divorce. Before his divorce, Henry believed that his dissatisfaction with his life stemmed primarily from his marriage. He thought his marriage had gone stale and that he needed a change—a younger, more lively female companion. Now, two years after his second marriage, he has recognized that the deterioration of his first marriage was a symptom rather than a cause of pervasive unhappiness.

Henry is worried about getting older and losing his vitality and zest for living. He feels that he doesn't have the energy he once had and sometimes gets angry with himself for "running out of gas at the end of the day." At work he feels an abnormally high degree of competition with the younger managers, largely because they seem to have so many opportunities for advancement while he fears that he has reached his peak. Sometimes his competitiveness takes the form of open hostility—he sometimes refuses to cooperate or explodes in angry outbursts. At meetings, he fears that his mind is not as sharp, his thinking not as creative, and his concentration not as good as that of the younger men in his division.

Henry looks tired. He has large pouches under his eyes and stands with slumped shoulders. Though he is not overweight, he is not physically fit. Two flights of stairs leave him winded. Henry's blood pressure and cholesterol level are within the normal range. However, he is a very heavy smoker, two packs a day, drinks eight to ten cups of coffee every day, and occasionally uses Ritalin (a stimulant prescribed by his doctor) if he feels very low. Aside from his concern about his age and lack of energy, Henry has two other complaints: migraine headaches (about three a month) and frequent chest colds. Bouts of the flu in the fall and again in the spring are routine. When the flu hits him, he misses at least three days of work. He is developing a chronic cough but thinks it's "no big deal."

Despite these concerns and symptoms, Henry believes that he is basically healthy because his doctor gives him a clean bill of health every year. Sure, his doctor tells him to cut down on his smoking, or stop altogether, but the doctor compliments him on his blood pressure, cholesterol level, and weight. Henry has quit smoking several times but never for longer than three months; a crisis hits and he is back to smoking.

Contrary to his belief, Henry is not healthy. He is a prime candidate for serious lung disease (cancer, emphysema, bronchitis) and will almost certainly begin showing symptoms before age sixty. Henry's concern about his decreasing vitality is entirely warranted—he is on the brink of very rapid deterioration. Over the next decade, Henry may experience a steady erosion of his energy level, his productivity, and his zest for living. Or he may take steps to halt this deterioration and even regain some of the ground already lost.

These seven cases give you a general idea of the kinds of health problems that this book can help you with. Of course, it is improbable that your level of wellness is identical to that of any of the individuals described. But if your health problems were touched on in one or more cases, then this book will in all likelihood be helpful to you. In many cases, our program can help to overcome:

—anxiety, tension, worry
—chronic fatigue
—"creeping obesity," poor physical fitness
—excessive drinking
—gastrointestinal distress, frequent indigestion, constipation
—high blood pressure
—insomnia

—irritability, poor concentration, distracted thinking
—low-grade depression, the
"blues"
—overweight
—poor self-esteem

—sexual difficulties
—smoking
—stress, strain, vague bodily
aches and pains
—tension headaches

By increasing your overall level of wellness, you will also significantly reduce your risk of falling prey to serious illness, including:

—arthritis
—cancer
—heart and circulatory disease
—kidney disease
—lung disease
—peptic ulcer, colitis
—severe depression and neurosis
—stroke

You should realize by now that ultimate responsibility for health rests with you and not your doctor. For this reason only you can decide whether you want to start making progress toward positive wellness. If your answer is yes, then your next step is to reassess your inner capacity for health, the healing silence.

PART II

A Powerful Prescription
for Your Health

All action begins in Rest . . . This is the ultimate truth.
                                    —LAO-TZU

Failure of existing rules is the prelude to a search for new ones.
                                    —THOMAS KUHN
                                    The Structure of
                                    Scientific Revolutions

4. The Holistic Health Revolution

If you have decided to make positive wellness your new health standard, you now need to know the techniques that will help you begin drawing on your inner capacity for health and resolving specific health problems. We will get to these soon, but don't be in a hurry to get started. Remember the tortoise and the hare. Your ultimate success will depend not on an initial burst of speed, but on regular, permanent advances. Time and again we have found that a thorough understanding of our program at the outset is a requisite for success.

Our program is new. It is rooted in a revolutionary concept of health care known as *holistic medicine.* Vital to this approach is the belief that you can go beyond feeling just "so-so" or "not bad" to a high level of energy, zest, and personal well-being. This emphasis on achieving high levels of wellness is the principal reason why holistic health care is being called revolutionary. Fundamental to the holistic approach is the participation of a wide range of health professionals in the healing-growth process. For this reason, holistic medicine involves cooperation between physicians and many allied health professionals such as experts in nutrition, fitness, Oriental medicine, growth-oriented psychotherapy, and meditation, to name a few.

While the holistic approach is new to modern medicine, the concept of holism has been influential for thousands of years. From the Greek *holos,* meaning whole, holism is a modern term for the ancient theory that the universe, and especially living nature (e.g., plants and animals) is correctly understood as more than the sum of its parts. The old saying "A house is more than a collection of bricks" expresses the holistic viewpoint well. Apply this principle to understanding living organisms and you must conclude that you can't understand a plant, animal, or human being just by looking at its parts. You have to look at all the parts together, as well as that which sustains harmony among the parts. This dimension is called *spirit*.

The holistic approach contrasts sharply with the mechanistic view that has dominated modern medicine. While holistic health care begins with the premise that all aspects of a person must be taken into account in treating disease, the mechanistic viewpoint pictures the body as a machine with parts that can be treated separately. Holistic medicine emphasizes the role of mental and emotional factors, but the mechanistic view downplays them. Whereas holistic care focuses on individual responsibility for prevention of illness through healthy living habits, the mechanistic approach stresses the importance of the physician's role in treatment of disease. Finally, holistic medicine recognizes spiritual health as an important dimension of a total health care program, but the mechanistic viewpoint discounts the relevance of spirit to medicine altogether.

Neither the holistic nor the mechanistic views of health care have claim to absolute truth. Both stem from philosophical ways of looking at the world, and neither can really exclude the other. The mechanistic view has its origins in the work of the seventeenth-century philosopher René Descartes, who compared the human body to the mechanical robots in Louis XIII's garden. You are probably most familiar with this world view because it has been crucial to the advance of science and technology. On the other hand, you are probably also aware of evidence (e.g., pollution, dehumanization of work, stress, urban decay, etc.) that our society has become one-sided in its mechanistic attitudes. We have lost harmony with nature in our efforts to master it. The holistic viewpoint promises to correct this imbalance. By restoring our respect for nature in its totality, holism may lead us forward to a comtemporary understanding of how to live long, fulfilling lives.

The evidence is clear that an exclusively mechanistic view of health underlies many of the problems of modern health care. The mechanistic model suggests that your doctor can get an adequate picture of your health by determining whether each organ is functioning properly. We have already pointed out the shortcomings of the resultant concept of health as the absence of abnormality according to diagnostic tests. The mechanistic approach encourages a disease orientation and medical specialization at the expense of teaching people how to prevent today's most serious illnesses. Consequently, the number of medical specialists and the costs of health care rise yearly because the epidemic of heart disease, emphysema, cancer, and the degenerative diseases continues unabated.

The ultimate achievement of mechanistic medicine is bionics, the replacement of living organs with mechanical ones. The dramatization of bionic medicine on TV romanticizes the mechanistic view to the point where trading in a living organ for a mechanical one appears enviable. What these shows fail to point out, however, is that bionics is no guarantee of zest, vitality, and happiness characteristic of high levels of wellness; in the real world, the need for bionics indicates a lack of wellness. There is no doubt that the mechanistic approach is leading to the replacement of diseased organs with mechanical ones. Bionics is real. But there is also no doubt that the mechanistic approach is not leading toward an understanding of how you can achieve genuine health, positive wellness.

This contrast of the mechanistic and holistic approaches is not meant to imply that one can replace the other. The mechanistic approach has been highly successful in developing specific treatments for disease. If, for example, streptococci attack the throat membranes, a doctor can administer penicillin to destroy the invading bacteria. If a tumor appears in the colon, the surgeon can excise it. Should a coronary artery become partially occluded, a coronary bypass may circumvent the blockage. In all these cases, however, the mechanistic approach reduces the person to a strep throat, a cancerous colon, or a bypass candidate. The whole person—including the habits, personality, feelings, and environmental stresses that may have predisposed him or her to illness—is ignored. As a result, the modern physician accomplishes miracles in treating disease but does little to promote and maintain health. Holistic health care resolves this paradox by employing the best of modern medicine as indicated but going further to show you how to achieve positive wellness.

In terms of your personal health care, the holistic approach means that you cannot expect to achieve and maintain optimum well-being simply by looking at the signs and symptoms of ill health one by one. You can't think of your body as a machine. Instead, you must look at all parts of yourself—body, mind, spirit, and environment—as an organic whole and determine what elements are out of balance. Your eating habits, nutrition, emotions, physical fitness and exercise routine, stress level, work or home environment, and even your sense of meaning and purpose in life must be taken into account. Improving your level of wellness may require attention to one or several of these areas in addition to traditional treatment of any illness.

The shift toward holism in medicine currently has no chief spokesperson. Nevertheless, there is no doubt that the holistic approach is rapidly gaining favor both in and out of the medical profession. The growing public interest in fitness, natural foods, nutrition, acupuncture and Oriental medicine, natural childbirth, humanizing death and dying, meditation, improved sexual functioning, and emotional growth all signal that holistic health is an idea whose time has come.

In 1975, the Rockefeller Foundation sponsored a groundbreaking conference of leading health professionals to discuss the basic issues of holistic health care. At that conference, it was clear that a cross section of leading health planners including physicians, government officials, and insurance company presidents has been asking the same question for some time: How can people achieve a level of well-being that will prevent the most serious and costly diseases? Their answers, often arrived at independently, converged on a common theme. Individuals must begin assuming repsonsibility for their health and learning ways to maximize vitality and longevity. The whole person, including physical, emotional, and spiritual dimensions of the personality, must be considered. These are the basic ideas behind holistic health care.

Since this first conference, several others have occurred, and thousands of health professionals have attended. The response to the ideas of holistic health care have been so enthusiastic that many more large conferences are planned for the future. A few of the eminent speakers at these conferences include Drs. Jonas Salk, Elisabeth Kübler-Ross, and Hans Selye. To nurture the growth of holistic health care, leaders in the field have formed a new professional organization called the Association for Holistic Health, headquartered in San Diego. Through their work, the first accredited program to train a new holistic health professional—the wellness resource guide—is under way at San Diego State University. A principal goal of this group is to assist in establishing holistic health centers throughout the country. Already, centers are operating in San Francisco, Los Angeles, San Diego, Chicago, New York, and Boston.

Despite its rapid growth, holistic health care is still in its formative stages. A full set of principles fundamental to holistic medicine is yet to be formally established. Nevertheless, most advocates of holistic medicine agree that the following eight principles are among the most important. We suggest that you study these principles carefully because they are crucial to everything that follows in this book.

1. Health requires an integration of mind, body, and spirit.

If there is a basic axiom of holistic medicine, this is it. Although many orthodox medical studies have documented the interdependence of physical and emotional health, conventional medicine treats either the body or the psyche, but rarely both at once. No one argues anymore about the impact of chronic anxiety or depression on classic psychosomatic illnesses such as asthma, peptic ulcer, and essential hypertension, but new evidence shows that mental-emotional states effect even what were once thought to be strictly organic illnesses.[32] One study shows a high correlation between cancer and the repression of chronic depression and anxiety; another demonstrates that feelings of optimism and well-being correlate highly with rapid recovery after surgery; many studies have shown that a placebo can sometimes produce significant improvement for emotional and physical illness alike.[61]

The proponents of holistic medicine insist that all illness involves a degree of imbalance between mind-body-spirit. Consequently, treatment must address the physical, emotional, and spiritual aspects of the personality. In practice, treatment at a holistic health center may involve conventional antibiotics, a nutrition and/or fitness program, a health habits improvement program, traditional or growth-oriented psychotherapy, Oriental medicine such as acupuncture and acupressure, biofeedback, vocational and marital counseling, and techniques to expand consciousness and broaden spiritual horizons. In other words, the holistically oriented physician draws upon the widest possible range of ancient and modern techniques to design a specific program to help each client achieve the physical-emotional-spiritual harmony of positive wellness.

Most people have an intuitive appreciation of how much their emotional state affects their physical health, but the treatment of the spirit by medical professionals elicits a general attitude of skepticism. Some people believe that the church is or should be the exclusive guide to spiritual growth. Others doubt the reality of spiritual growth altogether. And still others equate spiritual growth with mysticism.

Within holistic medicine, spirit is a pragmatic concept, not religious or mystical. Holism implies that human life is more than the sum of mental-emotional states, such as thoughts, perceptions, and feelings, and physical parts, such as brain, heart, and intestines. Spirit refers to that which gives meaning and direction to your life. Important signs of spiritual health are satisfaction with work, an untroubled home life, and a sense of deep inner happiness. Although spiritual growth may contribute to a religious life, it may also be experienced and understood in terms of the actualization of an inherent human potential. In any case, through spiritual growth you experience a personal connection to a greater reality, be it Nature, God, or History. Because Western medicine has only barely begun to explore the role of spirit in health, many advocates of holistic health care consider it a promising area of research.

2. Positive wellness rather than the mere absence of symptoms must be the goal of health care.

This second axiom is closely related to the first. Advocates of holistic medicine point out that poor integration between mind-body-spirit cannot necessarily be measured through conventional medical tests. Instead it might show up as boredom, frustration, poor productivity, destructive habits, or lack of meaningful life goals. All these emotional-spiritual symptoms may reduce energy levels, contribute to common physical symptoms such as headaches, insomnia, and gastrointestinal problems, and certainly undermine a person's ability to enjoy life. The long-term effects of this emotional-spiritual imbalance may be to weaken the physical system and make the body susceptible to disease. All of these factors point to the need for a new standard of health.

Proponents of holistic medicine believe that this new standard of health must be established carefully through scientific research. At the Langley Porter Neuropsychiatric Institute in San Francisco, Dr. Kenneth R. Pelletier and his associates are investigating the characteristics of unusually healthy people. Attention development, brain waves, muscle tension, and cardiovascular and respiratory function are a few of the factors under study. Psychologist David Orme-Johnson and his colleagues are carrying this research one step further in trying to identify the physiological characteristics of the enlightened person. According to ancient texts, enlightenment represents the highest level of mental-physical-spiritual development.

A complete scientific definition of positive wellness is still forthcoming, but leading physicians at holistic health conferences have agreed on its principal characteristics. Though we have already mentioned these characteristics, a review is worthwhile because understanding positive wellness is so important to achieving it. First and foremost, positive wellness insures a high level of general vitality and ample joy in living. Such a person is physically fit, free of health-destroying habits such as smoking, overeating, or excessive drinking. Enough sleep and adequate meals are a regular part of the person's daily routine. Work is meaningful and productive; love relationships are profound. All these factors contribute to a long, satisfying life not only free from the everyday complaints of tension and stress (as well as serious illness), but also able to express the highest values of the human spirit.

3. Everyday living habits are the basis of health.

This concept is neither new nor exclusive to advocates of holistic medicine. The American Cancer Society and the American Heart Association routinely present this idea in antismoking commercials. What holistic medicine adds to this idea is a strong emphasis on helping clients not just understand their destructive habits, but *effectively change them.*

The conventional scientific evidence that underscores the importance of living habits to health is now beyond dispute. Modern medical research has come a long way since the surgeon general's first report that cigarette smoking is harmful to health. For example, in a survey of seven thousand California adults, Dr. Lester Breslow, dean of UCLA's School of Public Health, found that seven basic living habits are crucial to health.[14,31] These habits are:

—no smoking
—moderate drinking
—seven or eight hours' sleep nightly
—regular meals with no between-meal snacking
—breakfast every day
—normal weight
—moderate, regular exercise

Dr. Breslow found that people with all seven habits are more healthy than those with six; those with six are more healthy than those with five, and so on. A forty-five-year-old man with zero to three of these habits has an average life expectancy of twenty-one years; if he has six or seven of the habits, he could anticipate another thirty-three years of life. At the University of Wisconsin, Dr. Robert Samp found similar results in his study of the habits and personalities of two thousand long-lived people. To Breslow's list of healthy living habits, Samp added desirable personality traits such as moderation, serenity, optimism, interest in others, and interest in the future. These large-scale, multifactored studies corroborate scores of smaller studies showing that the risk of lung cancer for a smoker is several times that for a nonsmoker; [86,87,233] the risk of heart disease for an overweight, competitive, aggressive man may be four or five times that of an emotionally balanced, easygoing individual who carries few excess pounds.[69]

Though these studies show how everyday living habits can shorten life, they tell only part of the story. Smokers may know that a pack-a-day habit shortens their lives by six years, but they may feel that they "have to die sometime" and prefer to spend what years they do have enjoying their cigarettes. What smokers fail to appreciate is that not only will they die six years sooner than nonsmokers, but they may spend the last ten years of their lives crippled by chronic lung or heart disease. (Emphysema, bronchitis, lung cancer, or coronary disease are often slow killers.) Furthermore, not only the individual smoker will suffer during these declining years of illness; his or her family will experience emotional anguish and medical costs that can be devastating.

4. The individual must affirm personal responsibility for his or her health.

How much can your doctor do to help you change your living habits and ultimately enjoy the vitality of positive wellness? Some believe that the doctor's role in the holistic health movement must necessarily be limited in order to foster the layperson's autonomy.

In *Medical Nemesis* Ivan Illich argues very convincingly that the average person has abdicated responsibility for his or her health to what appears to be an omnipotent health care system. Having developed an inordinate confidence in medical miracles, many people do not try to improve their health. Since the "all-powerful" medical establishment is on call twenty-four hours a day, many people seem to believe that they can eat to excess, smoke, drink without restriction, and drive carelessly. If illness should strike, doctors, nurses, and technicians will be there to pick up the pieces.

To correct this erroneous belief, physicians advocating holistic care point out that putting the pieces back together may keep a person alive but rarely restores a high level of wellness. A coronary bypass is no substitute for a healthy heart, and anticongestion medication cannot cure a diseased lung. The sooner you begin a program to achieve positive wellness, the more likely are you to avert serious illness and avoid premature death.

5. Illness provides an opportunity for growth.

This principle is a logical corollary to that about personal responsibility. If, as argued by proponents of holistic medicine, you significantly influence your susceptibility to illness through your emotional make-up and living habits, then the arrival of illness is a sign that you must change your habits and emotional responses. By studying how you get sick, you and your doctor can discover important clues to what changes you should make to regain your full capacity for health.

For example, if a thirty-five-year-old man begins to suffer from bronchitis, this may provide a chance to avoid irreversible lung disease later in life. He may recognize that he must change the habits, such as smoking, that contribute to his bronchitis. In doing so, he may also begin to deal with those emotional factors that fuel his smoking habit. The end result will be better living habits and emotional-spiritual growth, both leading to enhanced well-being and increased vitality.

6. Environmental factors play a major role in individual health.

Analysis of mortality records for the last two hundred years in Great Britain and one hundred years in the United States has shown that improvement of environmental factors (such as food, sanitation, and housing) accounted for almost 90 percent of the decline in infectious disease during that period.[155] The miracles of immunization and antibiotics accounted for only 10 percent. Today a new set of environmental factors is seriously threatening health. Pesticides, plastics, and some food additives are among the many substances that are suspected of being carcinogenic. It is estimated that as much as 90 percent of all cancer may be linked with these chemical carcinogens. Fluorocarbons may be destroying the protective ozone layer in the ionosphere. Exposure to a high level of air pollution over an extended period can cause or exacerbate emphysema and a variety of lung diseases. And on the job, many people are exposed to noxious agents such as excessive noise, toxic chemicals, and too much stress.

It is more difficult to isolate the emotional-spiritual elements in your environment. You probably spend most of your life interacting with other people in groups—your family, friends, co-workers. Each group generates its own emotional climate. If that climate is highly stressful, you may exhaust your physical-emotional resources in an attempt to adapt.[189] For example, the workplace may be calm and orderly or hectic and tension ridden. Several studies have shown that a stressful, anxiety-producing work environment increases the incidence of psychosomatic illness, accidents, and interpersonal conflict.[155] Similarly, an angry, unloving home environment promotes emotional distress and destructive behavior in the family members. Holistic health planning is directed toward eliminating all health-endangering factors, both physical and emotional-spiritual, from your environment.

7. All modalities of healing, ancient as well as modern, deserve careful scientific exploration and should be used where appropriate.

References to the art of medicine appear in the written records of many early civilizations. Many ancient medical practices have disappeared, but some, such as acupuncture and homeopathic medicine, are still practiced. Proponents of holistic medicine reason that a technique will survive hundreds of decades only if it produces substantial results. Recent study has suggested that acupuncture may relieve pain and even serve as an anesthetic. Clinical experience indicates that several homeopathic remedies may deserve more attention than they have been given by orthodox medicine.* And at the extreme, research on psychic healing, laying on of hands, and faith cures at religious shrines falls within the bounds of the holistic approach to health care.[103]

This emphasis on exploring ancient modalities of healing is one of the most exciting yet most potentially dangerous aspects of holistic medicine. On one hand, it may encourage indiscriminate use of the term "holistic." Well-intentioned "healers" may adopt this label to gain acceptance for methods that after scientific investigation may prove to have little or no benefit. Charlatans may exploit the term "holistic health" in promoting their useless remedies. Certainly, the public must beware of quackery and faddism. On the other hand, serious research into alternative healing modalities may result in significant advances in understanding health.

The undeniable results of some ancient techniques cannot be explained by conventional theories of how the body and mind work. For example, the energy channels outlined by acupuncture theory do

---

* Homeopathy is a healing system based on the belief that a small dose of a toxic substance can cure an ailment with similar symptoms to that produced by a large toxic dose of that substance. In other words, to cure your cold, a homeopath will give you a small dose of some substance that would in large doses cause a runny nose, sneezing, low-grade fever, and fatigue. For the most part, conventional medical practitioners have viewed homeopathy as a form of quackery. Recent reports that some homeopathic remedies may be useful in otherwise untreatable disorders such as chronic arthritis are prompting a few conventional investigators to explore several homeopathic prescriptions.

not correspond to any of the body's known chemical processes or anatomical structures. Nevertheless, acupuncture can produce some remarkable results. This anomaly suggests a need to rethink our basic assumptions about the workings of the body. Perhaps the body and mind are better understood as an energy system (the ancient view) rather than a chemical-mechanical one (the modern view). Or perhaps chemical-mechanical processes depend on underlying energy transformations (a view consistent with modern physics) that can be directly affected through ancient techniques. To some members of the medical profession, these speculations seem farfetched; to proponents of holistic medicine, they suggest the possibility of a breakthrough in understanding the fundamentals of health.

8. Your inner capacity for health is the foundation for achieving positive wellness.

Conventional medicine fails to help you achieve positive wellness because it focuses on the treatment of illness rather than you as a whole person. Without this eighth principle, holistic medicine would fall in the same trap. A new diet, some group therapy, a few acupuncture treatments, and life-enrichment classes do not in themselves lead to positive wellness. A piecemeal approach to health care will not work; an integrated program is necessary and your inner capacity for health, the healing silence, must be its foundation.

Referring to the lever, Archimedes said, "Give me a place to stand and I could move the world." This statement can also be applied to a health improvement program. Given the right techniques and guidance, you can substantially improve your health. You can figuratively "move the world." But these techniques will work easily and most effectively only to the extent that you have established an inner foundation of harmony and well-being. Your inner capacity for health will provide this foundation.

Your own experience undoubtedly confirms this need for inner change. No matter what diet you try, you will not be able to remain at your new weight unless you have established an inner harmony that will maintain healthy eating habits. No matter how well intentioned you might be at the outset of a fitness program, the odds are good that you will not keep it up unless you are also steadily increasing your inner strength and well-being. No matter what you do to recover from a deep backlog of fatigue, your fatigue will inevitably return unless you also improve your ability to handle stress and pressure. Whether you are trying to give up smoking, get rid of tension headaches, relieve insomnia, cope with depressions, resolve sexual problems, become more assertive, or give your life new meaning and direction, development of your inner capacity for health is essential to any health improvement program.

5. The Key to Positive Wellness

When an agitated, hallucinating, feverish, and dehydrated patient comes into the emergency room, no one has time to think about something so apparently unrelated to the situation as positive wellness. All questions must focus on the diagnosis of this medical emergency, and appropriate treatment must be swiftly implemented. Over the past thirty years, medical research has greatly enhanced the physician's ability to diagnose and treat acute illness. Not all medical researchers, however, have gotten caught up in the urgencies of studying disease. Some have recognized that medicine will never learn how to keep people healthy by studying them only when they are sick.

Among the first of these investigators was the eminent psychologist Abraham Maslow. In *Motivation and Personality*, he showed how psychological theories based on the study of neurotics did not explain the behavior of healthy people. Lacking a scientific standard of mental health, psychiatrists and psychologists could do little but develop their own, often conflicting visions of how the healthy person should function. For each vision of health there arose a brand of therapy to achieve it. After Freud discovered the unconscious, Jung developed methods to promote "individuation," Adler aimed at overcoming "inferiority," Sullivan sought ways of fulfilling "security needs" and increasing "self-esteem," Perls emphasized the importance of "awareness," and so on. As a result, according to Maslow, psychological research had developed a plethora of therapies but little understanding of mental health.

Maslow put his initial insights (many of which he credits to his teacher Kurt Goldstein) to work in the study of health. He began by identifying exceptionally creative, mature, and apparently fulfilled

individuals who agreed to undergo intensive interviewing and testing. His results indicated that certain traits were characteristic of the
healthy person. These are:

—superior perception of reality and clarity of thought
—acceptance of self, others, and nature
—spontaneity, liveliness, and expressiveness
—autonomy and sense of self-sufficiency
—freshness of appreciation and richness of emotional reaction
—frequency of ecstatic, peak experiences
—integrity and wholeness
—interpersonal competence
—nonauthoritarian, democratic personality
—exceptional creativity
—ability to fuse the concrete and abstract
—ability to express love and affection

Maslow marveled at how naturally and unself-consciously healthy
people exhibited these qualities. The healthy person apparently expressed them from deep within, as if they were inborn characteristics. This observation led him to a theory that synthesized his insights about the fundamentals of health. He concluded that every
person has a biologically innate "inner nature" that contains in seed
form what are usually thought to be outstanding human qualities.
This inner reservoir allows the individual to live with maximum vitality, health, and fulfillment. Maslow wrote, "If this essential core of
the person is denied or suppressed, he gets sick sometimes in obvious ways, sometimes in subtle ways, sometimes immediately,
sometimes later. . . . If it is permitted to guide our life, we grow
healthy, fruitful, and happy." (151, p. 4)

With this theory Maslow was among the first modern researchers
to assert the existence of a key to positive wellness, one factor that
supports comprehensive development of the individual. To distinguish this factor from the ego, emotions, body, and other elements
that make up the person, he called this inner nature simply the *self*.
Fully aware that his theory was not new, he pointed out parallels
between it and the work of many contemporaries such as Horney,
Sullivan, and Perls, to name a few. He also noted that this concept

appeared in the writings of many ancient philosophers, mystics, and saints.[95]

When Maslow first proposed his concept of the self, it met mixed reactions. Many Freudians, behaviorists, and other psychological and medical researchers rejected it or paid it little attention because there was no room for this new data in their disease-oriented model of human nature. However, a small but substantial group of psychologists, dissatisfied with the Freudian and behaviorist approaches, was impressed by the appearance, however vague, of the concept of the "self" in almost every culture throughout history.[162] These psychologists also recognized in the writings of some philosophers and many mystics who described the self a potential for human development that had been barely considered, much less systematically explored, by modern scientists.

Out of this interest grew what is now known as humanistic psychology and the human potential movement. Trying to put Maslow's theories to work, humanistic psychologists developed a wide variety of techniques aimed at helping their patients get in touch with the self and tap its healing potential. Nondirective therapy, T-groups, encounter groups, Gestalt therapy, bioenergetics, massage techniques, and nude groups are but a few of the methods that have become popular.* Along with the proliferation of these techniques have spread the ideas, first expressed in Western psychological thought by William James, that every person has an enormous untapped potential for vitality, creativity, and fulfillment and that consciousness can be expanded far beyond the level experienced by most people. In short, humanistic psychology has fostered the search for positive wellness.

The fact that positive wellness remains unachieved by most people has prompted criticism of the human potential movement. One observer has noted that humanistic psychology has given rise to a jungle of self-improvement techniques, many lacking scientific validation. Another has claimed that understanding of the self and the characteristics of the fully healthy person has not advanced much beyond Maslow's initial speculations. A third has suggested that anyone who comes up with a new method for "developing human po-

* See Chapter 20 for a brief explanation of these therapies.

tential," no matter how outlandish, is guaranteed an audience because people are desperate now that they have found that another new car, a third trip to Europe, or a new mate does not assure happiness.

Though some psychologists have voiced these criticisms, they have neither cast much doubt on Maslow's basic insights nor abated the search for positive wellness. On the contrary, scientific interest in the possibility of positive wellness is reaching a new height. No longer are psychologists the primary investigators of the human capacity for health; physicians and allied scientists, enthusiastic about the principles of holistic medicine, have joined the effort. At the same time, public interest in growth techniques continues to expand.

The Meditation Explosion

Over the past few years, hundreds of thousands of people have begun practicing meditation techniques. Thousands have learned Zen techniques of counting the breath, yogic methods of concentrating on various parts of the body or on mental images, and Western contemplative procedures of dwelling on profound ideas. Nearly one million people have learned the Transcendental Meditation (TM) technique alone. This makes meditation one of the most widely practiced methods for achieving maximum health, vitality, and personal development.

This ground swell of interest in meditation is particularly significant because philosophers and mystics from many cultural traditions have held that meditation is a key to health and personal development and can lead to higher states of consciousness. To some medical researchers this transcultural and transhistorical durability of meditation as a tool for achieving maximum personal development suggests that meditation is a key to achieving positive wellness.

Scientific research on meditation began in the 1930s when the French cardiologist Thérèse Brosse took a portable electrocardiograph to India where she found evidence that some yogis could control involuntary functions such as heart rate.[33] In the mid-1950s neurophysiologists M. A. Wenger, B. K. Bagchi, and B. K. Anand carted sophisticated research equipment four thousand miles across

India to study experienced meditators.[235,236] Though they studied only thirteen advanced meditators, these researchers concluded that meditation produces a unique state of rest, especially for involuntary bodily functions. The Japanese physiologists Y. Sugi and K. Akutsu confirmed these findings in a study of Zen meditators whose metabolic rate dropped about 20 percent during Zen meditation.[206] These and other early studies tended to confirm that a variety of meditation techniques produced a deep state of physical rest that could prove beneficial to health. Complicating this research, however, was the lack of large numbers of people practicing a single meditation technique that had been taught in a uniform manner.

With the popularity of the TM technique, the possibility of scientifically investigating the impact of meditation on health markedly improved. Drawing on an ancient, unbroken tradition of knowledge about meditation, Maharishi Mahesh Yogi developed TM as a simple and unique technique that could be effectively practiced by anyone after a few hours of instruction. As a result, scientists had available, for the first time since research on meditation began, a large number of experienced meditators who practiced the same technique, learned in a systematic and uniform way. Factors such as diet, lifestyle, emotional attitudes, and religious beliefs did not complicate research on the TM techniques as they had in the study of other techniques because the TM program required no changes in these areas. Consequently, scientists could be confident that any observed effects were due to the TM technique and not to changes in diet, beliefs, and so on. Finally, research was facilitated by the very mundane fact that scientists did not have to drag their equipment into the mountains but could invite TM meditators into their laboratories.

The Healing Power Within

Some proponents of meditation believe it is a cure-all that by itself will allow you to achieve positive wellness. But neither TM nor any other meditation technique will magically generate positive wellness. The rate at which you benefit from meditation depends on your initial level of wellness, your everyday living habits, and your motivation for self-improvement.

Another serious misapprehension is the belief that meditation can replace orthodox medical care. If you become acutely ill, you need expert medical attention, whether or not you practice TM or any other meditation technique. Meditation is no substitute for antibiotics in cases of severe pneumonia, insulin for the diabetic, or antidepressants for the acutely depressed. The person who learns a meditation technique and then decides to stop taking prescribed medication is foolhardy.

Given these limitations, what can meditation do for you? Through proper practice of meditation, you can achieve a profound experience of inner silence and tranquillity, the core of your self identified by Maslow as the key to health and well-being. Research has confirmed that this inner silence—free from pressure, concern, tension, and anxiety—has the power to nourish your body, mind, and spirit. From the more than four hundred published scientific studies on meditation, we have compiled the following table of results to illustrate the magnitude of this power. Many of these studies were conducted on practitioners of the TM technique because it is the most widely used meditation technique.

Effects on physical health:

—increases energy (25, 40, 184, 198a)
—increases resistance to disease (168, 184, 198a)
—improves autonomic stability—i.e., increases physical capacity to handle stress (167, 168, 235, 243)
—improves physiological efficiency—i.e., contributes to low pulse and breath rates at rest (183, 231)
—improves mind-body coordination and physical agility (168)
—reduces incidence of insomnia, tension headaches, and bodily aches and pains (158, 159, 237)
—helps reduce high blood pressure (15, 16, 21, 44)
—helps relieve psychosomatic conditions such as asthma, neurodermatitis, and gastrointestinal problems (24, 25, 91)
—helps normalize weight (234)

Effects on mental-emotional well-being:

—reduces anxiety, nervousness (29, 58, 80, 170, 197)
—reduces depression (58, 80, 197)

—reduces neuroticism and inhibition (58, 90, 190, 197, 226)
—reduces feelings of mental and/or physical inadequacy (40, 90, 197)
—reduces irritability (58, 170, 197)
—improves self-esteem, self-regard (40, 90, 190, 226)
—increases ego-strength (40, 80, 90, 190)
—improves problem-solving ability (198a)
—improves organization of thinking (117, 198a)
—increases creativity (47, 164)
—increases productivity (68, 117)

Effects on spiritual well-being:

—promotes self-actualization (46, 158, 166, 187, 197)
—fosters trust, capacity for intimate contact (90, 131, 166, 187)
—enhances ability to love and express affection (131, 166, 187)
—develops inner wholeness (6, 164, 187)
—increases autonomy and self-reliance (22, 40, 166)
—increases satisfaction at home and at work (27, 45, 117)
—reduces feelings of alienation and meaninglessness (26, 45, 187)
—strengthens religious affiliations (26, 117)

In light of these comprehensive health benefits, the healing silence appears to be a key to positive wellness. How this inner silence produces such a wide range of benefits remains for us to consider.

6. Stress, Silence, and Science

Medical professionals have long recognized that silence plays an important role in healing. Bed rest is the usual prescription for almost all illness, from the common cold to myocardial infarction. The more ill you are, the more emphatically will your doctor insist that you get rest and be quiet. Despite this age-old appreciation of the value of silence for healing, until recently medical and psychological researchers have paid little attention to states of internal silence.

The principal reason for this neglect may be the Western cultural bias against quiescence. The Western paradigm of success is the dynamic individual who works hard, enjoys life fully, and can withstand the pressure and tension of a fast-paced life. Even though wealthy, an idle person without inner dynamism is not highly esteemed. To many people, inner tranquillity suggests a lack of drive, a dull personality, and an inability to compete. To others, inner silence connotes an otherworldly, detached way of living suitable to monks and perhaps poets, but not to the down-to-earth person who wants to get the most out of life. Passion, joy, and all the other emotions that make living vibrant are wrongly thought to be antithetical to inner silence.

Recent medical research indicates, however, that this bias against inner silence is a serious mistake with major implications for your health and well-being. It has become evident that states of deep inner silence have tremendous power to restore balance and harmony to the whole range of your physical-emotional-spiritual functioning.

To appreciate how inner silence can strengthen your total health and well-being, you must first understand the principal causes of premature aging and physical deterioration. The gradual loss of vigor and vitality that occurs over the years cannot be traced to any single cause such as a virus, lack of exercise, poor health habits, or tension. These and other factors may all play a part. However, the principal mechanism of aging is reasonably well understood. This mechanism is simply the everyday wear and tear on the body, mind, and spirit.

Aging is a process of degeneration. Cells die and are not replaced; abnormal deposits form in the arteries and other tissues; organs gradually become less efficient; joints, muscles, and connective tissues lose their flexibility and elasticity; clusters of nerve fiber lose their sensitivity. This process is inevitable, but the rate at which it occurs is not fixed. You can speed it up or slow it down. For example, the more pressure, tension, and frustration you experience, the more rapidly will everyday wear and tear take its toll. Conversely, the more opportunities you give your body, mind, and spirit for natural regeneration, the slower will the permanent damage of everyday wear and tear occur. By stimulating innate regenerative mechanisms, you may even reverse degeneration that has not yet become irreparable.

Medical researchers define everyday wear and tear on the mind and body as *stress*. Though this term is often used loosely, it has an exact scientific meaning. Dr. Hans Selye, the leading authority on the subject, defines stress as "the body's non-specific response to any demand made upon it." In other words, stress refers to the uniform set of changes that occurs throughout your body whenever you meet *any* external or internal demand, be it physical or emotional. A viral infection, an injury, an argument, or a worry can all elicit the stress response. Some of the bodily changes accompanying stress include muscular tension, increased heart rate, accelerated breathing, mild to profuse sweating, cold hands or feet, and anxiety. A storm of chemical changes with long-term effects underlies these familiar physical signs of stress.

The stress response in itself is neither good nor bad. In fact, making value judgments about inborn responses is usually a mistake. Whatever nature has built into the body almost always has a useful function. Under certain circumstances, however, a response may cause damage. Such is the case with stress response. You could not repel a viral invasion, adapt to sudden temperature changes, work hard, experience great joy and excitement, or delight in sexual fulfillment without the stress response. Clearly, this response is fundamental to your survival and your enjoyment of living. But research has shown that when the stress response is prolonged, it may erode the foundations of your health. Prolonged stress seems to be the most important cause of premature aging, lowered resistance to disease, and emotional distress.

In the past, physical hardships such as cold weather, inadequate nutrition, and frequent illness caused excessive stress and resulting physical degeneration. Today these physical hardships are no longer prevalent in industrialized societies, but new causes of excessive stress—the by-products of modern civilization—have become commonplace. These include physical factors such as noise, foul air, and hurry to meet rushed schedules, and emotional ones, including financial worries, frustrations at work, marital strife, self-doubt, sexual dysfunctions, and neuroses. Equally important are spiritual problems such as inner emptiness, chronic boredom, and lack of fulfillment. With the increase in material well-being that accompanied the growth of modern industrial society, major infectious diseases have all but disappeared. The ravages of excessive stress, however, have never been greater.

What are the symptoms of excessive stress? One common symptom is feeling worn out at the end of the day. Another is difficulty falling asleep or sleeping through the night. Others include:

—tension headaches
—free-floating anxiety
—feeling all wound up
—feeling down in the dumps
—chronic fatigue
—pouches or dark circles under eyes
—worry
—inability to concentrate
—irritability
—frequent indigestion
—frequent constipation
—frequent colds
—frequent angry outbursts
—excessive drinking, smoking, eating

These symptoms warn that you are suffering excessive stress; they don't warn you of its long-term consequences. Insight into these long-term effects is fundamental to understanding the healing power of inner silence.

How Excessive Stress Kills You Slowly

Since Hans Selye first discovered the stress response more than three decades ago, it has become a major concern of medical and psychological research. Today its principal components and the mechanics of its long-term effects are well understood.

The stress response begins when the central nervous system registers a demand on your physical-emotional-spiritual resources. Because everyday living places many demands on you, the stress response occurs frequently with varying degrees of intensity throughout the day. When a loud noise, an angry memo from the boss, a disobedient child, or other common occurrence registers as a stressor, the first stage of the stress response, the alarm stage, begins automatically. You know this stage well by the surge of energy, the acceleration of your heartbeat and breathing, and the tension that are its principal signs. Regulating this mobilization of your energies are the sympathetic branch (energy expending) of your autonomic nervous system (that trunk of the central nervous system which controls involuntary functions such as digestion, heart rate, and breath rate) and your adrenal glands. Your sympathetic system sends alarm signals throughout your body, and your adrenals pour the hormone adrenaline into your blood to increase your available energy.

Nature seems to have designed this first stage of the stress response with the intent that it should suffice for handling most of the everyday demands that you might face. This alarm stage is called the "fight-or-flight reaction" because it allows massive mobilization of energy. It helps fuel your excitement in a pleasurable situation and your anger in a frustrating one. If while crossing the street you have to dodge an unexpected automobile, the alarm response provides the burst of energy you need. This ability to mobilize energy is critical to athletic pursuits such as tennis and explains how an average person can in the case of an emergency perform unexpected feats of strength.

After the demanding situation passes, your physical-emotional system automatically seeks rest in order to restore inner balance and "recharge your batteries." If the external demand remains or if you continue to trigger the stress response through worry or frustration, you soon enter the stage of resistance. At this point the body mobilizes itself for long-term battle against the stressor. This second stage is like a double-edged sword. It helps you survive in the face of illness, injury, or prolonged physical hardship. But if it can't be turned off and becomes chronic, its biochemical effects will erode the foundations of your physical-emotional-spiritual well-being.

When prolonged high levels of adrenaline, along with signals from the hypothalamus (a small master control center in your brain), activate the pituitary gland, the resistance stage gets under way. This master gland secretes hormones that mobilize your whole physical-emotional system for a long-term battle. One of these hormones, vasopressin, raises your blood pressure by causing your arteries to narrow. Another, thyrotrophic hormone (TTH), stimulates your thyroid gland to increased production of the hormone thyroxine, thus accelerating your metabolism. A third pituitary hormone, called adrenocorticotrophic hormone (ACTH), further activates your adrenal glands to produce the adrenocortical hormones (cortisol, cortisone, aldosterone, etc.), which among other effects raise your blood sugar level, control inflammation, and alter your immune system.

The second stage of the stress response need not be damaging. It will naturally give way to the third stage, exhaustion, during which the body can replenish its biochemical resources, and you can return to a state of natural balance and attunement. Should you be unable to get adequate rest because you remain chronically tense, fatigue will persist and serious damage will ensue. The mechanics of this damage are complex, but the principal effects include:

1. Chronic elevation of your blood pressure with slow but steady damage to your heart, kidneys, and entire cardiovascular system.
2. Tearing of your arterial walls and elevation of clotting elements in your blood, both of which increase plaque formation (clogging) of your arteries.
3. Increases in your blood sugar levels which in turn raise cholesterol levels.
4. Lowered resistance to disease through a reduction in certain critically important white blood cell levels.

5. Increased stomach acidity and changes in the stomach lining which contribute to gastrointestinal distress and ulcer formation.
6. Increased inflammation in joints, aches and pains, and ultimately chronic arthritis.
7. Hyperactivity of your whole system, resulting in mental-physical exhaustion, chronic fatigue, and insomnia.

One or more of these processes are probably already eroding your health. Noise, hurry, frustration, and worry are the daily companions of most people today. These pressures of modern living can cause prolonged, excessive stress, not necessarily at extremely high levels, but enough to accelerate the aging process, sap your vitality, and make you susceptible to serious illness.

The emotional consequences of excessive stress are as harmful as the physical ones. In fact, they may be even more dangerous because they inhibit your coping ability and reinforce the stress response. Excessive stress keeps you in a keyed-up, hyper-aroused emotional state, to the point where you rarely rest well, even when you are asleep. As a result, your psyche has difficulty regaining its natural state of harmony, ease, and well-being. You may experience unpredictable mood shifts and a whole range of abnormal emotional states—from anxiety, tension, and irritability to fatigue and depression—that will undermine your ability to function well and enjoy yourself.

How Stress Reinforces the Bias Against Silence

Ironically, excessive stress militates against rest and inner silence—what your system needs to recover from the damaging effects of stress. The keyed-up state of chronic stress makes it difficult to enjoy quiet pleasures. Instead, our culture has become dependent on excitement as a primary source of enjoyment. Hollywood offers a steady diet of sex, violence, occult fantasy, and terror because the producers know what most people have come to need in order to enjoy a movie. TV producers and book publishers are equally well attuned to what our culture demands.* Recent research indicates that the addiction to excitement has become so great that some people cannot endure a half-hour (or even minutes for others) of complete silence without becoming edgy and nervous. Sitting quietly may seem to be a waste of time, especially when there is always so much to do and so little time to do it. This attitude explains why so few people take time to meet their own inner needs and nourish their total physical-emotional-spiritual health.

A distinction must be made between the silence of emotional tension and that of inner well-being. If you are so angry, depressed, lonely, or afraid that you are unwilling or unable to speak, you may appear outwardly quiet, but within there seethes frustration and distress. On the other hand, if you are deeply absorbed in meditation, your outer quiet reflects a silent well-being that emanates from the deepest recesses of your personality. The silence of emotional distress has a pathological quality and, in keeping with the disease orientation of modern medical research, has attracted much more scientific attention than the silence of well-being.

Nevertheless, a cross section of mental health professionals, from psychoanalysts to humanistic psychologists, has begun to recognize that the unique silence of well-being is crucial to health. Maslow, among others, has asserted that periods of solitude are critical to the continued vitality and well-being of the highly creative, self-actualizing person. Studies of exceptionally healthy, self-actualizing people show that they make time in their busy schedules for some quiet solitude. University of Louisville psychiatrist Mohammed Shafii points out that genuine inner silence, not the silence of repressed emotion, serves a regenerative and integrative function.[192] At this level of deep inner silence, the psyche can, according to Shafii, heal itself quietly and naturally without the need to verbalize or examine long-buried emotional traumas. This new view of silence was well summarized by psychoanalyst Sacha Nacht: "Human life needs at

---

* These may seem shopworn observations but recent research has verified the stressful impact of much of what we call entertainment. Dr. Lennart Levi, noted stress researcher at the Karolinska Institute in Stockholm, has shown that violent and pornographic movies increase adrenaline secretion. Dr. Bozzuto at the University of Connecticut has reported what he calls "cinematic neurosis." This condition refers to the complex of symptoms including insomnia, irritability, and hyperactivity that develops in some people after viewing violent and terrifying movies.

moments to steep itself in silence, from which it draws essential nourishment and in which it develops its deepest roots." (163, p. 302)

The Antidote to Excessive Stress

Recent research on the effects of meditation confirms that a twice daily experience of inner silence can be of immense benefit to your health and total well-being. Inner silence has profound effects upon body and mind. You experience a state of very deep rest, marked by decreases in heart rate, breath rate, oxygen consumption, perspiration, muscle tension, blood pressure, and levels of stress hormones. You also achieve a state of heightened mental clarity and emotional ease, possibly a result of increased coherence of brain-wave activity.

One way to appreciate the significance of these effects is to contrast them with those of the stress response.

	Stress Response	Healing Silence
Respiration rate	UP ↑	DOWN ↓
Heart rate	UP ↑	DOWN ↓
Metabolic rate (O_2 consumption)	UP ↑	DOWN ↓
Blood pressure	UP ↑	DOWN ↓
Muscle tension	UP ↑	DOWN ↓
Skin conductance (perspiration)	UP ↑	DOWN ↓
Stress hormone production (ACTH, TTH, cortisol)	UP ↑	DOWN ↓
Brain-wave coherence	LOW	HIGH

While stress saps your vitality, the healing silence restores it. While stress causes physical and emotional strain, the healing silence neutralizes strain and increases inner ease and natural attunement. While stress lowers your resistance to disease, the healing silence raises it. While stress accelerates aging, the healing silence restores a youthful appearance and retards physical deterioration. Sleep is not enough to neutralize chronic stress because stress disturbs sleep, and even undisturbed sleep does not produce rest as complete as the healing silence. The healing silence also reduces tension and the other causes of insomnia, thereby restoring natural balance to your whole rest-activity cycle.

Silence and Your Emotional-Spiritual Well-being

When made a regular part of your daily routine, the experience of inner silence increases your capacities for adaptation and enjoyment. The physiological changes that neutralize the physical effects of stress also affect your emotional health. Consequently, the healing silence reduces stress-related emotional states such as anxiety, tension, irritability, chronic fatigue, and depression. The positive feelings that accompany the experience of the healing silence also contribute to personality development. Self-esteem grows, sociability develops, and doubts and insecurities fade.

To explain these effects, several researchers hypothesize that the healing silence permits the natural unconscious resolution of repressed traumas and conflicts. Two factors apparently contribute to this process. First, the extreme reduction in metabolic rate that accompanies the deep experience of the healing silence may allow a wholly physiological resolution of preverbal psychic conflict.[190,192] Second, should the conflict surface during meditation, the accompanying relaxation permits a natural desensitization to occur. The conflict gradually loses its anxiety-provoking character as it emerges against a background of physical relaxation and psychological security and well-being characteristic of the healing silence.[45,46,47]

The spiritual effects of the healing silence have received little scientific scrutiny, but they are evident in reports of increased inner harmony and feelings of wholeness among meditators. It is common to hear the healing silence associated with an expanded ability to love and appreciate, two important dimensions of spiritual growth. Meditators also report an increased feeling of self-worth, with a concomitant reduction of fear, envy, and jealousy, and growth of empathy and compassion. In addition to emotional sensitivity, meditation may also foster determination, purposefulness, and discrimination.

This comprehensive personal development seems to occur because the healing silence taps the strengths of the deepest core of the personality.

Meditators report that feelings of ease, security, vitality, and fulfillment accompany the experience of inner silence. Some people also report at times slipping into a state of awareness free from any thoughts, desires, or sensations. Sometimes referring to this state as "perfect silence," meditators describe it as limitless, blissful, and unchanging. Though these reports may suggest a trance state, there is no evidence that this experience is anything like a trance. On the contrary, in the laboratory, meditating subjects show signs of exceptional alertness and mental clarity incompatible with trance states.

Descriptions of this silence vary, but the following three reports contain recurring elements. A forty-two-year-old woman who has been meditating for two years says:

When I meditate after a long day at work, it's like going on a vacation. The worries of the day quickly fade as I get back in touch with the quiet place in my mind that I can always count on to restore, refresh, and revitalize me. Sure, thoughts come and go—the neighbor's whining dog, an anticipated promotion, what to cook for dinner—these and lots of other thoughts come and go, but underneath it all there is a deep tranquillity. It's like drifting on a rubber raft in the pool with the warm morning sun relaxing every muscle. I can just feel the life streaming into me and my spirits rising.

A fifty-six-year-old meditator of five years describes an even deeper silence:

When in full wakefulness, all inner activity comes to a stop, all thinking, all fantasy, all feelings, all images—everything, even the urge to think or to feel or to act—when all this stops on its own, without suppression, one thing remains—a vast, inner stillness, a clear peace, and the realization that this, at the very best, is how it feels to be simply alive.

A thirty-three-year-old, eight-year meditator added:

At certain points my sense of time and space entirely disappears. I lose awareness of my body and surroundings, and my breathing becomes so shallow that it almost seems to stop. The overwhelming feelings are security, peace, contentment, and a sense of vastness, an inner dimension of experience without any limits. I'm aware only of awareness itself—silence, full and unbounded—and in this stillness, this deep unfathomable quietness, there is the inescapable sense that this silence is the eternal, unchanging essence of my being.

These descriptions echo the testimony of mystics, philosophers, and sages who have lauded the healing silence throughout history. Today, however, scientific research has lifted the veil of mystic-religious ambiguity that has long obscured the healing silence. It is now evident that at least one reason why this experience has been esteemed throughout history is its enormous positive effect on health. We believe that current scientific research provides persuasive evidence that the healing silence can provide a firm foundation for achieving positive wellness.

How to Make the Healing Silence Part of Your Life

The time has come for you to start including the periodic experience of the healing silence in your daily routine. But how? There are many techniques, both ancient and modern, from which to choose. You can learn some from books, while mastering others requires personal instruction from a trained teacher. From the outset you should understand that the techniques vary considerably in their effectiveness. A given technique, especially one taught by a qualified instructor, may provide a deeper and more potent experience of inner silence than others. Nevertheless, nearly all techniques have some value for simple relaxation.

The easiest way to begin including more inner silence in your life is to close your eyes and relax for at least ten minutes once or twice a day. Harry Truman and Winston Churchill were but two of many world leaders who used brief rest periods of this sort to sustain their energy and vitality. For this procedure to be most effective, you should set aside a quiet period each day. All you need is a room where you won't be disturbed and a comfortable chair or sofa.

Positive imagery is often used to create a relaxed mood. Dr. Mike Samuels and Hal Bennett have developed a technique they call the *feeling pause*.[184] Again, you need a comfortable chair and a quiet environment. The technique is simple. They recommend that you sit down, take off your shoes, loosen your clothes, get comfortable, and do as follows:

1. Close your eyes and take three or four slow, deep breaths, preferably through your nose rather than mouth. Notice the soothing effect of the air filling your lungs, then flowing out through your nostrils.
2. Gently direct your attention to your toes and feel them relax. Let your attention glide slowly up your body—feet, ankles, calves, knees, thighs, hips, abdomen, back, chest, hands, arms, neck, face—and stop at each part to feel relaxation taking place. In this way, a warm heaviness will suffuse your entire body and you will become deeply relaxed.
3. Now imagine that you are floating on a peaceful, remote lake, or, if you prefer, far out in space. By letting your imagination go, you will be able to leave troublesome worries behind and enjoy a pleasant calm.
4. After ten minutes, come out of your reverie. Bring your attention back to your body, then slowly open your eyes. Take a few minutes to orient yourself. When ready, slowly get up.

Whereas the feeling pause relies on imagery and mood, another widely used relaxation technique works through systematic reduction of muscular tension. This technique, called Progressive Muscular Relaxation, was developed in the 1930s by Dr. Edmund Jacobson.[99] Today it is an important part of behavior therapy and is often recommended by psychotherapists for general relaxation. While the technique is best learned from an instructor, you can master it on your own. What distinguishes this technique from others is the careful attention you must pay to relaxing each major muscle group one by one. Jacobson taught that relaxing a particular muscle group required only three simple steps. In *You Must Relax,* he illustrates his technique by suggesting you try the following steps to relax your hand.

1. Clench your hand into a fist as hard as you can. Hold it for a few seconds and feel the tension. Noticing the tension is very important; it helps you become fully aware of the muscle.

2. Now let go. Let your hand relax. Feel the warmth and ease suffusing your palms and fingers.
3. Keep your attention on your hand muscles for another minute or two. Your awareness will help the relaxation deepen until your hand is completely relaxed.

Tension—release—awareness, these are the three basic components of Jacobson's technique. To relax your whole body, Jacobson recommends that you apply these three steps to the following muscle groups. Remember Jacobson's rule that each preceding muscle group must be fully relaxed before you go on to another:

—dominant hand and forearm
—dominant upper arm
—nondominant hand and forearm
—nondominant upper arm
—forehead
—eyes and nose
—cheeks and mouth
—neck and throat
—chest, back, and respiratory muscles
—abdomen
—dominant upper leg, calf, and foot
—nondominant upper leg, calf, and foot

The whole process should take between twenty to thirty minutes and can be practiced lying down as Jacobson recommends or sitting in a comfortable chair. Again a quiet environment is essential to avoid distractions. If the process seems tedious or boring, that's OK. Many people report this experience, but the technique can produce deep relaxation nevertheless. Many psychotherapists have found that the boring, tedious nature of progressive relaxation is a serious drawback because people stop doing it.[80,125] The key to long-term results is regular daily practice.

Cardiologist Herbert Benson has developed a summary derivative of various ancient and modern relaxation techniques. He believes that his technique, popularized through his book *The Relaxation Response,* is simpler than many others and can be mastered without the help of an instructor.[15] The technique he advocates involves four steps.

1. Sit comfortably in a quiet room.
2. Close your eyes.
3. Relax your muscles systematically, starting with your feet and working up to your head.
4. Repeat the word "one" (or any simple word or syllable you might choose) to yourself with each exhalation of breath.

Because Benson's technique is a composite of various meditation and relaxation techniques, it has become cause for controversy. Some experts in meditation question its effectiveness. While these criticisms will take time to explore in the laboratory, we have observed that the technique is evidently not as simple as claimed. Our observations suggest that perhaps as many as 80 percent of those people who have tried the technique report that after a while it no longer produces the relaxation they desire. However, some people do report benefits.

The oldest and we believe the most practical and effective technique for experiencing the healing silence is meditation. While there are many meditation techniques that you might learn, you should recognize that the techniques vary in important ways, such as the amount of time required for results, the ease of practice, and the availability of qualified instructors.

Meditation is traditionally considered a process that requires expert personal instruction for maximum benefit and understanding. If you have tried to learn a meditation technique from a book or magazine article and have been disappointed with the results, you should not be discouraged or surprised. Your experience is that of many and testifies to the age-old maxim that to learn to meditate properly you need a qualified teacher.

Among the various meditation techniques available, we recommend TM. Five reasons explain our preference.

- It is easy to learn and to practice.
- It is an ancient time-tested technique whose benefits have been well established through modern scientific research.

- Qualified teachers are widely available to teach the technique and provide necessary, supportive follow-up.
- Should you be interested, the full TM program, including regular follow-up and advanced courses, provides not just deep relaxation, but also unfolds your full potential for dynamic, successful living.
- Unlike most relaxation techniques, it can be practiced anywhere—on the subway, riding in a car or airplane, amidst noise or quiet. You don't become dependent on a particular environment to achieve the inner silence you need.

The TM technique has not been passed down through the centuries as a means of reducing high blood pressure or relieving insomnia. The holistic effects of the technique extend beyond those of muscular relaxation or a calm, soothing mood. The TM technique allows you to experience the deepest level of the healing silence, the nonchanging field of awareness that underlies all activity of the mind. This experience nourishes creativity, self-confidence, and self-worth. These effects take time, but they are important to long-term growth to positive wellness.

While enrolling in the TM program will cost you money, you may find that it will be money well spent. Our recommendation is to investigate carefully. You might first read one of several books written about the technique and its benefits.* Or you can attend an introductory lecture (no admission charge) at your local TM center; the address and telephone number are in your local telephone directory.

In the next chapter, we will begin explaining how to design a holistic health program to help you resolve specific complaints and to progress toward positive wellness. It should be clear at this point that we believe maximum success in following your program depends on regular experience of the healing silence.

---

* Our books, *TM: Discovering Inner Energy and Overcoming Stress* (New York, Dell, $1.95) and *HAPPINESS* (New York, Pocket Books, $1.95), as well as *The Transcendental Meditation Program*, by Jack Forem (New York, Bantam, $1.95), are widely available.

7. How to Design Your Own Holistic Health Program

Now you are ready to begin permanently solving those common health problems that keep you from enjoying your full measure of vitality and well-being. These problems include:

—smoking
—overeating and overweight
—inadequate exercise and poor physical fitness
—excessive drinking
—high blood pressure
—chronic fatigue, low energy, lack of vigor
—low-grade depression, the "blues"
—worry, tension, anxiety
—insomnia, a disturbed rest-activity cycle
—low self-esteem, lack of self-confidence
—sexual dysfunction
—lack of meaning, spiritual malaise

Even if you suffer from eight, nine, or more of these problems, take heart. You will still be able to design a step-by-step plan that will help you make substantial progress toward positive wellness.

At this point, you may be saying to yourself, "I've tried to give up smoking [or lose weight, stop worrying, etc.] before, and none of my efforts have worked."

Our response is, "Congratulations on your honesty. Your willingness to see yourself honestly is half the battle in the programs we will outline."

Solving everyday health problems isn't easy; at times it can be slow, demanding, or tedious. A measure of self-discipline will be just as necessary to the strategies we will outline as to any other you may have tried. This time, however, there will be a critical difference. The healing silence will give you the full support of nature in your efforts. Without this help, you would require enormous willpower and motivation to adopt our recommendations and would therefore probably benefit little. But if you draw on the healing silence, you should soon find yourself feeling better than you have in years and without suffering the frustration so often part of other health improvement plans.

It Can Work for You

We are confident that our strategies will work for you because they were developed through our experience with patients at the Center for Holistic Health in San Diego, California, as well as that of experts at other health centers worldwide. Our center was established in 1974 to meet the need for professional health care that treats disease with the best of modern medical therapeutics but goes on to help patients achieve positive wellness through the holistic approach. Since we opened our doors, we have been very active and now treat hundreds of clients annually. With our recent expansion, our professional staff includes three physicians, a psychiatrist, a clinical psychologist, and a director of research. Additional staff including nurses, a social worker, physical therapists, and wellness resource guides helps us provide a wide range of services. Among these services are:

—the Holistic Health Survey
—comprehensive medical and psychiatric evaluation
—modern medical therapeutics
—traditional and growth-oriented psychotherapy
—physiotherapy and massage
—nutritional counseling and optimal weight program
—life enrichment and physical fitness classes *
—the Transcendental Meditation program

* These classes range in their goals from helping participants eliminate specific negative habits to improving overall fitness and developing a more active and enjoyable life-style. We often refer clients to outside groups such as Alcoholics Anonymous, Lamaze, Make Today Count, Parent Effectiveness Training, Sierra Club, and Smok-Enders.

A Visit to a Holistic Health Center

Understanding the basic steps you would follow were you to visit a holistic health center will be helpful in designing your own health improvement plan. Soon holistic health centers will be operating throughout the country; currently, you will find them primarily in California and many large cities, including Boston, New York, and Chicago. Because you may be hundreds of miles from the nearest center, we will use a case history to help you visualize the steps involved in the holistic approach.

When you think of a health center, images of stark examining rooms, doctors in white coats, X-ray machines, and other elaborate equipment probably come to mind. When you visit a holistic health center, the sophisticated equipment is there, but the feeling is very different. The atmosphere is warm, the staff is friendly, and the tone is relaxed and open rather than cold and formal. You are meant to feel at home, not as if you were entering an alien world. This warm tone helps you recognize from the outset that you play a more important role than your doctor in maintaining and improving your health. You are expected to ask questions, express your feelings, and play an active role in your treatment.

Your first task at the center would be to complete the Holistic Health Survey, which gives you and the medical staff a broad picture of your medical history, health habits, current complaints, and overall level of wellness. This survey includes the standard items in a conventional medical history (i.e., childhood illnesses, family medical history, etc.) in addition to an extensive series of questions unique to a holistic medical evaluation. These items include questions about your occupational satisfaction and environment, physical exercise habits, rest-activity cycles, nutrition, social behavior, personal and household care, and environmental awareness. (A sampling of these questions is listed in Appendix I.) After completing this survey, you would see your primary care physician for a physical exam and a discussion of the survey results. Your doctor may then begin formulating a health improvement plan with you, or he or she may recommend additional tests such as blood and urine analyses or the Minnesota Multiphasic Personality Inventory (MMPI) to aid in physical and /or psychological diagnosis.

Holistic and conventional medicine begin with many of the same diagnostic procedures, but holistic medicine goes beyond conventional medicine. The holistically oriented physician wants you to feel "great," not just "OK." The practical differences between the two approaches are best illustrated with a case history. We have chosen one that is very common and particularly suited to the holistic approach.

Dorothy

When Dorothy, an attractive thirty-three-year-old housewife, first visited our center, the Holistic Health Survey, an initial interview, a physical exam, and an MMPI gave a clear picture of her health status. She sought our help primarily because her long-standing feelings of depression and insecurity had intensified and were disrupting her second marriage. Since early childhood, she had been troubled by feelings of insecurity, which tended to make her shy and somewhat withdrawn. Her inability to form close friendships undermined her self-esteem and self-confidence. Despite her obvious intelligence and charm, she felt unattractive, incapable, and "not like the kind of person anyone would want to get to know, much less love." Lacking the confidence and initiative to make friends, she had few and depended heavily on her husband. In addition to these emotional symptoms, she suffered from migraine headaches, cold feet and hands (Raynaud's phenomenon), and a long history of gastrointestinal sensitivity.

Dorothy felt that her life "was not going anywhere" and that her husband was getting tired of her. Her husband's work as an airline pilot often required that he be away from home, and his absences became a critical focus for her feelings of self-doubt. Every time he left on a trip, she slipped into an emotional tailspin of worry, "the blues," and crying spells. When he returned, she felt better, but this respite lasted only until his next trip. With no friends or family from whom to draw support, her periodic depressions grew steadily worse, making her more and more difficult to live with and putting increasing pressure on her husband, who in fact loved her deeply. With her deepening emotional distress, her physical symptoms grew worse. Migraines, frequent colds, and "freezing" hands often kept her at home, thereby adding to her feelings of isolation and low self-regard. Though her personal and household care remained excellent (indicating that she was not severely depressed), she rarely participated in any sport or exercise program, and her rest-activity cycle was disturbed by sleeping problems.

The conventional diagnosis of Dorothy's illness is depressive neurosis, and the conventional treatment is antidepressant medication along with individual psychotherapy. The shortcoming of this treatment, evident in thousands of patients, is that it rarely results in permanent relief; the depressions and concomitant psychosomatic symptoms recur cyclically. With appropriate medication and psychotherapy, the patient will get through a period of depression and may function well for a few weeks, months, or even years. Eventually, however, something—a failure at work, a fight at home, or even a bout of the flu—taxes the person's emotional resources enough to precipitate another period of depression, which again can be "gotten through" with appropriate treatment.

Because Dorothy was quite depressed when she first visited our center, her initial treatment consisted of antidepressant medication and individual psychotherapy, but we were not satisfied with merely continuing that treatment and pinning a label (depressive neurosis) on her complaints. From a holistic standpoint, we viewed Dorothy's depressions as the expression of imbalances in her total physical-emotional-spiritual functioning. Her low self-esteem indicated a deep emotional distress that had disrupted her ability to appraise herself. This distress contributed to an emotional-physical imbalance resulting in migraine headaches, a disturbed rest-activity cycle, and her other somatic symptoms. Her lack of friends and social contact also indicated an imbalance with her social environment. All these factors were interrelated and mutually reinforcing. For example, her self-contempt contributed to her migraines, which in turn triggered more feelings of worthlessness. Her physical symptoms added to her difficulties in making friends, thus lowering her already poor self-regard.

To raise Dorothy's level of total wellness, we devised a team treatment program that addressed each of the principle imbalances in her health. This program was designed for her step-by-step participation, accommodating her own rate of growth. Because her depressive crisis obstructed any immediate attempts to resolve her deeper imbalances, getting her out of that crisis with medication and individual psychotherapy was the first priority. After six weeks of weekly psychotherapy and moderate antidepressant medication, her depression began to lift. Her crying spells subsided and she was once again recognizing her positive qualities and potential for a productive, happy life. These feelings signaled her readiness for the next stage, which involved experiencing the healing silence.

At her doctor's recommendation, she and her husband began the TM program. This was a critically important step. Psychotherapy could help her improve her self-appraisal, but it alone could not resolve the deep emotional distress that fueled her poor self-esteem. By bathing her childhood conflicts and stresses in the healing silence, she mobilized the natural healing forces capable of resolving her deep-seated emotional distress. This inner silence allowed her emotional wounds to begin healing just as naturally as the body heals a physical wound, without the need for prolonged intellectual exploration of these deep stresses through psychotherapy.

In the first month after beginning the TM program, Dorothy reported that she had never felt better in her life. But she soon hit a plateau and began feeling discouraged with her progress. She could not help noticing, however, that despite her discouragement she was not slipping into another depressive crisis. Her anxiety, crying spells, and despair had all diminished substantially. Throughout this period, psychotherapy was important to help her understand the ups and downs in the growth process and improve her self-appraisal.

When it became clear several months later that she was established in the TM program, we started treating her imbalance with her social environment. She took assertive training classes and began couples therapy. With the healing silence stimulating and stabilizing her overall development, it did not take many sessions before she was discovering her social self and making new friends. She started working part-time and taking two courses at a local college. Each success in getting out on her own and enjoying other people boosted her self-esteem. A few months later she asked to begin a program (to which she had been quite resistant) for correcting her physical imbalances. She had long since started sleeping better, but she needed a thermal biofeedback program to reduce her migraine headaches and attacks of "freezing hands." She also took advantage of a massage and exercise program to reduce muscle tension and improve her physical fitness.

Sixteen months after her initial visit, Dorothy had completed a holistic health program that included individual psychotherapy, medication, couples therapy, assertive training classes, thermal biofeedback, life enrichment classes, massage, and exercise. Along with these treatment modalities, Dorothy continued her regular experience of the healing silence. In a short time she had grown from a very depressed woman troubled by physical complaints and cut off from her social environment to a happy person enthusiastic about living. Visits to our health center were gradually reduced as Dorothy came to realize that the most important health center is within.

Do's and Don'ts of Designing Your Own Program

There are seven important principles that you must keep in mind in formulating your own health improvement plan.

- Take responsibility for your health. Don't just stay home and complain if you have symptoms, feel "blah," or know that you're not fully healthy. Complaining puts tremendous pressure on those around you and makes you hard to live with.
- Your program to achieve positive wellness must move one step at a time. You can't solve all your health problems at once. Have patience; with a well-designed plan, your total wellness will grow steadily. On the other hand, trying to do too much too soon is a sure way to meet failure and frustration.
- Establish priorities. Some health problems are more damaging than others. Your doctor is the best person to help you decide which health problems to address first.
- Integrate your own efforts to raise your level of wellness with your doctor's care and advice. If you have any of the symptoms listed on pages 25–26, you may be seriously ill and should see your doctor as soon as possible. Your doctor's help is essential in diagnosing and treating high blood pressure, an illness that you may be unaware of. He or she can also help you with chronic depression. You should consult your doctor before starting a fitness or a weight reduction program.
- Enlist the support of family members in your program. No one can more quickly undermine a health improvement program than an uncooperative spouse. On the other hand, the whole

family can participate in a program to achieve positive wellness. This will increase harmony and help open channels of communication among family members. One way to begin a family program is to have everyone read this book.

- Recognize and accept the fact that plateaus will occur. The body does not readjust its functioning in a smooth and continuous fashion. It proceeds through a series of stages until normal functioning is re-established. At each stage, there is a period, sometimes long and other times short, when no change appears to be taking place. Don't be discouraged—these plateaus are natural. Stay on your program. Soon you will again see pounds melting, blood pressure dropping, your vitality increasing, worry lessening, and so on.

- Be regular in your twice-daily experience of the healing silence. With the steady improvement in your feelings of well-being and enjoyment of living, you may soon feel that you don't need to take the time for inner silence. This is a serious mistake. Stress is a constant part of everyday living. With all the pressures you face, you owe it to yourself to take time (even on your busiest days) that is really all your own, a brief interlude with the sole purpose of nourishing your body, mind, and spirit.

The Role of the Healing Silence

We and others have conducted clinical research on the role of the healing silence in health programs. We have reached several major conclusions.

1. The healing silence is among the best available treatments for the relief and prevention of everyday stress and strain. It has been estimated that stress and tension play a role in the symptoms of nearly 80 percent of all people seeking help from their family doctors. When you complain of headache, insomnia, anxiety, or any number of other common health problems, and your doctor finds no evidence of serious illness, you both face a serious dilemma. You clearly need relief, and mild medication (along with some advice about taking it easy) may help; however, your doctor knows that medication will only mask and not relieve the underlying causes of your symptoms. The healing silence, on the other hand, gives your

body's healing mechanisms a unique opportunity to resolve the stresses underlying your complaints. It helps you cope with and ultimately rid yourself of the effects of everyday stress and strain. Unlike tranquilizers and sedatives, the healing silence is natural and therefore when properly applied has no negative side effects such as slurred speech, drowsiness, and nausea.

2. The more serious psychosomatic disorders—hypertension, bronchial asthma, ulcerative colitis, rheumatoid arthritis, and so on—require expert conventional medical care, and appropriate medication is usually essential to effective treatment. From a holistic medical perspective, however, the healing silence can play two important roles. First, it may contribute directly to improvement in these conditions. We have seen the healing silence help in normalizing blood pressure, alleviating chronic insomnia, reducing asthmatic symptoms, easing the irritable colon, and decreasing allergic reactions. Second, it may serve as a natural "vaccine" against recurring psychosomatic illnesses. If you have a psychosomatic disorder, you are familiar with the cyclical exacerbation of your condition. When the pressures of living are mild, so are your symptoms. But if pressures at work or at home increase, the troublesome symptoms reappear, only to add more stress to an already tension-filled situation. The healing silence short-circuits this cycle by increasing your capacity to cope with pressure.

3. To the extent that inner silence mobilizes healing processes throughout the body, it is also useful in the treatment of what are considered purely organic illnesses—from simple sore throats to recovery from an acute pneumonia. The healing silence allows your body to concentrate its energies and resources on fighting infection and repairing tissue. At our center we have found that patients who practice the TM program recover faster from respiratory infections, sore throats, and other common illnesses than those who do not. This is especially true if the patient sick enough to require bed rest meditates as much as is comfortable in addition to the two regular meditation periods.

4. A substantial number of the people visiting our center want help with emotional rather than physical problems. The intensity of their complaints ranges from what may be called problems of living—mild anxiety, low-grade depression, worry, boredom, and simple discontent—to acute emotional illnesses such as psychotic

depression, manic-depressive illness, and schizophrenia. Though evidence indicates that the healing silence can be useful in treating this whole range of disorders, it is particularly helpful in relieving mild emotional distress. People with so-called "problems of living" usually get very little out of psychotherapy because their emotional distress is rooted in the chronic tension of everyday living rather than in deep-seated psychological conflicts. We have found that these problems are alleviated not through a tedious probing of the psyche, but through a direct experience of ease and inner well-being that allows the psychoemotional system to regain its natural harmony. The healing silence effectively provides this experience.

5. We have observed that the healing silence has a significant impact on our clients' abilities to change destructive patterns of living and adopt healthy ones. This effect undoubtedly has many causes, including:

—decreased tension that fuels habits such as smoking and over-eating
—increased sensitivity to the noxious aspects of unhealthy living habits
—increased interest in health that accompanies generally heightened well-being
—increased willpower
—increased autonomy and self-sufficiency, decreased dependency on "crutches" of all sorts
—increased sensitivity to your real needs

In summary, the healing silence can help you solve some specific health problems, while serving as a foundation for your holistic health improvement plan.

PART III

Strategies for a Better Life

I have heard that in ancient times human beings lived to the age of a hundred. In our time, we are exhausted at the age of fifty. Is this because of changes in the circumstances, or is it the fault of men?
—SU WEN
From the *Nei Ching*, oldest ex-
tant medical text, circa 4500 B.C.

Your every separate action should contribute to an integrated life.
—MARCUS AURELIUS

8. The Life You Save Will Be Your Own

The evidence that life habits play a critical role in the genesis of nearly all major modern illnesses is overwhelming. So if you want a long, healthy life with maximum vitality and optimum functioning, you must develop sound health habits. Unfortunately several living habits that destroy health and well-being are ingrained in our culture. Among these habits are smoking, overeating, high fat and cholesterol consumption, excessive drinking, speeding, driving after drinking, and inadequate exercise and/or rest.

Why do people persist in life-threatening behavior? The simple answer is that people enjoy their cigarettes, high-cholesterol meals, and double martinis too much to give them up for the promise of better health and a half-dozen extra years of life. In addition to providing immediate sensory gratification, these habits exert a particularly strong pull on your behavior because they have become ingrained in your personality over a period of years. And many of these habits (such as smoking or overeating) may meet basic psychological needs for tension reduction, security, stimulation, and so on. If these needs go unfulfilled, you may feel irritable, anxious, or even depressed.

This in no way means that all habitual behavior is a sign of psychological weakness or immaturity. Habits such as tying your shoes, brushing your teeth, and driving safely, allow you to perform routine tasks without wasting time and mental energy. They free your mind from mundane concerns, thus increasing your vitality and creativity. Habits originate in your needs and provide a degree of enjoyment. This cycle of need-enjoyment is what makes habits both highly functional and very resistant to change.

A New Strategy for Better Health Habits

In the past you have probably tried the two most common methods for changing habits:

—avoiding the behavior through willpower alone
—breaking the habit cycle by reducing the enjoyment you derive from it.

You can forget these approaches right now—they don't work. Willpower is all too often in short supply when the craving for a cigarette or a second helping of dessert is the strongest. And it is almost impossible to block your enjoyment of a cigarette by telling yourself about the health risks of smoking.

In the next sections we will present a new strategy for improving your health habits. In each section we will review the principal cause of a specific habit pattern or troublesome complaint. Then we will present one or two case histories to illustrate how you can free yourself from destructive habits and bothersome symptoms of stress through a holistic health program. We will outline specific steps you can follow to focus your growth on the resolution of specific health problems.

You will succeed because you will enjoy every step along the way. You may find this surprising because, like most people, you may believe that attaining and maintaining health is difficult and tedious— eating vegetables you don't like, doing exercises you find boring, and denying yourself a cigarette that you crave. But a holistic program will cause your tastes, desires, and anxiety level to change. Dependency will lessen and autonomy increase. This growth will make it not just easier but actually enjoyable to follow a strategy aimed at increasing your level of wellness.

Another critically important element in success is timing. No matter what we, your friends, or your doctor might say, it really doesn't matter (unless you are now very ill) when you lose weight, quit smoking, start exercising, or solve any of your everyday health problems. You can start today, next month, or next year. The important thing is that when you do focus on a specific health problem, you succeed in resolving it permanently.

With this idea in mind, you should not be in a hurry to start tackling your health problems. You should begin to work on a particular health problem only when you have a clear and strong desire to end it forever. Guilt or worry should play no part in your decision. A health improvement program motivated by worry or guilt will soon be derailed; frustration and self-recrimination will be the only results. Your only motivation should be increasing your enjoyment of living and pleasing yourself. If, for example, you don't honestly feel that losing weight will increase your enjoyment of living, then don't start our weight reduction program. It's as simple as that. The same principle applies to each of our strategies for solving your health problems.

Growth takes place in small, steady increments. If you focus on enjoying each small step rather than agonizing about the final destination, you'll arrive at your goal before you know it. This is essential to success in your holistic health program. You can't expect to achieve positive wellness by punishing yourself, so get this attitude out of your mind. Once you start enjoying each step of progress, the whole program becomes self-reinforcing. The discovery of new pleasures at each step keeps you going. You'll soon pick up momentum, and progress will become easier. Of course, you may have trouble getting started, so you'll have to put out some extra effort in the beginning. But soon the various elements in your program (i.e., running, meditation, better nutrition, and so on) will start having their complementary effects; benefits will begin to appear in many areas of your life at once, and you'll be well on the way to positive wellness. Let's look at some strategies for a better life.

9. Natural, Easy Weight Reduction

Losing excess pounds and then maintaining your ideal weight can be enjoyable!

If you are among the forty million obese Americans (20 percent or more overweight) or one of the additional eighty million more who carry only ten or fifteen extra pounds, this statement may seem hard to believe. For you, *dieting* and *enjoyment* are probably antithetical concepts. But losing weight *can* be pleasurable. The secret is simple: you must increase your natural sensitivity to the unpleasant effects of overeating and the enjoyable rewards of eating according to your real needs.

For most people, the struggle against overweight begins as a skirmish around age twenty-five but escalates into full-scale war by age forty. Two facts make this battle so difficult. First, between age twenty-five and forty-five, your caloric requirement for maintaining good health and a stable weight *drops* from 10 to 20 percent. Between ages forty-five and sixty-five, it drops another 20 percent. Second, our culture brainwashes you into eating even when you don't feel hungry.

This brainwashing began early in your life when your parents, concerned about proper nutrition, insisted that you clean your plate despite your protests. Soon you learned that eating brought approval; so you ate even when you weren't hungry. Later you became habituated to eating to have fun at most social occasions. Going to a party or the movies or just staying home to watch TV with family or friends involved eating, not just to the point of satisfying your hunger, but often to the very borderline of indigestion and sometimes well beyond (e.g., stuffing yourself and not just the turkey at Thanksgiving).

Today, you are bombarded by radio and TV advertisements telling you that you are not really enjoying yourself without a potato chip, a soda, or a beer in your hand.

Those two facts, your decreasing need for food and cultural brainwashing about eating, explain the creeping weight gain that inevitably leads to obesity. If you continue at age thirty-five to eat the same amount as when you were twenty-five, you will gain at least three pounds per year. Your weight gain will continue steadily until you cut down on your food intake, or (more likely) increase your calorie need to carry around your extra poundage. When you notice that your clothes fit too snugly because you are carrying ten or fifteen extra pounds, you have two choices. You may adjust your food intake and increase your exercise, or you may continue in your old eating pattern while your body demands less and less food each year. Remember that the path of creeping obesity is paved with resolutions such as, "I'm only fifteen pounds too heavy, I can take it off any time I want." The hooker is that if you don't do something about those first fifteen pounds, you'll probably be thirty pounds too heavy when it finally dawns on you that you've gotten fat. To paraphrase an old proverb, an ounce of weight reduction now can save you struggling with pounds later!

A mistake too often made by people anxious to reduce is a hasty attempt to start the latest diet. We caution you against treating our program this way because we don't want you to suffer another frustration. At the outset you should realize that people respond differently to the same program and may lose at different rates. You must tailor our program to suit your needs and have confidence and patience.

You must also make sure that your weight problem is suitable to the self-help approach. If you are 30 percent or more overweight and one or both of your parents have had lifelong weight problems, we suggest you consult your doctor. You may have a strong genetic predisposition to overweight, such as an abnormally high percentage of fat cells, and require a highly structured weight loss program. If you have been overweight since childhood but under 30 percent, then you may also need a special program, but everything we say still applies to you. You will simply have to make a greater effort than the person battling middle-age spread. You will also have to be vigilant about your weight for the rest of your life. One further caution is necessary. If you suffer from a major medical disorder such as kidney disease, a heart ailment, or an underactive thyroid, you should also consult your doctor before undertaking any weight reduction program.

The Secret of Weight Control

The decision to lose weight or remain plump is yours. You may enjoy yourself as you are. A little extra weight is highly esteemed in many cultures. If you are happy with your weight, go ahead and enjoy it as long as you do not get dangerously obese (30 percent overweight or more). Unless you have firmly decided that you want to lose weight and stay thin the rest of your life, your efforts at weight reduction will probably be unsuccessful. The resulting frustration and weight fluctuations will be more harmful to you than remaining at a heavy but stable weight. On the other hand, if you do want to lose weight, read on.

The human body has a built-in mechanism for regulating its food intake. When you need energy (i.e., calories from food), you feel hunger pangs. This biological mechanism, believed to be in the hypothalamus, is often called an *appestat*. It signals—with hunger pangs and satiety feelings—when to eat and when to stop eating. If you maintain a stable weight, your appestat is helping you gradually reduce your food intake each year. If you are on the path of creeping weight gain, you have become insensitive to your appestat or have rendered it inefficient.

Once you have lost this sensitivity, you won't know when you are really hungry. You eat not only when you are hungry, but also whenever you feel bored, tired, or anxious, or whenever you watch television or go out with friends. You may frequently eat to the point of feeling stuffed. Just satisfying your hunger, which often takes only a small amount of food, isn't enough; you've got to have that good, solid, full feeling before you can push yourself away from the table.

Having lost this sensitivity, you also weaken your ability to handle the mild hunger feelings that accompany any restriction of food intake. Eating has become a reflex response to so many feelings that the slightest hunger becomes a disproportionately strong stimulus.

Mild hunger combined with mild boredom, mild anxiety, mild fatigue, or any other mildly unpleasant feeling develops into a major impulse—you have to get something to eat.

To lose weight easily and maintain your ideal weight comfortably, you must regain your natural sensitivity to your appestat. This is the secret of weight control. No matter how overweight you may be, you can regain sensitivity to your appestat. By restoring your natural sensitivity to food intake, you will achieve the single most important step in breaking your habit of overeating. You will discover (or rediscover) that overeating is unpleasant, and eating just to the point of satisfying your hunger is enjoyable. You will also realize that feeling slightly hungry is far more conducive to your full enjoyment of living than being constantly full.

How do you reattune yourself to your appestat? You can use willpower. At the dinner table, simply force yourself to have only one small serving of each dish. You may not feel full, but you won't be hungry—an important distinction you have to learn. If, two hours after dinner, you think you are hungry, you should eat one-half of an apple. This should satisfy your hunger; eat no more. Again, you may not feel satisfied at first, but eventually you will discover that half an apple is a satisfying snack. If you keep up this discipline for three or four months, you will gradually reawaken your sensitivity to your appestat.

Sound difficult? Even hopeless? It probably is. For all but the exceptional person, willpower alone will never work. The habits you have acquired through years of overeating are almost certainly more than a match for your willpower. But there is another way.

The healing silence enhances your sensitivity to the natural rhythms of your life. An integral part of this process is a growing awareness of your real needs, including your need for food. In other words, the healing silence increases your sensitivity to your appestat in a completely natural and effortless way.

We have found that moderately overweight clients in treatment for nonweight-related problems often lose a significant amount of weight within a year after beginning the TM program. In some cases, this loss occurs without conscious effort by the individual. We have also found that the healing silence can significantly enhance an obese person's ability to succeed at a weight reduction program. Individuals who have struggled to lose weight in the past discover that they can reduce and maintain their new weights. Several cases will help shed light on this process.

How the Healing Silence Helps

Joan is a forty-one-year-old housewife who sought medical attention for a sore throat. Her initial examination revealed borderline hypertension and obesity. At 5' 4" tall and 154 pounds, she carried an extra thirty-five pounds of fat and was almost 30 percent overweight. A year later she had lost thirty-eight pounds. She explains:

> Ever since our second child was born I had become a big snacker. I don't know whether it was boredom, fatigue, or tension that kept me going at the potato chips and pretzels, but I ate them all day long. Six months after I began TM for my blood pressure, my doctor asked if I wanted to reduce. I took it as a good omen because I had had the same idea for several days. I went home, thought about it, and came back for a weight reduction plan. Today, I'm really surprised how I've changed, especially since I had failed on every diet I'd ever tried. This time, I was able to see my compulsive eating for what it was. I guess I was just ready to lose, because it wasn't a struggle at all.

Ted is thirty-four, 5' 10", and weighed 172 pounds, or about twenty pounds too much. The effect of the healing silence on his weight is typical.

> Twenty-eight was the critical year for me. I started to gain and before I knew it, I was in the stratosphere above 170. My suits had to be let out and I had to buy pants with larger waistlines. I didn't like it but I also lacked motivation to diet. I'd never dieted and hated the idea. Anyway, I started TM for relaxation. One benefit that I didn't expect was a change in my eating habits. I started saying no at the table because I didn't like feeling stuffed. It fogged my brain and made me uncomfortable. I also lost my hunger between meals, which I suspect was really nervousness, and stopped snacking. One other factor in my weight loss was probably my getting back to tennis. All this is in retrospect, so I can't really explain it. What I do know is that I'm back down to 156 and I didn't even try.

Ted lost sixteen pounds in seven months, an impressive loss considering that he was not trying to control his food intake.

An accountant, Sam is fifty-two and had been thirty to thirty-five pounds overweight for the last twenty years. He sought our help specifically for weight reduction.

> I've tried every diet, you name it, high-protein, liquid, even fasting, but I just couldn't stay on them. My problem was that I'd cheat and try to convince myself I wasn't. My first mistake was skipping breakfast; I never was a breakfast eater until recently. Then I'd have a small lunch. Dinner would be reasonable with no dessert. Up to that point, I'd think I was doing fine; then the clock would strike eleven, and I'd become Mr. Hyde. I'd make my way to the fridge, stand there and eat anything. Next I'd take something "small" back to my den, maybe a piece of pie because I was so good all day. Then I'd go get another to help me stay awake while I worked. By the time I went to bed, I had resolved to skip breakfast and lunch the next day to make up for my excesses. Actually, I wouldn't be hungry in the morning anyway. But once I made the TM technique part of my life, my whole eating pattern changed. I started having breakfast, lunch, and dinner. My nightly urge to gorge gradually faded. It took some willpower, but soon it was gone. I lost twenty-eight pounds in four months, and I've finally won the battle of the bulge.

Four effects of the healing silence appear to be most significant in weight reduction.

• Increased sensitivity to the appestat helps in distinguishing real hunger from boredom, fatigue, tension, and other feelings that often lead to overeating.

• Generally increased feelings of inner harmony along with a reduction of fatigue, anxiety, and stress tend to strengthen the will and the ability to restrict food intake.

• Heightened natural attunement increases sensitivity to the negative effects of overeating such as drowsiness, a sluggish mind, and a heavy stomach.

• Growing well-being fosters an active orientation to living. The sedentary person tends to rediscover the joy of physical activity and starts exercising. The chronic snacker learns to cope with boredom through creative self-expression—writing, gardening, music lessons, sports, etc.—rather than sitting passively in front of the tube and munching.

A Step-by-Step Weight Reduction Plan

The first key to success in weight reduction is not to start before you are ready. If you have been heavy for years, another few months won't matter. You should give yourself ample time to begin enjoying the benefits of the healing silence. Once you notice a reduction in your anxiety level, an increase in your energy, and a general improvement in your sense of well-being, then you are ready to go ahead. You won't have to force yourself to start the program; your desire to begin will grow naturally from within. This inner commitment is very important and cannot be forced or intellectually manufactured. So go ahead and enjoy the healing silence and eat all you want until you decide that you are going to win the battle of the waistline once and for all.

When you have decided, there are many good food intake plans you can follow. We do not recommend those that restrict your choice of food. This approach makes weight reduction unpleasant and boring, two effects that can quickly lead to failure. Our plan involves five basic steps and incorporates what we have found to be the best elements of various good plans. Before you begin our weight reduction program, you should consult your doctor to make sure there are no medical reasons why you should not reduce.

STEP 1. Are you overweight? You can best determine whether or not you are overweight by using yourself, not a weight table or a fashion ideal, as a standard. Take off your clothes and look at yourself in a full-length mirror. Are you pleased? If so, then you don't need to lose weight, even if the tables say you do. But if you are too thick around the middle, in the thighs, or on the buttocks, or have rolls of flesh on your body, then you should lose weight. You can verify your conclusion with the "inch of pinch" test. Using your thumb and forefinger, pinch up your skin at the back of your upper arm, your waist, your buttocks, and your thigh. If you can pinch up more than an inch of flesh anywhere, then you should probably reduce.

If you've decided that you should reduce, you must now determine your desirable weight. This will be your goal. One way is to recall what you weighed at age twenty-five. If you weren't overweight then, you should return to that weight and maintain it for the rest of your life. But maybe you were overweight at twenty-five or at fifteen for that matter. If so, a weight table can be helpful.* Notice that the following table gives a range of weights for each height and body-build category. Even among people of the same height and build, ideal weight varies.

MEN

Height in Shoes (1" heels)	Weight in Pounds (In Indoor Clothing)		
	Small Frame	Medium Frame	Large Frame
5' 2"	112-120	118-129	126-141
3"	115-124	121-133	129-144
4"	118-126	124-136	132-148
5"	121-129	127-139	135-152
6"	124-133	130-143	138-156
7"	128-137	134-147	142-161
8"	132-141	138-152	147-166
9"	136-145	142-156	151-170
10"	140-150	146-160	155-174
11"	144-154	150-165	159-179
6' 0"	148-158	154-170	164-184
1"	152-162	158-175	168-189
2"	156-167	162-180	173-194
3"	160-171	167-185	178-199
4"	164-175	172-190	182-204

WOMEN

Height in Shoes (2" heels)	Weight in Pounds (In Indoor Clothing)		
	Small Frame	Medium Frame	Large Frame
4'10"	92- 98	96-107	104-119
11"	94-101	98-110	106-122
5' 0"	96-104	101-113	109-125
1"	99-107	104-116	112-128
2"	102-110	107-119	115-131
3"	105-113	110-122	118-134
4"	108-116	113-126	121-138
5"	111-119	116-130	125-142
6"	114-123	120-135	129-146
7"	118-127	124-139	133-150
8"	122-131	128-143	137-154
9"	126-135	132-147	141-158
10"	130-140	136-151	145-163
11"	134-144	140-155	149-168
6' 0"	138-148	144-159	153-173

* This table is adapted from the 1960 Metropolitan Life Insurance study of over-weight.

Now you have set your goal. If you have fifteen, fifty, or a hundred pounds to lose, it can be done without a struggle. Before you go on, write down your present weight and your goal and take nude measurements of your chest (at your nipples), your midsection (at your navel), and your hips (at your hip joint). Watching yourself lose inches as well as pounds reinforces motivation.

STEP 2. How fast do you want to lose? Overnight, of course! Though you can't reduce that quickly, the next best thing is to establish a plan whereby you lose weight steadily but hardly feel you're trying.

To lose weight you must force your body to draw on its fat stores for energy. Nutritionists measure your energy needs in terms of the *calorie* (the amount of energy needed to raise one gram of water one degree Centigrade). You can estimate your daily calorie need from the following table.

Daily Calorie Need per Pound of Body Weight

Infants	0–3 years	40–50
Children and teens	4–19 years	30–40
Adults	20–65 years	18–30
Elderly	65 years and up	10–18

Though these figures are averages and vary depending on your level of activity and rate of metabolism, they can give you a rough idea of your calorie needs. For example, if you are thirty years old and weigh 130 pounds, you need roughly 2,600 calories each day to maintain your weight. If you eat more, you will gain; if you eat less, you will reduce.

Fat is very rich in energy. Each pound of body fat contains 3,500 calories. If you consume 500 calories less than you expend each day, then you will lose one pound of fat per week ($7 \times 500 = 3500$).

Another way to produce a calorie deficit is to increase your calorie expenditure through exercise. The table on page 108 lists several activities that will force your body to burn 100 calories.

We suggest that you use both methods in designing your weight reduction plan. For example, you can increase your energy need by 200 calories daily and decrease your food intake by 500 calories. The result will be a deficit of 700 calories each day, or 4,900 per week—

Activity	Minutes
Walking	20
Tennis	14
Gardening	20
Bowling	22
Swimming	9
Washing, showering, shaving	31
Running	7

in other words, a weekly weight loss of almost one and one-half pounds.

It's evident that how fast you reduce is up to you. We strongly recommend, however, that you do not try to lose more than two pounds per week. In other words, you should not try to produce a calorie deficit of more than 1,000 per day. We also recommend that you not expect to increase your energy need by more than 200 calories daily; more is unrealistic.

We have found that a reduction in food intake of 600 calories and an exercise plan that increases energy need by 200 calories make for effective and relatively easy weight loss. You won't find it strenuous or restrictive, and you will lose at least six pounds per month. And if you exercise more, you will reduce more quickly.

Now take a large piece of graph paper and draw two coordinates. Write your desired weight at the bottom of the vertical axis. Add two pounds to your goal and write this weight on the first line across the vertical axis. Continue up the vertical axis, recording weight in two-pound increments, until you reach your present weight. Next divide the amount of weight you have to lose by the number of pounds you plan to lose each week. This will tell you how long it will take to achieve your desired weight. For example, if you have thirty pounds to lose and you plan to lose one and one-half pounds weekly, it will take you twenty weeks to reach your goal (30 ÷ 1.5 = 20). Enter the number of weeks in your reduction plan on the horizontal axis (see example).

Now make a dot where week zero and your present weight intersect. Make another dot where your desired weight and your final week cross. Draw a line connecting the points. This line gives you a picture of your weight loss plan. Each week you will weigh yourself and record your weight on the graph with an X. You will also take your measurements and record them on your graph as well. You will

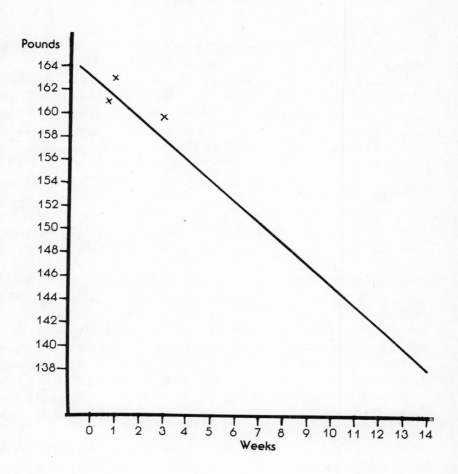

Inches

Chest	42	42	42	41.5
Waist	35	35	34.5	34
Hips	40	40	39.5	39.5

be amazed at how pounds translate into inches. Soon you'll be able to go back to the mirror with pleasure.

STEP 3. How should you begin? Eat! For the next two weeks, enjoy yourself and don't even think about calories.

This may sound like an unusual way to begin a diet, but it has a purpose. For the next two weeks, you won't just eat: you will learn what you eat, how much, when, where, and why. This learning period is essential; it will give you the understanding necessary to plan a strategy that allows you to reduce your food consumption naturally and enjoyably.

There is a simple way to learn about your eating habits. Buy a spiral notebook and keep an eating diary. For the next fourteen days, you must write down some basic information about everything you eat. The sample diary page opposite shows what you should record. (You will need a calorie counter listing the caloric values of common foods.)

Don't worry about calories. Just record the foods you eat, where (e.g., in the kitchen, in the car, at work, in front of TV), your position (e.g., standing in front of the refrigerator, sitting on the living-room sofa, sitting with a complete place setting at the dinner table), your mood (tired, contented, bored, frustrated, excited, etc.), and whether or not slowly and with enjoyment. Above all you must be honest. Don't worry about what it means while you're doing it. Just record this information as objectively and completely as possible. Each evening record the caloric value of everything you ate that day; then add up your figures for a daily calorie total.

After this two-week period is over, analyze your diary. First, look at your daily calorie totals. You may be surprised to see that you ate very nearly the same number of calories each day. If you did not gain or lose any weight in that two weeks, you have discovered how many calories you need to maintain a stable weight. Just take your average daily calorie total for these two weeks. This is the figure you will use as an upper guideline in reducing your calorie consumption to create your daily calorie intake deficit. If you gain or lose more than two pounds during this period, you should continue keeping your diary for another two weeks because you have probably increased or decreased your normal food intake. This sometimes occurs because keeping a diary makes you conscious of what you eat. After the first two weeks, however, the diary becomes a habit and your weight will

Calorie Count	Meal	Place/ Position	Mood	Slow with Enjoyment?
	Breakfast			
____	____	____	____	
____	____	____	____	☐ Yes
____	____	____	____	☐ No
____	____	____	____	
	Lunch			
____	____	____	____	
____	____	____	____	
____	____	____	____	☐ Yes
____	____	____	____	☐ No
____	____	____	____	
	Dinner			
____	____	____	____	
____	____	____	____	
____	____	____	____	☐ Yes
____	____	____	____	☐ No
____	____	____	____	
	Snacks			
	After Breakfast			
____	____	____	____	☐ Yes
____	____	____	____	☐ No
	After Lunch			
____	____	____	____	☐ Yes
____	____	____	____	☐ No
	After Dinner			
____	____	____	____	☐ Yes
____	____	____	____	☐ No
	Before Bed			
____	____	____	____	☐ Yes
____	____	____	____	☐ No

TOTAL

stabilize even while you continue to record your food intake. Don't be distressed if you must keep your diary for two extra weeks. In the long run, it will prove to be an advantage. You will have had extra time to identify your eating habits, especially those that keep you overweight.

Now look for other patterns. First consider the mood entries. Most people tend to overeat when they are bored or tired. Depression and anger less frequently contribute to overeating. Does it appear that eating is one of your ways of coping with boredom, fatigue or feeling blue? If so, then you know that you have to learn to distinguish real hunger from these feelings; you also have to learn new ways to cope with them.

When do you eat? Do you do a lot of snacking? How many calories do you consume in snacking alone? You may find that you can reduce your intake by 500–700 calories just by cutting out snacks. Studies show that most people snack during routine activity. You probably do most of your between-meal munching while cleaning, studying, watching TV, reading, or driving. If you become aware of when you snack and what you eat, you will be prepared when the urge to snack strikes by having a low-calorie, delicious food at hand. When you look for a snack you don't want to take long or work hard. You can use this principle in your favor by making sure that low-calorie snacks are the only ones available. Over a period of weeks, your snacking will taper off as you increase your sensitivity to your appestat. You won't even have to work at it.

In what position do you do most of your eating? Standing is the most common way heavy people fool themselves into thinking that the calories they are eating don't count. If TV is your downfall, stop eating while watching unless you use a complete place setting—knife, fork, spoon, tray, plate, glass, and napkin. Do this even if you just eat a peach so that you become conscious of what you eat. In general it's a good idea to do as much of your eating as possible at a table with a complete place setting.

How do you eat? Rapidly or slowly? Do you chew your food thoroughly? Do you enjoy your food? Or has it happened that you've been eating cookies in front of TV, and reached deep into the box for another, only to discover that you've finished them all? You've got to stop this habit of unconscious eating and begin to enjoy every bite you eat. Several studies have shown that you will eat much more if you eat quickly rather than slowly. Your appestat does not work instantaneously; it takes a few minutes after you've eaten for the satiety feelings to register. If you eat quickly, you may down hundreds of excess calories before your body can tell you to stop. No more gulping or bolting food.

You should delight in your food; savor every mouthful. Eating *must* be enjoyable if you are to succeed with this plan. *Enjoyment is absolutely essential to the process of regaining your natural sensi-*

tivity to your appestat. By making sure to eat slowly and with enjoyment, you will give your mind a chance to re-establish a harmony between your hunger, i.e., your physiological need for food, and your appetite, i.e., your desire to enjoy eating. Perhaps to your surprise, you will eventually find that food, no matter how attractively prepared, is not appetizing unless you are hungry. Once you re-establish harmony between your hunger and appetite, you will have freed yourself from slavery to food. You will be able to eat whatever you want and not get fat because you will eat in response to your real bodily needs.

STEP 4. How do you cut calories? Above all, try not to deny yourself. One of the big myths of weight reduction is that you must go on a diet consisting almost entirely of rabbit food and give up everything you like. If you try to cut calories that way, you'll never become sensitive to your appestat.

For the most part we want you to eat what you have always been eating.* We hope that you now eat a balanced diet, which means that your daily calorie intake includes food from the four basic food groups:

Dairy: skim milk, cheese	2 times daily
Protein: meat, fish, nuts, beans	2 times daily
Cereals: grains, bread, crackers	3 times daily
Fruits and vegetables: citrus; red, green, or yellow vegetables	3 times daily

To reduce your calorie intake, continue eating from these food groups but follow four important principles.

• Substitute low-calorie food you like for high-calorie food whenever possible. There are many excellent low-calorie cookbooks on

---

* Issues in nutrition are complex and hotly debated. For this reason, we have chosen not to include a whole chapter on better nutrition. Throughout this book, however, you will find basic recommendations that most experts now agree upon. In addition to eating a balanced diet, you should eat less sugar, less fat, and less white flour. Eat more fresh fruits, vegetables, and fibrous foods. We recommend two books for a balanced view of the current health-food movement: *Are You Confused?* by Paavo Airola (Phoenix, Health Plus Publishers, 1971) and *Panic in the Pantry: Food Facts, Fads and Fallacies* by Drs. E. Whelan and F. Stare (New York, Atheneum, 1977). In this modern age of processed and fast foods, we do urge you to become nutrition-conscious. People are different, especially when it comes to food; find out what is best for you.

the market that can help you.* The following table shows you how easy it is to cut your calories significantly without sacrificing your enjoyment.

High Caloric	Calories	Low Caloric	Calories	Calories Saved
Milk, whole, 8 oz.	166	Milk, skim, 8 oz.	87	79
Beer, 12-oz. bottle	170	Liquor, 1 oz., with carbonated water	85	85
Hard cheese, 1 oz.	105	Cottage cheese, 1 oz.	34	71
Cupcake, iced	200	Cupcake, plain	150	50
Cookie, 3″	125	Vanilla wafer	25	100
Ice cream, 4 oz.	167	Frozen yogurt, 4 oz.	60	107
Chef salad with oil	180	Chef salad with dietetic dressing, 1 tbsp.	40	140
Peanuts, salted, 1 oz.	170	Apple, large	76	94
Peanuts, roasted, 1 cup	800	Grapes, 1 cup	102	698
Potato chips, 10	110	Pretzels, 10	40	70
Chocolate bar, milk, plain	143	Marshmallows, 3	60	83
Lima beans, 1 cup	150	Asparagus, 6 spears	22	128
Winter squash, 1 cup	90	Summer squash, 1 cup	33	57
Succotash, 1 cup	264	Spinach, 1 cup	45	219
White bread, 1 slice	70	Whole-wheat bread, 1 thin slice	40	30
Oatmeal (cooked), 1 cup	150	Puffed rice, 1 cup	45	105

• Eat smaller portions. You don't need a second helping of meat; three or four ounces should satisfy your hunger. You also don't need extra mashed potatoes. Again, three or four ounces will do. Slow down, chew your food, enjoy it. Wait a few minutes after you've finished to see how you really feel. You'll be surprised to learn that you're not really hungry. Resist the temptation to have more, and eventually the temptation will fade away.

• Cut down on your snacking. Most people can easily drop 500

* Low-calorie cooking has even reached an art form in France. See Michel Guerard's *Cuisine Minceur* (New York, Bantam, 1977). The *Weight Watchers International Cookbook* (New York, New American Library, 1977) is also noteworthy.

calories from their diets simply by eating low-calorie snacks and reducing the total number of snacks per day. To do this, you must make it a point to establish new ways of coping with boredom, fatigue, and frustration. Food is a passive coping mechanism; overeating makes you a weaker not a stronger person. Growing inner silence, on the other hand, enhances your inner strength. Use your new strength to develop an active approach to coping with boredom or frustration. You don't have to be ruled by food.

• Cut down on your sugar consumption. We are a nation of sugarholics. Americans consume annually more than 100 pounds of refined sugar per person. In addition to the obvious sugar intake through cakes, pies, pastries, soft drinks, and sugar added to coffee and tea, we engorge our bodies with sugar in unseen ways. Look for the ingredient sugar on canned food labels the next time you shop. You'll find it in soups, baked beans, ketchup, salad dressings, and hundreds of other products you eat every day. The reasons for cutting down on sugar are many. Not only does excessive sugar consumption contribute to overweight, it also leads down the path to degenerative disease. High sugar consumption increases your risk of diabetes, atherosclerosis, and heart disease. It also causes tooth decay. Because sugar provides calories empty of vitamins and proteins, it drains your long-term energy and vitality after giving you a brief energy boost. To reduce your sugar intake, you don't have to become a fanatic. An occasional dish of ice cream is fine if you have planned it in your diet. However, you do have to discover the joys of natural foods and substitute them for sugary processed foods whenever possible. Try mineral water instead of soft drinks, an apple rather than a doughnut, and a mixture of dried fruits and seeds in place of a candy bar. You'll soon see for yourself that natural foods are just as tasty and far more energizing than the sugary processed snacks.

If you implement these four suggestions, you should be able to meet the goal of your weight reduction program without sacrifice or struggle. Periodically you will experience mild hunger, especially before mealtimes. But you should welcome these feelings as a joyful new dimension in your life. You will begin to discover and enjoy the positive effects of mild hunger such as increased energy, heightened alertness, and a lean, light feeling. You will start to enjoy periods of "the hungry feeling" throughout the day and will derive extra relish from your meals because they satisfy genuine hunger. Be proud of your newfound strength to enjoy hunger feelings rather than eating at the slightest provocation. Within a short time, you will find yourself much preferring to be slightly hungry than slightly too full. You may even want to try a one-day juice fast. (More about that later.) So go ahead and start enjoying your weight loss plan and your new active approach to living.

STEP 5. How do you measure progress? Don't weigh yourself too frequently. Daily weighing makes little sense while you are reducing. Because of changes in fluid intake, bowel movements, and humidity, your daily weight can vary from one to three pounds. Rather than weigh every day, you should establish a weekly schedule, preferably on a Saturday or Sunday.

The reason for weighing on your day off is simple. If you are losing too quickly or too slowly, you will need time to re-examine your calorie intake plan and make necessary adjustments. If you are losing more quickly than planned, and enjoying it, go ahead and continue. But a loss of more than ten pounds per month is not desirable; you must give your body a chance to adjust to its new weight. If, on the other hand, you hit a plateau for two or three weeks, something has gone wrong. Stay on your plan, but get out your food diary and record everything you eat for the next week. Include mood, position, place, and so on. When you examine your diary a week later, the cause of your problem will jump out at you. Somehow you have inadvertently increased your calorie intake. Correct the problem, create a calorie intake deficit again, and your weight will start going down once more.

While you are losing, you should make it a point to drink at least six eight-ounce glasses of water each day *in addition to your normal liquid intake*. This water will help flush out the waste products that result from your body burning its own fat. Have a glass of water as soon as you get up in the morning. Then, before each meal, have a glass of ice water. This will provide the water you need and will slightly deaden your hunger, a simple but effective way to help yourself eat less at the table. Do it! It works!

Record your weight on your weight reduction graph every week. You should also take your measurements weekly. You can also record your measurements on your graph.

The months will pass, your weight will drop, and soon you will reach your goal. When this occurs, you should recalculate your daily calorie need to maintain a stable weight. An active adult needs about twenty calories per pound of weight. You should increase your calorie intake to that level but not beyond it unless you find yourself still losing weight. If so, add 100 calories to your diet. Don't try to reduce below your desired weight simply to conform to a distorted ideal of beauty. It will be damaging to your total wellness.

Now that you have reached your new weight, you must become more friendly with your bathroom scale. You should weigh yourself daily to make certain that your weight never fluctuates more than three or four pounds. Monitoring your weight daily is absolutely essential. If your weight rises slightly, go back to your diary and record your eating pattern for a few days. You'll be able to see the problem and correct it on your own. Your calorie requirement to maintain a stable weight may be lower than you originally thought.

Having achieved your desired weight with this plan, you will never again be a slave to food. Enjoy your new vitality and your new figure for the rest of your life.

Some Final but Crucial Tips

• Make sure to count calories in the supermarket. Don't bring high-calorie food home unless you have carefully fitted it into your calorie intake plan. Never bring home high-calorie snacks. Never go food shopping when you are hungry. With all that food so beautifully displayed, all you need is a little hunger to tempt you to stock up on high-calorie food you don't need and haven't planned for.

• Keep a bowl of fresh-cut vegetables in the refrigerator at all times. A mixture of cauliflower, green peppers, celery, carrots, and radishes is one possibility. You should prepare this when you fix dinner so it's available when the urge for a snack arises. Unwashed vegetables in the back of the refrigerator are no help at all.

• Stop believing in the myth about food waste. You don't have to clean your plate because children are starving in India. You can only save food by preparing less in advance. The worst way to waste food is to clean your plate when you are not hungry. All you do is get fat. It's better to throw out what you can't eat—your garbage pail can't gain weight.

• If you are bored or frustrated and can't think of anything to do but eat, *take a walk*. Walking is a marvelous tonic that soothes and enlivens. It will also burn up 100 to 200 calories. You might put this sign on your refrigerator:

DON'T EAT TO CLEAR YOUR HEAD,
ENJOY A WALK INSTEAD!

• Don't be too concerned about how fast you reduce as long as you lose at least four pounds per month. The overweight person's lament—it goes on so fast but comes off so slowly—really isn't true. If you gained thirty pounds between the ages of thirty and forty, you gained an average of only three pounds per year. If you lose four pounds per month, you'll be back at your old weight in less than eight months.

• If you want to do some fasting, try a one-day juice fast on a Saturday or a Sunday. Be sure to cut down the amount of meat and increase the portions of vegetables you eat the day before and the day after your juice fast. The key in fasting is to start it properly and come off it slowly. If you want to do longer fasting, we suggest you do so only under medical supervision.

• If possible, close your eyes for a few minutes before you eat your meals. This will help you settle down and become aware of your real level of hunger. It will also help you slow down and enjoy your food. As a result, you will eat less and enjoy it more.

• If you occasionally want a milk shake or a piece of pie à la mode, go ahead and relish it. Just recognize that you are consuming 500 calories and adjust your other food intake accordingly. There is no reason to feel guilty about your milk shake. It is high in protein and very nutritious if made from natural ingredients. While you enjoy your shake, you should be proud that you are strong and sensible enough to have it and still lose weight.

• If you overeat one evening, don't worry. You won't be very hungry the next day, so you can easily adjust your calorie intake to make up for your previous excess.

• If you are going to a party, prepare for it. Eat lightly that day to give yourself an extra calorie allowance for the occasion. Before you go, have a glass of skim milk to cut your hunger. Once you're there, have two or three hors d'oeuvres and sip your drink slowly. No one will force you to clean your plate, so don't. You can also ask for a small portion of dessert but still enjoy it thoroughly.

• If you have difficulty following your plan and cutting calories, the ongoing group support provided by Weight Watchers, Tops, Overeaters Anonymous, or similar groups can be very helpful. Don't hesitate to join one of these groups, especially if obesity and overeating have been lifelong problems. These organizations are usually listed in your local telephone directory and meet weekly. Meetings focus on helping you learn how to plan delicious low-calorie meals and how to avoid your old temptations to overeat.

On a closing note, forget the word "diet." It's an awful word that conjures up unhealthy feelings such as frustration and self-denial. Try using the phrase "holistic health program" instead. When your friends ask you how you lost so much weight, don't say you were on a diet, because in actuality, you changed your life-style. Losing weight is a matter not just of the calories you take in, but also of the energy you put out, and you have become more active. You replaced overeating with healthier, more enjoyable ways of living. As a result, you did not just lose weight; you increased your level of wellness, which is the goal of holistic health.

10. Fitness Without Frustration

Whether or not you are physically fit, you are probably aware that regular exercise is important to good health. Regular exercise contributes to a radiant appearance, an erect posture, and a positive mental outlook, in addition to maintaining strength, coordination, and endurance. Numerous authorities report that exercise reduces fatigue, tension, and minor aches and pains. It also helps in controlling overweight.

Nature has designed your body for the enjoyment of physical activity. If you fail to take advantage of this gift, you not only short-change yourself of many wonderful experiences, but also invite extensive physical degeneration. You're familiar with this degeneration. You see it often as the signs of aging—slumped shoulders, sagging flesh, loss of vitality, stiff joints, weakness, a colorless, wrinkled complexion, fatigue, decreased libido, and frequent illness. To some degree, these changes are inevitable. But you can influence when and how severely they will strike, whether you will begin growing old at age forty-five or seventy-five.

What you may not understand about exercise is its effect on your circulatory system and aging process. To maintain optimum health, your tissues must receive fresh nutrients and excrete wastes efficiently. If you are sedentary, your circulatory system will maintain a level of efficiency that will supply your tissues with enough oxygen and nutrients to sustain your low level of physical activity, but no more. You have practically no reserve capacity, so you may find yourself panting after a brief romp with your children or a short walk uphill. You have not developed a level of circulatory efficiency that will accommodate moderate exercise. To increase your circulatory efficiency, you must do regular exercise that is moderately more vigorous than your daily routine activity.

If your circulatory system will automatically accommodate a sedentary life-style and you have no interest in playing sports, why should you develop a reserve of circulatory efficiency? The answer is simple: to help you avoid illness and delay the onset of physical degeneration and the crippling effects of aging. With a reserve of circulatory efficiency, your body can accommodate the wear and tear of everyday living without difficulty. Without this reserve, everyday wear and tear will cause gradual physical degeneration and pave the way for early aging. You can compare the value of reserve circulatory efficiency to that of savings and investments. Without any savings, you are living hand to mouth, and the ups and downs of life will cause you a good deal of strain and pain. But with even a small nest egg and a regular savings plan, you can take the ups and downs in stride.

Another name for reserve circulatory efficiency is *fitness*. Its three principal components are flexibility; strength and muscle tone; and endurance. Flexibility is the natural elasticity of your body tissues, which allows freedom of movement. Strength depends upon three elements—muscle mass, muscular coordination, and the amount of energy stored in your muscle tissue. Endurance is the ability of your circulatory system to provide your body with sufficient oxygen and nutrients and to eliminate wastes with relative ease during prolonged moderate exercise.

How Exercise Develops Fitness

Moderate regular exercise develops the components of fitness by triggering far-reaching biological changes. It promotes the growth of blood vessels, especially the small capillaries that carry blood deep into your tissues. Exercise strengthens your heart. The muscle fibers of your heart not only become stronger but also work together more efficiently. As a result, your whole circulatory system increases its ability to suffuse your tissues with blood. Exercise develops strength by increasing muscle mass and energy reserves and by stimulating tissue regeneration. Finally, by exposing your body to a wide range of movements, exercise restores and maintains the elasticity of your tissues and the smooth, painless functioning of your joints.

In short, exercise can do much to enhance your level of wellness and is a critical component of any holistic health improvement program. You don't have to run yourself ragged to benefit significantly. Simply by maintaining the minimum level of fitness sufficient to prevent premature physical degeneration, you can expect the following effects:

—increased energy
—reduced fatigue
—fewer bodily aches and pains
—fewer colds and increased resistance to disease
—improved self-esteem and self-regard
—improved sleep
—increased self-confidence and assertiveness
—increased libido and enhanced sexual vitality

For a more detailed explanation of how you will benefit from exercise, you can consult any one of a dozen fitness books on the market. Our concern here is wholly practical: to help you start exercising. To do that, you must clear the exercise hurdle.

The Exercise Hurdle

If you're like most people, you have an aversion to exercise programs. You may enjoy tennis or golf on the weekend, but you don't like to work at getting yourself into condition. We don't blame you. Physical fitness programs are usually boring and exhausting. But this aversion to programmed exercise may grow into a distaste for all exercise. Rather than walk ten blocks to the store to pick up something small, you take the car. Given a choice between an elevator and two flights of stairs, you always take the elevator. Your kitchen is filled with labor-saving devices—electric can opener, knife sharpener, mixer, and dishwasher. If you work at a desk during the day and frequently watch TV or go to a movie in the evening, you may soon be spending less than two hours a day on your feet. If this occurs, and if you have no formal exercise program, you have crossed the boundary from an active to a sedentary life-style, and your level of fitness will begin to decline.

One of the most insidious aspects of this shift to a sedentary life-style is that it can happen without your noticing it. At twenty-three, you may be in fairly good shape. But the pressures of work, home, or your social life gradually cut into your daily physical activity, and by age thirty your level of fitness begins to slip. This reduction in activity leads to a modest weight gain that further reduces your enjoyment of exercise. Finally, by age forty-five, you have let your fitness deteriorate significantly. You look in the mirror and see your face beginning to sag and soft flesh hanging from your arms and abdomen; you're winded by climbing two flights of stairs. You resolve to do something about it, but you don't. You may pick up a fitness book and start a program, perhaps a modest one that requires only thirty minutes a week. You may give it a try for four, five, or six weeks; but then you will probably give up on your program. You have encountered the exercise hurdle.

What we call the exercise hurdle is a lack of the sustaining motivation that is necessary for you to change from a sedentary to an active orientation to living. Once you have adopted a sedentary life-style, the grip of inactivity is difficult to break through willpower alone. Your biggest problem is time. You just don't seem to have time to exercise. The pressures of work demand your full attention, problems at home come up, and there's that TV program you want to see; you just don't have time to walk to the store to get some exercise. You don't have the time to do the dishes by hand. Paying a neighborhood boy or girl to wash the car or mow the lawn seems to be a good investment in light of all you have to do. After all, you don't want to miss Sunday-afternoon football on TV just to get some exercise.

How to Clear the Exercise Hurdle

Though a busy schedule can be a stumbling block to regular exercise, lack of time isn't the real essence of the exercise hurdle. If it were, hundreds of thousands of busy people, including business executives, doctors, congressmen, and indeed people from all walks of life, wouldn't be running five to ten miles every day just to get some exercise. But they do. For them, getting up forty-five minutes earlier or skipping cocktails in the evening in order to run is worth it; so they find time for exercise even on their busiest days. Avid tennis players, squash enthusiasts, and bicycling addicts are the same way.

If you are sedentary, you may be wondering what these people have discovered that you haven't. To you, running five miles may sound like pure self-punishment. You probably feel you work hard enough without adding another apparent burden to your life. If you feel this way, you are not alone. Most people still agree with you, but there are a growing number who see the matter differently. They don't view their exercise as work. They acknowledge that it is demanding, strenuous, and sometimes even agonizing, but they also say it is one of the most satisfying and exhilarating parts of their lives.

Could it be that exercise is only for the privileged few who have the rare ability to derive some intense joy from it? Unlikely, for the simple reason that a renewed interest in exercise is slowly sweeping the country, and hundreds of thousands of previously sedentary people are getting back into shape and loving it. They are jumping the exercise hurdle successfully and, once on the other side, discovering enormous physical and psychological benefits. Mike, a thirty-eight-year-old advertising executive sums it up well:

> Two years ago, I was in sad shape, 230 pounds on my six-foot frame, sagging shoulders, insomnia, several colds every winter, and I would get winded just watching the Super Bowl on TV. When a friend said I looked fifty, I decided to do something, so I got a book on running and gave it a try. Within four months, I was hooked. Now I run at least five miles every day, sometimes eight. I'm down to a lean 170, eat whatever I want, don't smoke anymore, and have never felt better. I sleep well and have lots of energy. Even more important, I enjoy a feeling of calm inner power that I have never known before. I won't bore you with stories about the agony of my first few months. I made mistakes, pushed too hard, and got hurt. It didn't have to be that way. Anyway, now I enjoy the running itself as much as what I get out of it. After the first mile or two on a quiet country road, my mind slips into a serene, joyous state. My experience isn't unique. Lots of runners report it.*

* For a further discussion of this experience, see *Positive Addiction* by William Glasser, M.D. (New York, Harper & Row, 1975).

Energy, sound sleep, freedom from tension, self-confidence, and even spiritual growth—these are the benefits of regular vigorous exercise. But to achieve them, you have got to get started.

Here in a nutshell is the essence of the exercise hurdle. Getting into shape is a slow process. During the first few months, you may work hard and only gradually notice benefits. You may be so out of shape to begin with that you get discouraged with your progress. This discouragement, coupled with lack of enjoyment of your exercise program, is the hurdle. No doubt it is a formidable one; it has tripped millions of men and women who started exercising with the best intentions of getting fit. You may already be among them. Don't be discouraged. Your problem is most likely one of approach. The key to jumping any hurdle, either on a track or in your head, is the right approach. The following pointers will help.

• Start with a decision not just to get fit but also to have fun. Exercise doesn't have to be work even though it is strenuous. Half the problem is just getting out the door. When you're sitting in front of TV, running may seem like work. Once you get out there, you can get the same charge you experienced as a child when you ran out to play. Be open to it.

• Build up slowly. Remember that your purpose is to have fun and not run yourself into the ground. This doesn't mean you shouldn't push yourself or get winded. You have to get a good workout in order to progress, but you don't have to suffer. Pain and injury from overdoing it may derail your whole program, so stop and rest when you feel you should. Your body knows—so listen.

• Choose an exercise that you enjoy. Running in place, push-ups, and sit-ups may keep you fit, but they are also likely to bore you to death. Running outdoors is an excellent way to get in shape because you can enjoy the scenery and pace yourself easily. If you like tennis, squash, or other competitive sports, do some running as well. Running is the best exercise for getting in shape and will help you in your sport.

• Restrain your competitive zeal at least for the first four months. You aren't out there to prove yourself or win a race against yourself or your neighbor, so don't set yourself up to get discouraged. Competition can wait until you are really in shape and on the other side of the exercise hurdle.

We cannot say how soon after you start exercising you will clear the exercise hurdle, because we do not know what priority you will give it. All we can be sure of is that with the right approach, you will—and the benefits will be enormous. Experts on holisitc health agree that fitness should be a high priority.

How to Test Your Fitness

Before starting a fitness program, you have to determine your present level of physical conditioning. Testing your level of fitness needn't involve sophisticated measuring equipment. A reliable method was discovered 4,500 years ago in China. That ancient discovery was the arterial pulse and its relation to overall wellness. A slow, strong resting pulse indicates vitality, a high level of fitness, and wellness. A fast, weak one indicates lack of vitality, poor fitness, and possibly illness.

The best place to take your pulse is along the radial artery of your wrist. This artery comes close to the surface of your skin just inside your wrist bone and about one inch below the base of your thumb. You can locate your pulse by placing the middle and index finger of your dominant hand (i.e., right hand if you're right-handed) on this point and pressing lightly. Shift your fingers toward your thumb or away from it slightly until you find your pulse. Once you have it, sit in a straight-backed chair and count the number of beats in a fifteen-second interval. Multiply this number by four; the result is your average resting pulse rate per minute. To get an accurate reading, you should avoid stimulants such as coffee or cigarettes for several hours before the measurement.

To interpret your pulse rate, compare it to the norms for men and women. The average adult woman has a pulse rate of 75 to 80; the average adult man has a rate of 72 to 76. (It is unclear why men have lower average resting pulses than women.) In any case, if you are a woman and your pulse rate is 80, you are maintaining a barely adequate level of fitness. Your circulatory system does not have to work too hard to provide your tissues with adequate nutrients. If you are a man, a resting pulse of 76 indicates barely adequate fitness, below 72 is good, and below 68 is excellent. For a woman, a pulse below 76 is good and below 72 is excellent.

Of course, these figures are only averages. Your resting pulse may be higher than average and you may be reasonably fit. In most cases, however, a man's resting pulse over 76 and a woman's over 80 indicates a sedentary life-style and a need for improved fitness. The higher your resting pulse, the harder your whole system is working just to maintain itself. If your resting pulse is in the high 80s, you can be almost certain you need to improve your fitness. You can be equally certain that you should begin your fitness improvement program slowly to avoid placing too much strain on yourself. If your pulse rate is 100 or higher, you should see your doctor. You may be ill or you may have a circulatory problem.

Your resting pulse gives you an initial estimate of your fitness, but it does not indicate your circulatory system's reserve capacity and its ability to handle moderate exercise. To test this aspect of your fitness, take a fairly brisk two-mile walk (in thirty-two minutes or less) on flat ground. Don't run or jog; it isn't necessary and could be dangerous if your fitness is very poor. If you finish the walk and don't feel fatigued, have plenty of energy to spare, don't feel any aches or pains (especially in your legs or feet), and were never short of breath, then your fitness is adequate. If the walk had any unpleasant effects, you could benefit by developing a more active life-style and improving your fitness.

Warning! If at any time during this walk, you feel pain, heaviness, or heartburn in your chest, light-headedness, weakness, shortness of breath, or numbness and tingling, stop immediately and sit down. When you have recovered, walk home slowly and see your doctor at your earliest convenience. You may just be severely deconditioned, or you may have coronary artery disease. In either case, your doctor's help is warranted.

Your common sense is enough to interpret the results of your walk. If you handled it easily, you are probably already an active person. If you had some difficulty, you may be surprised by your poor condition. You may have thought you were more active than you actually are. If the walk wore you out or left you panting, then you are in poor condition and should begin a fitness improvement program slowly.

Another measure of fitness is flexibility. Can you bend over and touch your toes easily? Can you lie on the floor, do a sit-up, and touch your elbows to your knees? Can you stand and twist your torso 90 degrees in each direction? If you can't, then you are allowing your body to lose its natural elasticity and asking to grow old quickly.

There are more elaborate and precise ways to measure your physical condition. One well-known method is the Harvard Step Test in which you step up and down a step at a prescribed rate, then measure your pulse. Even more precise readings can be obtained by measurement of your oxygen consumption and the electrical activity of your heart while you run on a treadmill. These tests should be performed only under medical supervision. If you are over thirty-five and want to play competitive sports, these tests are a wise investment.

How fit do you want to become? At the very least, you should become fit enough to enjoy yourself and maintain a high level of wellness. This, in fact, is an excellent goal because you can achieve it easily.

How to Get Fit

What is an active life-style? How do you know if your daily routine is active enough to keep you fit? The answers to these questions show how easy it can be for you to develop and maintain fitness.

An active life-style has five elements:

—enough stretching, twisting, reaching, and bending to maintain flexibility and elasticity
—at least two hours of standing every day
—a few minutes daily of moderate exercise that pushes your pulse rate up to 120 and thereby forces your circulatory system to maintain a reserve efficiency
—exertion of moderate physical effort once or twice daily, thus maintaining your strength and energy
—enough daily physical activity to burn at least 300 calories

To meet these requirements, you don't have to make major changes in your daily routine. In fact, you may be surprised at how little you have to do to shift from a sedentary to an active and fit life-style.

An active approach to getting dressed in the morning can be enough to maintain your flexibility and elasticity.

• When you get out of bed in the morning, don't stumble to the bathroom. Wake up by enjoying a good stretch, first in bed and then standing up. Bend over and let your arms dangle for a moment. Try to touch your toes.

• Before you put on your suit or dress, move your arms up, back, and around in a circular motion once or twice. Roll your head around and limber up your neck.

• While you're getting dressed, exaggerate your motions a bit. Turn your torso once far to the right and once again to the left.

• Stand up and bend over to put on your socks and tie your shoes.

Although you will have met your stretching and bending requirement before you leave your bedroom, take opportunities to stretch and bend during the day. During a midafternoon break, you can stretch your neck by slowly rolling your head three times to the left, then three times to the right. You can give your torso a good stretch by sitting forward in your chair and twisting as far as you can in both directions to look behind you. Bending over to touch your toes even while seated in a chair will be good for your back, and standing up and then bending to touch your toes will be even better. Your arms and shoulders can benefit just by reaching as far as you can above your head, one arm at a time.

To meet your standing requirement, you have got to be a bit more willing to learn new habits. If you're sedentary, you probably don't realize how little time you are spending on your feet. A stopwatch can help you change your behavior. Every time you stand, start the watch; when you sit, stop it. At the end of the day, you'll see how much time you have spent standing. Remember to stand whenever you can!

• When you get up in the morning, try to stand as much as possible before breakfast. Stand while getting dressed, shaving, putting on make-up. You can probably get in forty-five minutes of standing before you go to work.

• If you work at a desk during the day, don't spend your coffee break sitting. Get up to talk and sip coffee. You might also try standing occasionally when on the phone.

• When you go out to lunch, find reasons to walk. Go shopping, go to a restaurant ten blocks away, or if there's a park nearby, just go for a walk to enjoy yourself. You'll feel a lot fresher and be much more productive when you return.

• During the day, look for opportunities to be on your feet. Park several blocks from the store when you go shopping. If you can, get up during meetings; you'll fulfill your standing needs and make your point more forcefully as well.

• When you come home from work, you still may be short of your requirement by a half-hour or so. You can work around the house. Or you can take a leisurely half-hour walk. Don't treat this walk as exercise or you'll miss half its tonic effect. Let your mind wander, take it easy, and the pressures of the day will fade. If you get into the habit of walking, you'll never give it up because it refreshes not only your body, but also your mind and spirit.

Meeting your exertion need is quite easy. Any activity that provides a brief period of muscular exertion will do.

• Carry two bags of groceries from the car at the same time.

• Open a vacuum-sealed jar. Don't bang the lid with a knife until you have tried two or three times with all your might first.

• If you have small children, lift them over your head a few times. You're helping yourself, and they'll love it.

• Move some furniture, change a tire, lift a bag of fertilizer, or do some other strenuous activity around the house.

Meeting your need for a brief acceleration of your heart rate is equally easy. Remember that you should force your pulse up to 120, so check this rate after exercise. Once you discover the right level of exertion, you won't have to take your pulse every time. You will know how much effort to expend.

• Walk rapidly up two flights of stairs, or one flight twice.

• Plan your evening walk to include a modest hill and take it at a brisk pace.

• Romp with the kids for a few minutes.

• Run with your dog.

• Run in place for two minutes.

Your final need is to burn calories in physical activity. If you walk for an hour every day in order to meet the other four requirements, you will fulfill this need automatically. You won't have to do anything else. If you do enough standing during the day and don't like to walk in the evenings, you could try any one of a variety of activities to burn calories.

• Run for twenty minutes.

• Swim for twenty minutes.

• Bicycle for thirty minutes.

- Play thirty minutes of tennis.
- Play forty-five minutes of table tennis.

This brings us to the question of training to play competitive sports such as tennis, basketball, handball, or squash. One of the worst ways to abuse your health is to be sedentary from Monday through Friday, play a sport competitively on the weekend, and wake up Monday morning stiff and sore. If you want to play sports *competitively and wisely,* you've got to achieve an above-average level of fitness. This requires a regular training program at least three times per week in addition to your sports activity. There are many books on the market that will help you achieve that level of fitness.* If you are overweight or over thirty-five, consult your doctor before starting an intensive program. To achieve a very high level of fitness, you must do so gradually.

Fortunately you do not have to achieve an exceptionally high level of fitness to enjoy a high level of wellness. The program we have outlined will meet your exercise needs. And you don't really have to try very hard. It's just a matter of changing your attitudes and orientation from sedentary to active. Great rewards are in store for you. Why not give it a try?

* See Laurence Morehouse and Leonard Gross, *Maximum Performance* (New York, Simon and Schuster, 1977). Also see Kenneth Cooper, *Aerobics* (New York, Bantam, 1968).

11. Cooling the Smoking Habit

If you smoke, the next pages may save your life. They present a strategy that will allow you to quit smoking permanently. The odds are good that you have already tried on one or more occasions. One recent survey indicated that nine out of every ten smokers want to quit and eight of ten have tried at least once.

You may be tempted to stop reading at this point because you know how difficult it is to stop smoking. Don't! We're not going to lead you down another path to frustration, the almost inevitable result of trying to quit through willpower alone. Instead we will show you how to enlist your body's healing capacities to help win the battle against the weed. With this inner support, your chances of success, small up to now, will be vastly improved. You may even find yourself quitting with little effort because your desire for cigarettes will wither from within.

The first step in giving up smoking is to nourish your intent to quit. If you throw away your cigarettes on mere impulse, sooner or later you'll probably find yourself starting again. Make your decision carefully.

Reasons for quitting are many. The federal government requires cigarette manufacturers to warn you about the danger of smoking because the scientific evidence of this fact is overwhelming.[225] Research indicates that by smoking one pack of cigarettes per day, you:

—shorten your life by eight to nine years
—significantly increase your risk of cancer, heart disease, and stroke
—reduce your vigor and vitality by as much as 50 percent

—significantly increase the number of colds and respiratory infections you get each year

Smokers suffer much more illness than do nonsmokers. In 1974 alone, smokers spent 88 million more days in bed, lost 77 million more working days, and endured 306 million more days of restricted activity due to illness than did nonsmokers.[222] These statistics make it clear that you pay for a nicotine high with your vitality, health, and capacity to enjoy living. That's not a good buy.

Aside from the health consequences, there are other reasons for quitting. Your habit is expensive, especially if you add your medical bills to the cost of cigarettes. Smoking fouls your breath, your hair, and your clothes. Beyond that, your habit undermines your autonomy. You are dependent on cigarettes; without them, you become uncomfortable. Finally, smoking deadens your sensitivity. It erodes your ability to taste and smell. It also dulls your emotional sensitivity by disturbing your natural inner attunement. You can probably cite other reasons to stop smoking. It's important for you to decide *why* you want to quit. You may find it helpful to write down your reasons.

Don't throw away your cigarettes until you have firmly decided that you want to stop forever. As long as you enjoy your cigarettes or feel you can't do without them, go ahead and smoke. Another three, six, or twelve months of smoking may be necessary before you stop permanently. You needn't feel guilty or anxious about your habit. Self-recrimination won't help you quit. When your natural desire to quit becomes strong, however, go ahead and decide to stop and don't underestimate your ability to succeed.

Why You Smoke

Let's assume that you have decided to quit. You are enjoying the healing silence through regular practice of the TM technique and now feel confident that you can break your habit. The next step is to understand why you smoke. People smoke for different reasons, and your particular reasons will determine which strategies will help you quit.

There is one common factor behind every smoker's habit—nicotine addiction. Whether you realize it or not, your physical need for nicotine is the strongest force that keeps you smoking. Ironically, the introduction of "safer" low-tar, low-nicotine cigarettes has been instrumental in proving this fact. Studies show that when heavy smokers switch to one of these brands, they tend to increase their daily cigarette consumption to compensate for the low level of nicotine in each cigarette. By facing your nicotine addiction squarely, you can minimize the inevitable though temporary discomfort of withdrawal. If you don't face your addiction, you will misinterpret your initial nervousness, irritability, and discomfort as psychological, and you may conclude that you need cigarettes for your psyche. This is an all-too-common self-deception.

We do not mean to imply that psychological factors play no role in smoking. On the contrary, they play an important one that also must be faced. Here the variety of reasons for smoking becomes apparent. Among the most common are:

—to get a stimulating lift, to get through a tedious job, to wake up in the morning, to clear the mind
—to reduce tension, to control anxiety, fear, "nerves," or other uncomfortable emotions
—to facilitate relaxation, e.g., after a meal, while reading a book, taking a walk, or watching TV
—to fight boredom, e.g., while waiting in line, caught in traffic, or riding on an airplane or train
—to be sociable, e.g., at parties, over coffee, in a meeting

To learn what motivates you to smoke, keep a smoking diary for two weeks before you try to quit. Smoke whenever you want to, but take a moment to record when and where you smoke each cigarette. Examination of this diary will show you which times and situations will be most difficult for you during the first months after you quit. This self-knowledge will help you meet your needs in healthier ways and avoid falling back into smoking.

Though willpower will be essential, you will not have to rely on it alone. The healing silence will weaken your desire for cigarettes and increase your sensitivity to the noxious aspects of smoking. Several cases will illustrate why we advise that you make the healing silence a regular part of your daily routine if you want to quit smoking for good.

Three Who Quit Easily

George H., a thirty-six-year-old, hard-driving executive, was under treatment at our center primarily to control his high blood pressure. We put him on medication, recommended the TM program, and tried to help him adjust his living habits, especially his diet and cigarette intake. Saying he needed cigarettes to manage his emotions, George did not heed our advice to lay off his one and one-half packs per day. Over a period of six months, however, his cigarette smoking gradually tapered off until he finally quit completely. In an interview, he explained:

> I used to smoke because it gave me a lift. I had to have a cigarette when I rolled out of bed in the morning or I couldn't get going, and once I had that first one, I dragged on one cigarette after another all day long to keep myself in high gear. But with TM you're not supposed to smoke until after your morning meditation. Well, I decided that I could hold off for a half-hour while I meditated and I did. Within a few weeks, I started to notice that my cigarettes weren't giving me the lift that they used to. I thought it might be my brand, so I tried another, but that didn't help, and I guess I began to cut down without even thinking about it. About two months later, when I had my first cigarette in the office one morning, it dawned on me that the cigarette was making me a little edgy and clouding up my mind. That did it; I threw the pack out and haven't smoked since. It was rough for a while but now I'm functioning a lot better for it.

Other clients have reported a similar pattern of gradually reduced need for cigarettes. Jack, a forty-four-year-old auto salesman, smoked because he enjoyed relaxing with a cigarette, especially after meals. In treatment to resolve marital problems, he and his wife were in couples therapy, and both started the TM program at their therapist's recommendation. Three months after starting the TM technique, Jack found that his cigarettes were no longer relaxing him but instead were producing a moderate level of tension. This tension was unpleasant enough to prompt him to quit smoking.

Connie, a thirty-two-year-old lawyer, was under treatment for a chronic cough and frequent colds and was told that she would have to give up smoking. She had already tried to quit many times but got very anxious if she could not have a cigarette when she wanted one. Having smoked at least a pack a day since age sixteen, she wanted tranquilizers to help her quit. The TM program was the first step in her treatment, and she was neither told to force herself to stop smoking nor was she given tranquilizers. But within a year she had quit smoking. She explained, "It really wasn't that bad. I started to feel more at ease at work and with friends, the two situations in which cigarettes had always been a necessity, so I started exercising a little self-restraint in my smoking. It went well; I felt better; and I finally quit."

These cases illustrate the powerful impact of inner silence on smoking. By increasing psychological well-being and reattuning the body to its natural rhythms, the healing silence gradually reduces the need and the enjoyment that sustain the desire to smoke. This does not mean that the desire for cigarettes magically disappears and that willpower plays no role at all. But once the healing silence becomes a part of your life, your own growth rather than willpower will prompt a reduction in your smoking.

How Long It Takes

How long does it take to stop smoking after starting the TM program? The answer to this question depends on how long you've been smoking and on your own psychological make-up. In one group of smokers, 22 percent quit within three months of starting the TM program. After nine months, 40 percent had quit. And after two years, more than 70 percent had stopped.[168] These observations are supported by the findings of other independent investigators. Harvard cardiologist Herbert Benson and physiologist Keith Wallace found that 26 percent of a group of smokers quit within three months after starting the TM program. Forty percent quit after nine months, and 66 percent after thirty-three months were no longer smoking.[17] In another study, psychiatrist Mohammed Shafii reported that 57 percent of a group of smokers had stopped smoking within twenty-four

months of beginning the TM program and 71 percent had significantly decreased their use of cigarettes.[193]

How to Quit Successfully, Step by Step

• Keep a diary before you quit so you know when your urge to
smoke is the strongest. By doing this, your craving for a cigarette
will never catch you by surprise and overcome your commitment to
stop.

• With the healing silence you will find your taste for cigarettes
diminishing, but be careful not to fool yourself. Eventually you will
have to quit cold turkey. When quitting time comes, there is no reason to prolong your nicotine withdrawal or the process of learning
new ways to enjoy yourself without a cigarette. Trying to continue
cutting down gradually will drastically reduce your chances of success and significantly increase the frustration of quitting.

• Make it difficult to smoke. Don't just throw away your cigarettes.
Pitch your matches, lighter, and ashtrays into the trash (or give them
to an enemy). This includes smoking paraphernalia at work.

• Face your nicotine addiction intelligently. For the first seven to
ten days after you quit, you will go through withdrawal. This means
you should expect to be nervous, edgy, irritable, tense, or just plain
hungry for a cigarette. This also means you should not try to quit
during a pressure-filled time, i.e., before exams, at the outset of a
new project at work, when looking for a job, when changing your
residence, during the breakup of a relationship, and so on.

• To get through withdrawal as quickly as possible, drink plenty of
fresh vegetable juices and eat lots of fresh fruit and plentiful salads.
These foods will help flush the nicotine from your system very rapidly, probably in a week or less.

• To satisfy your oral cravings, keep sugarless gum at home and at
work and in the car. Keep a bowl of fresh raw carrots, cauliflower,
radishes, and celery in the refrigerator to satisfy your desire to snack
without putting on pounds.

• If a friend offers you a cigarette, refuse. Explain that you have
quit smoking and that you are happy about it, but don't make a big
deal of your efforts or get into a long discussion. You are quitting for
yourself, not your friends.

• When you travel, sit in the no-smoking section of airplanes, trains, and buses.

• Don't be hesitant to assert your wish to avoid smoke-filled environments. In a cab, you have the right to ask the driver not to smoke. If he complains, you get out. In a crowded restaurant, you can also ask people at a table near you not to smoke or ask to be seated away from the smokers. A "Thank You for Not Smoking" sign displayed conspicuously in your home saves you the trouble of asking your guests not to smoke. You will be surprised at how people respect you for expressing your wishes courteously but firmly.

• Set a series of goals and reward yourself when you reach them. For example, after one month treat yourself to a meal in a fine restaurant. After three months give yourself that silk blouse, pair of shoes, tennis racket, or whatever else you have had your eye on. Six- and nine-month goals are also helpful. After a year you might take an extra vacation—a weekend in the Caribbean, for example. The money you will save in just the first two years of not smoking will more than pay for your "rewards."

• Recognize that you have an opportunity to develop new, healthier, more enjoyable ways to cope. Smoking is passive as well as unhealthy. It offers no opportunity for self-expression. Instead of lighting up when you're bored, write to a friend, take music lessons, or take a bubble bath. Instead of smoking while you watch TV, draw, doodle, or do needlepoint. Don't sit at the table after meals if that's when you crave a cigarette most. Go for a walk or move to another room. On your coffee break, read a book or magazine article rather than smoke. The principle is simple: Substitute an active, interesting way of coping with your feelings as you drop your old passive habit of lighting up.

• Above all, don't worry. Have confidence in your ability to quit. The healing silence will help you stop and will normalize your system rapidly. Your coughing will decrease, your senses of taste and smell will sharpen, your sleep will improve, and your energy will increase. Soon you will find smoking distasteful; you may even find the odor of cigarette smoke unpleasant. By breaking your addiction, you will enjoy a significant boost in your sense of autonomy.

In short, you have much to look forward to by ending your enslavement to tobacco. Instead of the inevitable degeneration that results from smoking, you will enjoy a steady increase in your total well-being and natural attunement. Each year the benefits will increase because your level of wellness will continue to grow. Don't underestimate yourself. By increasing your level of wellness through physical fitness and meditation, you can quit *now*.

12. High Blood Pressure and Heart Disease: How to Beat These Silent Killers

Do you know your blood pressure? If it is elevated, are you under a doctor's care and are you following your treatment program to the letter? Do you know your personal risk of a heart attack? Are you aware that your risk can be calculated with a high level of accuracy? If you answered no to any one of these questions, you should have reason for concern. A few facts will explain why.

• You may be one of the at least twenty-four million Americans, including one in three adult men, who have definite or borderline high blood pressure. Without proper treatment, your life expectancy may be reduced by up to sixteen years! You may encounter crippling health consequences in your early fifties and death before age sixty.

• One of the peculiarities of high blood pressure is its lack of symptoms. Even severe high blood pressure may be present for years, and you may not know you have it unless you have your blood pressure checked. Despite this lack of symptoms, elevated blood pressure slowly and steadily damages your arteries, kidneys, and heart.

• In most cases high blood pressure appears between the ages of thirty and thirty-five and its consequences may kill or cripple before age sixty. There is little likelihood of getting high blood pressure after age fifty-five.

• Fewer than half of all people who have high blood pressure know they do. And only half of these people are getting treatment. And only half of those in treatment follow their doctors' instructions well enough to control their illness adequately. In other words, only three million of the twenty-four million Americans with high blood pressure are doing enough about it to avert its serious consequences.

• Heart attack is only one of the many ways that high blood pressure kills or cripples. Others include kidney failure, congestive heart failure, and stroke.

• Research has pinpointed several factors that promote the development of heart disease. They are: a high-fat and high-cholesterol diet, high blood pressure, cigarette smoking, an excessively aggressive-competitive personality, overweight, and lack of fitness. The evidence is now incontrovertible that these factors predispose you to clogging of your coronary arteries (atherosclerosis) and ultimately a heart attack. Each factor raises your risk by a precise amount, but some increase it more than others. The presence of several factors has a multiplying effect. For example, if you smoke, your risk of heart attack is twice the average. If you smoke and are also not fit, then your risk is four times the average. If you also have a high cholesterol level, then your risk is sixteen times above normal. If you exhibit all six factors, you will almost certainly have your first heart attack before age sixty.

Obviously, there is much you can do to avoid falling prey to heart disease. Let's first look at your blood pressure because understanding and controlling it is a crucial first step toward circulatory health.

How to Measure and Interpret Your Blood Pressure

Your blood pressure is simply the amount of force your blood exerts on the walls of your arteries. A good analogy to it is the pressure of water in a garden hose. If you turn on the faucet hard and narrow the nozzle, the water pressure in the hose increases; if you turn the faucet down and open the nozzle, the pressure decreases. In the same way, your blood pressure increases when your arteries narrow or you increase your blood volume by retaining fluid.

Your blood pressure is defined by two pressure readings. Between heartbeats, your blood exerts what is called *diastolic* pressure. When the heart beats, blood spurts into your arteries and your blood pressure increases sharply. This higher reading is called your *systolic* pressure. Blood pressure is measured with a sphygmomanometer, which is simply a pressure cup attached to a pressure gauge, usually a column of mercury in a glass tube. When the cup is strapped around your arm and inflated, the pressure raises the column of mercury a certain number of millimeters. The two pressure readings,

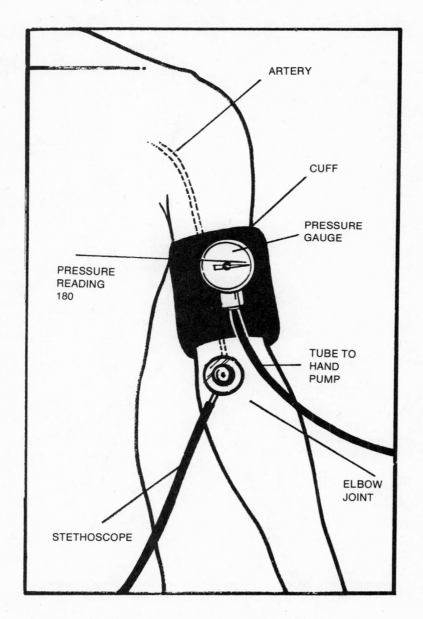

Blood pressure cuff is inflated by squeezing hand pump until pressure gauge reads 180. Arterial blood flow in the arm is momentarily blocked.

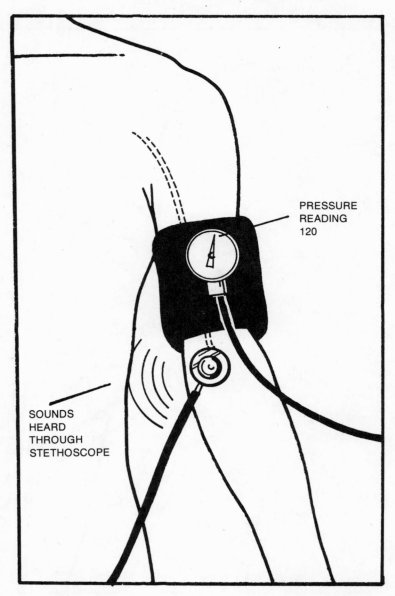

PRESSURE
READING
120

SOUNDS
HEARD
THROUGH
STETHOSCOPE

Blood pressure cuff is deflated slowly and steadily until blood begins to squirt through the artery, creating sounds heard through the stethoscope. Whatever pressure reading appears at this point is the *systolic* blood pressure.

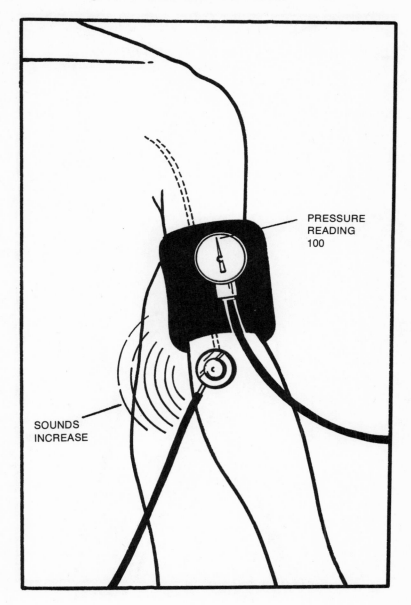

PRESSURE
READING
100

SOUNDS
INCREASE

Sounds heard through the stethoscope increase as cuff pressure
continues to diminish.

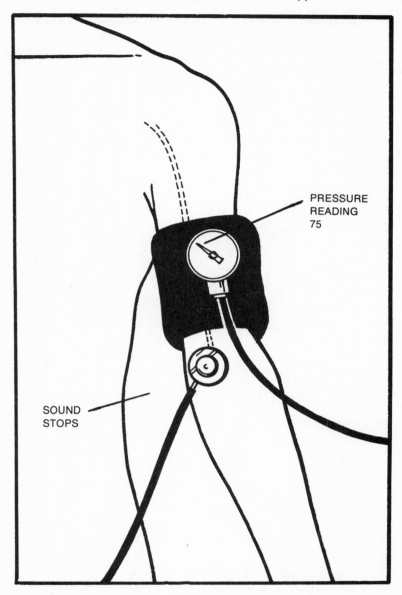

PRESSURE
READING
75

SOUND
STOPS

Finally, the pressure in the cuff decreases enough to allow un-constricted flow of blood through the artery. Sounds previously heard through the stethoscope stop. Whatever pressure reading appears at this point is the *diastolic* blood pressure.

usually written systolic/diastolic, are expressed in terms of the number of millimeters the mercury rises during the two phases of your heartbeat. A reading of 120mmHg/80mmHg means that you have a systolic pressure of 120 millimeters of mercury and a diastolic pressure of 80 millimeters of mercury.

You have probably had your blood pressure taken many times. It's a simple procedure, and you can easily learn to do it yourself. In fact, learning how to measure your own blood pressure should be a part of any holistic health program. All you need is a sphygmomanometer, which can be purchased for about forty dollars from a medical supply house, and a stethoscope.

First, wrap the cuff around your upper arm, midway between your elbow and shoulder. Put on the stethoscope. Pump up the cuff until the gauge reads about 180–200. This stops the flow of blood to your arm.

Place the stethoscope face over the crease in your elbow. Let the air out of the cuff slowly and listen carefully for a thumping sound. As soon as you hear this sound, you have found your systolic pressure. Look at the pressure gauge and remember the reading.

Continue to slowly let out the pressure in the cuff. The thumping sound will become a quiet murmuring. Keep watching the dropping pressure on the pressure gauge.

When the murmuring sound stops completely, you have found your diastolic reading. Write down your systolic reading over your diastolic in a fraction form, and you have your blood pressure.

To determine if your blood pressure is elevated, check it against the following table of normal blood pressures for men and women based on age.

NORMAL BLOOD PRESSURE

Age	Men	Women
6–8 years	100/60	100/60
20–25 years	122/76	116/72
30–35 years	127/80	124/78
40–45 years	132/82	129/80
50–55 years	137/84	134/83
70 and over	146/81	159/85

Although blood pressure tends to rise gradually with age, you needn't worry if your blood pressure is slightly higher or significantly lower for your age as defined by this table. Doctors were once concerned about low blood pressure but now do believe that the lower your blood pressure, the better, as long as you don't feel inordinately fatigued, get suddenly drowsy upon standing, or faint easily.

There are, however, well-defined standards of elevated blood pressure. These standards apply to men and women and are given in the table below.

STANDARDS OF HIGH BLOOD PRESSURE

Degree	Systolic Range/Diastolic Range
borderline	140–160/90–95
moderate	160–180/95–115
severe	above 180/above 115

If your blood pressure is elevated, see your doctor. He or she will want to determine how much damage has already occurred. One way to do this is to perform an eyeground examination. By looking into your pupil with an ophthalmoscope, your doctor can see whether the small arteries feeding your retina have been damaged. If they are injured, it is fairly certain that arteries in the rest of your body have been similarly impaired.

Especially when caught early, damage can be reversed. The first step is to halt further injury by reducing your blood pressure and eliminating other risk factors in heart disease, especially high fat and high cholesterol consumption. The second step is to start a fitness program that encourages the gradual growth of new arteries, veins, and capillaries to blood-starved areas. Of course, it is far wiser to prevent this damage from occurring in the first place.

Causes and Treatment

High blood pressure is a mysterious illness; in nine out of ten cases the cause is unknown. The known causes that explain the tenth case include kidney disease and reduced blood flow to the kidneys by a tumor or a mechanical defect. These cases frequently respond well to surgical treatment. In the other nine cases, however, the doctor cannot aim at a specific cause. Instead, he or she must prescribe a multifaceted treatment program that addresses several or all of the known contributing factors.

What are these factors? An important one is heredity. If one or both parents were hypertensives, you have an above-average risk of developing high blood pressure and you should watch your blood pressure between ages twenty and fifty-five. You should also inform your pediatrician so he can pay special attention to your children's blood pressures. Another factor is obesity. Every pound of fat requires miles of extra blood vessels which place strain on your circulatory system. Weight reduction can be a key element in reducing blood pressure. A third factor is salt intake. Salt causes your body to retain fluid, which in turn increases your blood volume. This increased volume elevates blood pressure. By reducing salt, you reduce fluid retention and therefore blood pressure. A fourth factor is stress. We have already explained how the stress response triggers the secretion of several hormones that raise blood pressure. When stress becomes chronic, blood pressure may become chronically elevated.

The mainstay of current medical treatment is antihypertensive medication. Over the past twenty years, medical researchers have developed a variety of potent drugs for lowering blood pressure. Because these drugs work in different ways, your physician has a large arsenal from which to choose the right medication or combination of medications to suit your needs.

The pharmacological treatment of high blood pressure has two principal drawbacks. First, the drugs often produce undesirable but bothersome side effects. And second, patients find it difficult to accept a lifelong program of medication. If you have no symptoms and your doctor discovers your high blood pressure in a routine checkup, you may be disturbed by the prospect of pharmacological treatment. You went to your doctor feeling fine, but you left with a prescription for a drug that may make you sleepy, dry-mouthed, light-headed, even impotent, just because you have an illness that may kill you twenty years hence if you don't do something about it. Unfortunately, many individuals in treatment decide to stop taking medication when they are told that their blood pressure has dropped. They mistakenly believe that they don't need it or their doctors' supervision anymore. This faulty reasoning almost guarantees an early stroke or heart attack. Once medication is stopped, the blood pressure goes back up and begins again to wreak its silent destruction on arteries, heart, and kidneys.

Rx: Medication plus Meditation

Because it is difficult to keep patients on a pharmacological treatment program, a number of cardiologists have been exploring the value of meditation techniques in reducing blood pressure. The basic reasoning behind this research is simple: if a meditation technique reduces stress along with the neurological and hormonal activity that raises blood pressure, then the regular practice of an effective meditation technique might gradually lower blood pressure and lessen the need for long-term medication.

With the recent publication of several studies, the evidence is now conclusive that the healing silence can often be of significant value in the long-term reduction of high blood pressure.[16,21,44,174] We prescribe the TM technique regularly at our health center *with the proviso that our patients absolutely not reduce their medication without careful supervision from their doctors.* Using this careful clinical approach, we have found that the healing silence can produce dramatic results in some individuals, moderate but significant (i.e., enough to reduce medication intake substantially) results in others, and limited results in long-term, severe hypertensives. The healing silence also appears to help nonhypertensive individuals maintain exceptionally low-normal blood pressures, even as they get older.

A few cases will illustrate why we feel the healing silence should be at least an initial part of any treatment program for high blood pressure and why we feel it may be one of the best ways to prevent the onset of this illness.

Stan G. is forty-eight years old and the chief executive of his own building company. Six years ago he learned that his blood pressure was 160/105 and reluctantly began taking medications that he feared he would have to take for the rest of his life. The medication brought his blood pressure down to 140/90, and he suffered few side effects. Nevertheless, he sought other modes of treatment in hopes of eventually reducing his need for medication. Three years ago he began a holistic treatment program that included weight reduction, a salt-restricted diet, exercise, and the TM technique. Six months later his blood pressure had dropped to 130/83. His doctor then gradually reduced his medication over a four-month period. Stan's blood pressure is now stabilized at 135/88 without medication. He keeps his weight down, watches his salt intake, and experiences the healing silence regularly. He periodically checks his blood pressure at home and sees his doctor regularly.

Henry N. is fifty-eight years old. He began meditating (the TM technique) thirteen years ago. His blood pressure is 110/75, that of a twenty-year-old man in excellent physical health. Many factors may play a role in Henry's low blood pressure, but the healing silence is undoubtedly a supportive one. This case is by no means unusual. Our clinical evidence indicates that by making the healing silence a part of your life, you can expect to maintain the blood pressure characteristic of a much younger person.

Audrey M. was thirty-seven when she first learned of her elevated blood pressure during a routine medical exam. Her doctor prescribed medication, and she had been taking a diuretic and an arterial-dilating drug, hydralazine, for more than a year when she began a holistic treatment program that included weight reduction and the healing silence. Medication had reduced her pressure from 145/100 to 135/85, but the hydralazine caused headaches and joint pain, and she was taking additional medication to relieve these side effects. Three months after she began losing weight, vigilantly watching her salt intake, and meditating regularly, her doctor decided to reduce her intake of hydralazine. Within three months, she no longer needed hydralazine and required only half her original diuretic dosage. She now takes a mild diuretic once a day, meditates, and watches her salt intake. Her blood pressure is stable at 135/85.

How to Reduce and Control Your Blood Pressure

The serious consequences of improperly treated high blood pressure along with the possible need for medication in controlling it make your doctor's assistance absolutely essential in any treatment program. All too often, however, doctors rely too heavily on medication alone when a holistic approach might produce better results without the side effects of medication. To persuade your doctor to help you go on a holistic treatment program, you have got to show motivation and some understanding of what will be required. A holistic approach will never work unless you shoulder the responsibility for it. The following suggestions will help you understand what you must do and how to encourage your doctor to view your problem holistically. If you have normal blood pressure now, these suggestions will help you keep it that way.

• Get your blood pressure checked regularly. You obviously can't deal with your blood pressure unless you know what it is. A blood pressure check takes less than three minutes. Check it yourself, have it done at work or at a public health clinic, or see your doctor.

• Keep your weight down. Even if you are only ten or fifteen pounds overweight, you may lower your blood pressure by reducing. Ten or fifteen pounds may not seem like much, but were you to try carrying around a fifteen-pound lead weight all day, you would see how much strain this extra weight can cause.

• Reduce your salt intake significantly. You need about one-quarter gram of salt per day in addition to what you get naturally from food. Unless you are now on a salt-restricted diet, you are probably consuming about ten grams of salt daily, *or forty times as much as you need.* You should cut down on salt, especially if high blood pressure runs in your family. Several studies indicate that with a hereditary predisposition, excessive salt consumption and mild overweight may be enough to bring on high blood pressure. Northern Japan, where large amounts of salt are used in food, has the highest incidence of hypertension in the world. A similar picture is emerging in the United States. To reduce your salt intake follow these simple rules: Avoid salty snacks such as potato chips, pretzels, salted herring, and hard cheeses; salt your food *lightly* while cooking; keep the salt shaker off the table; substitute other seasonings for salt.

• Keep fit. There is reason to believe that exercise opens capillaries in your muscles and reduces the pressure required to suffuse your muscular tissue with blood. Exercise also helps build collateral circulation—new channels that allow blood to bypass clogged, constricted arteries.

• Make the healing silence a part of your life. This is the best natural way to reduce stress-related physiological factors that contribute to high blood pressure. By increasing your capacity to handle pressure, it will also help you avoid overloading your system with hormones that raise blood pressure. Your blood pressure peaks at five or six in the evening. If you meditate then, you can lower this peak.

• Get enough sleep and take regular vacations. Your blood pressure will go up whenever you are under strain. Lack of sleep and too much work without a vacation cause physical and emotional strain.

• Stop smoking. The correlation between smoking and high blood pressure is not clear-cut. However, the presence of smoking along with high blood pressure dramatically increases the risk of stroke and heart disease.

Additional Steps to Stop Heart Disease

• Reduce your consumption of cholesterol and fat. Ever since the link between cholesterol and heart attacks was first proposed in the early 1950s, physicians have debated its truth. Some debate persists today, but most now agree that the evidence is conclusive. High cholesterol and fat (both saturated and unsaturated) consumption is a leading factor in atherosclerosis and heart attacks. Reducing your blood cholesterol level clearly lowers your risk of a heart attack. If you can maintain a blood cholesterol level of 150, which is well below the American average of 220, your risk of heart attack is *ten times less* than average.

In this light, we find it intriguing that over a period of years meditators tend naturally to eat fewer high-cholesterol, high-fat foods (e.g., beef, pork, lamb, eggs, liver) and more low-cholesterol, low-fat foods (e.g., fish, fowl, fruits, vegetables). To help you reduce your fat and cholesterol intake, you may want to use one of the many cookbooks that will show you how to do so and still enjoy a very satisfying diet.* In Appendix II, we give broad guidelines for reducing your cholesterol and fat intake. If you don't know your blood cholesterol level, we strongly urge you to have it checked. The test is relatively inexpensive, but your doctor must order it. If your blood cholesterol is above 220, you should definitely reduce it. To achieve maximum wellness and reduce your risk of heart disease to a mini-

---

* Myra Waldo, *The Low Salt, Low Cholesterol Cookbook* (New York, Berkley Medallion, 1972). Michel Guerard, *Cuisine Minceur* (New York, Bantam, 1977).

mum, you would be wise to lower your cholesterol level to 175 or below. It can be done much more easily than you might think.

• Develop a balanced personality and a high level of inner harmony. At the turn of the century, the great physician William Osler postulated that an aggressive, competitive, overworked person is especially vulnerable to heart disease. Seventy-five years later, cardiologists Meyer Friedman and Ray Rosenman presented highly convincing evidence that the excessively aggressive-competitive Type A personality has a far higher risk of heart disease than the well-integrated, balanced Type B person. From what we have already said about the healing silence, its implications for reducing Type A and developing Type B personality characteristics should be clear. Turn to Chapter 15 for more detailed instructions on what you can do about modifying the personality characteristics that can destroy your heart.

Before reading this chapter, you may not have realized that you determine how long you'll live. The facts, however, are clear. Your decision about how you care for your heart and circulatory system largely determines your life span. If you wouldn't mind a heart attack before age sixty, ignore these silent killers we have discussed. Otherwise, you can squelch them easily. All you need do is follow a few simple steps that will not just protect you from heart disease, but will vastly enhance your vigor and vitality. The decision about what level of wellness you want to enjoy is yours.

13. Good Night to Insomnia

Do you toss and turn for hours before falling asleep? Do you wake up in the middle of the night and have difficulty getting back to sleep? If you suffer from insomnia, you are not alone. A recent Gallup poll indicated that more than 100 million Americans regularly have difficulty falling asleep or sleeping soundly through the night. Another study indicated that one in four Americans are sufficiently troubled by sleeping irregularities to require sleeping medications periodically.

You may have already tried a variety of folk cures. Counting sheep is among the most well known and least effective. Another is a glass of warm milk, a solution that usually accomplishes little alone but can prove quite helpful in a holistic plan of sleep regulation. Still another approach is reading long into the night until you finally can't keep your eyes open. This technique usually works quite well . . . by three or four in the morning. Reading late is no solution at all if you have to be at work by eight or nine. The last resort is a prescribed or patent sleeping medication. Like most last resorts, this one is unsatisfactory. But don't despair! With a holistic approach to regulating your sleep cycle, you can lick the common forms of insomnia within a matter of weeks and without pills.* You will also sleep better and awake more refreshed than you have in years.

* Most cases of insomnia respond well to the holistic approach because they result from simple nervous tension and excess stress. In a small minority of cases, however, insomnia may indicate an incipient psychosis, severe depression, organic illness, or more obscure causes that may only be diagnosed in a sleep research laboratory with elaborate equipment such as that necessary for all-night monitoring of brain waves. If distressing emotional or physical symptoms such as withdrawal in your personal life, disorientation in your thinking, or loss of appetite accompany your insomnia, you should consult your doctor.

Although insomnia is unpleasant and worrisome, it appears to pose little real threat to your health. The first step in beating insomnia is to stop worrying about it. Even if you lie awake half the night, you will in all likelihood get enough rest to avoid illness. So when you have insomnia, don't worry about it. Just turn the lights out and relax. You will be getting a good deal of rest if you don't struggle to fall asleep. Once you begin a holistic plan to regulate your sleep, you will find that this relaxed, unconcerned attitude will give way to sleep easily and quickly.

Your Sleep Need

To adjust your sleep cycle, you have to understand your sleep need. Most people require about seven and one-half hours of sleep each night, but your sleep need may vary substantially from this average. A significant percentage of the population reports a nine-hour sleep need and an almost equal percentage needs only six hours per night. A small percentage of the population gets along well on four to five hours nightly.

If you need more than ten hours per night, your abnormally high sleep requirement may stem from a physical or emotional problem. Excessive sleep may be symptomatic of depression, a troubled marriage, or frustration at work. It may also be due to an organic disorder such as an underactive thyroid, infectious mononucleosis, or hepatitis. If you sleep excessively, you should mention this pattern to your doctor.

You need less and less sleep as you grow older. The declining sleep requirement from infancy to adolescence is obvious. Infants may sleep twenty hours per day. The normal adolescent needs at least nine hours. By age twenty-four, the typical adult has established a seven-and-one-half-hour sleep cycle. At age fifty-five, however, he or she may need but six hours and may be sleeping less at age seventy-five.

You may have noticed an interesting pattern to the statistics on average sleep requirements. They are all multiples of one and one-half. People tend to sleep four and one-half, six, seven and one-half, or nine hours. Sleep researchers have achieved some insights that help explain this pattern. They have found that sleep is an active process that proceeds cyclically through a series of distinct stages. At each of these stages there are changes in the electrical activity of your brain and sometimes in your respiration, heart rate, and muscle tension. You often shift body position as you shift from one sleep stage to another. The typical ninety-minute sleep cycle proceeds as follows:

STAGE 1. Light sleep. The electrical activity of your brain slows down to four to six cycles per second from the thirteen to twenty-six cycles per second characteristic of focused mental activity in the waking state. Your breathing tends to be irregular and your heart beats as rapidly as if you were awake. You also dream during this stage and show the most noticeable sign of dreaming, rapid eye movements back and forth beneath your closed eyelids.

STAGE 2. Medium-depth sleep. The electrical activity of your brain slows further, and characteristic brain wave patterns, called *sleep spindles,* appear. Your breathing becomes more regular and your heart rate begins to slow down.

STAGE 3. Deep sleep. The electrical activity of your brain shows an increased voltage. Sleep spindles persist but are somewhat slower than in Stage 2.

STAGE 4. Deepest sleep. Your brain waves become high in amplitude and very slow, usually about one or two cycles per second. Sleep spindles disappear. Your breathing is slow, deep, and regular. Your heart rate is also slow and regular.

Having attained Stage 4 sleep, you don't remain there very long. After as little as five or ten minutes, you return to light sleep. The change is so abrupt that it might appear to an observer that you are about to wake up. But you don't. Instead, your muscles relax completely, almost as if you are getting settled to watch a movie. Then you dream. Once your dream show is finished, you return again to the deeper levels of sleep, only to return to light sleep and dreaming about ninety minutes later.

The length of this cycle explains the pattern of sleep needs. Some people (the four-to-five-hour sleepers) need three complete sleep cycles to wake up refreshed. Others (the six-to-seven-hour sleepers) need four complete cycles. Most people seem to require five cycles, or seven and one-half hours' sleep. And still other people need six cycles, or nine hours.

Sleep research indicates that both the quality and the quantity of your sleep are important. To say good night to insomnia forever, your efforts to regulate your sleep cycle must address both these dimensions of sleep. Sleeping medications are not an adequate solution because they satisfy only one half of your sleep need, quantity. By inhibiting your tendency to dream, hypnotics undermine the quality of your sleep. You may sleep for eight uninterrupted hours after taking a sleeping pill but may wake up in a complete fog. Numerous studies have demonstrated the negative consequences of this hangover effect on your performance the next day. Moreover, all sleeping medications lose their effectiveness within a short period (two to three weeks) of use, and dosages must be increased to induce sleep if insomnia persists. Due to this addictive effect of sleeping medication, severe and debilitating insomnia (much worse than that experienced before treatment) may result once the drugs are withdrawn.

With a holistic approach, however, you can fulfill both dimensions of your sleep need and lick your insomnia without pills or gimmicks.

The Roots of Insomnia

Insomnia has been called "midnight madness" for good reason. When you lie in bed unable to fall asleep, you may toss, turn, and feel like jumping out of your skin. You might also feel angry and start berating yourself. No matter how you may feel, one fact is certain. Your mind is churning incessantly, and you are unable to turn it off. Here is the key to understanding the roots of insomnia.

Though sleep itself is an automatic process, going to sleep is a conscious one. You must choose to get ready for bed, climb under the covers, and let the concerns of the day float through your mind without your paying attention to them. Insomnia results when you are unable to let your mind drift idly and lazily into sleep. A variety of factors can contribute to the incessant mental activity at the root of insomnia. Frustration at work, financial worries, marital problems, concerns about your health, excitement about a new project, and fears about the future are a few of the common emotional ones. Certain foods, especially those high in sugar or a stimulant such as caffeine, can also keep your mind going. Other factors that make it difficult to let your mind idle include stimulating mental activity right before bedtime, chronic muscular tension, and aches or pains.

How to Quiet Midnight Madness

The effect of a holistic health program on a disturbed sleep cycle can be dramatic.

Charles W., a thirty-four-year-old headmaster at a small private school, began awakening several times each night after he took the headmaster's job two years ago. Invariably, he would wake up with a financial problem, a student, or a teacher on his mind, and he might spend a half-hour trying to get back to sleep. He sought medical help and followed his doctor's recommendation to meditate and begin jogging. Within a month, he had regained his natural ability to sleep through the night. He also reported awakening more refreshed in the morning.

Steven B., a forty-five-year-old insurance salesman, suffered from bouts of insomnia off and on ever since his marriage at age twenty-six. During these bouts, which lasted two to three months, he took one to two hours to fall asleep. When he was transferred to a new city, he consulted a new doctor for a prescription for the sleeping pill he had used for years. His doctor recommended the TM program and counseled him on adjusting his sleep cycle naturally. For the past eighteen months, Steven's insomnia has not recurred and appears to have been cured for good.

Claudia M., a thirty-two-year-old dental technician, began taking sleeping pills at her doctor's recommendation to control her chronic insomnia. Before taking medication, she sometimes spent two or three hours lying awake at night. Though Dalmane (a widely prescribed sleep agent) helped her sleep, she did not wish to continue relying on her medication. After reading a magazine article about holistic medicine, she decided to look for a natural solution to her problem. She sought help and began a carefully designed program including the healing silence, gradual reduction of her sleeping medication, and a series of activities designed to increase her relaxation before bedtime. Within three months, she was falling asleep easily without medication and waking up refreshed in the morning.

Research indicates that these cases are the rule rather than the exception. In one study, a group of individuals with chronic insomnia required an average of seventy-five minutes to fall asleep each night. Within thirty days after learning the TM technique, this average time had dropped to fifteen minutes. One year later, the average was still fifteen minutes.[159]

How the healing silence helps relieve some basic sleep irregularities is not altogether clear. Several factors seem to be involved. One likely element is anxiety reduction. We know the healing silence dramatically reduces anxiety, and we also know that anxiety reduction tends to help relieve insomnia. Another probable factor is decreased muscle tension. The most important factor, however, is learning to allow an effortless mental flow. Through regular exposure to the healing silence, you learn how to let your mind experience thoughts in a neutral, noninvolved way. This learning experience carries over to bedtime, when falling asleep requires that you treat thoughts in the same way. As a result, instead of getting caught up in "midnight madness," you will let thoughts come and go as they please while you slip into delightful, soothing sleep.

Ten Strategies

The healing silence should be a significant part of your sleep program, but it alone may not be enough to conquer insomnia. A holistic approach would also include the following important strategies.

• Stop all activity that requires intense concentration or critical thinking at least one hour before bedtime. This includes writing letters, reading, doing crossword puzzles, and any activity having to do with your work. This slowdown is absolutely essential. You must give your mind a chance to begin settling down and disengaging itself from attentive thinking.

• Occupy yourself with boring mundane activities for at least one-half hour before going to bed. Late movies, the *Tonight Show*, and anything you find interesting or stimulating are out. Washing, brushing your teeth, polishing your shoes, arranging your clothes for the morning, or straightening your desk are suitable activities. Let yourself get bored.

• Set regular hours for sleeping and waking; then stick to them. If necessary, use an alarm clock to wake you in the morning. When the alarm goes off, get up no matter how tired you feel. This will help establish your natural body rhythms in a regular cycle conducive to maximum wellness.

• When you feel sleepy, go to bed, even if it is before your planned bedtime. If you force yourself to stay up and shake off your sleepiness, you may not be sleepy later when you want to be. Remember the old saw, "Early to bed, early to rise . . ."

• You might try taking a *very leisurely* twenty-minute walk about an hour before bedtime. This will help take your mind off your daily concerns and unwind any knotted muscles. Enjoy the silence and peace of this walk. It can be very soothing and healing.

• Sex is fine. In fact, it is among the best antidotes to insomnia.

• When you put your head down on the pillow, remind yourself that there is *nothing you can do about any of your problems right now*. Everything can wait until morning. You've worked hard all day, and now is your time to enjoy a rest.

• A warm bath can be very relaxing. Make sure the bath is not too hot, and don't stay in more than twenty minutes. Above all, don't read. Listen to some soothing music instead. You'll find yourself getting quite snoozy. When you get out of the bath, pat yourself dry; save brisk toweling for the morning.

• A small amount of warm milk sweetened with a little honey and cardamom seed may help you sleep. All sugary, high-carbohydrate foods are out at this time because these foods provide instant energy, exactly what you don't need when going to bed. If you don't like milk, another high-protein food such as a few nuts or a piece of cheese (no cracker) will do. Remember, the quantity should be very small. You may find a cup of herb tea soothing. Be careful which tea you choose. Some are stimulants; others have sedative properties. A mixture of chamomile, lime flower, and lemon verbena is a good choice for bedtime. You can find it already mixed at most health-food stores.

• Increase your physical activity during the day. A sedentary lifestyle and poor level of fitness can be major contributors to insomnia. If you add just a half hour of jogging, swimming, or squash (or any vigorous sport you enjoy) to your daily routine, you may soon be sleeping better than you have in years.

With a holistic approach, you stand a good chance of licking your insomnia in a matter of weeks. The longer insomnia has been troubling you, the longer it may take to end it. In any case, don't worry about it. Your doctor can assure you that you have no serious medical problem. Just keep up your program; you will soon be saying goodnight to insomnia.

PART IV

The Heart of Wellness: How to Become the Person You've Always Wanted to Be

Let each become all that he was created capable of being; expand if possible, to his full growth; and show himself at length in his own shape and stature.

— Thomas Carlyle

Everyone is familiar with the phenomenon of feeling more or less alive on different days. Everyone knows on any given day that there are energies in him which the incitements of that day do not call forth. . . . Compared with what we ought to be we are only half awake. Our fires are damped, our drafts are checked. We are making use of only a small part of our possible mental and physical resources.

— William James

14. You Can Change

Are there aspects of your personality that you would like to change? Perhaps you get nervous under pressure, or maybe you occasionally suffer from depression. If you are shy or unassertive, you might want to become more outgoing. Lack of energy, low self-esteem, sexual anxieties, or guilt and inhibition may trouble you. These are the common problems of living today, and they are so widespread that few people indeed are entirely free from them.

Don't be afraid to admit a personality weakness. After all, you are not alone. But more important, recognizing a trait that you would like to change is the first step toward becoming the person you have always wanted to be. And becoming such a person is an important part of your plan to improve your level of wellness.

The Holistic Approach

In this chapter, we want to discuss briefly how the principles of holistic health apply to personality growth. Above all, you should be aware that the holistic approach asks more from you than most self-improvement books and even a good number of therapists. Many people in the therapy business give the erroneous impression that you can simply think your problems away. Since you can control your thoughts, they reason that you can control your feelings and behavior just by changing your thoughts. It sounds easy, but it isn't. Were personal growth so simple, no one would have any hang-ups and we would all would be enjoying the heights of wellness without even trying.

Our point is not that these therapists are entirely wrong. You can benefit from understanding your self-defeating thoughts or behaviors and using your will to change them. We are simply saying that this is not enough. You would be naive to believe that some form of positive thinking alone would be sufficient to resolve all your anxieties and open the door to lifetime happiness. The holistic approach recognizes the importance of will and positive thinking. But we emphasize that focusing on just one part of your personality is likely to produce small returns for the effort you expend. A growth program that instead aims at improving your level of total wellness (physically, emotionally, and spiritually) offers potentially greater and more permanent results. The principle is simple.

You have already looked at your fitness, weight, smoking, and sleep patterns. Because your mind and body are so intimately connected, changes you make in these areas will probably contribute significantly to your emotional growth. For example, just getting out and running every day may do more for your self-esteem, self-confidence, and assertiveness than a dozen self-help books or as many sessions of psychotherapy. In fact, running may produce emotional benefits that you might not be able to achieve any other way. On the other hand, running regularly *and* putting some effort into reducing your tendency to worry may yield even greater results. If you have a weight problem, working on that too would yield still more growth. This is the essence of the holistic approach—a multifaceted program that incorporates a variety of strategies for growth. The total effect is more than the sum of its parts.

What should be clear is that there are no panaceas. You can't become the person you want to be just by relying on one technique, principle, or idea, no matter how true or effective it might be. You also can't rely solely on what you learn from others. The best therapist does not solve your problems for you but helps you discover that you can solve them yourself. A holistic approach will do the same.

The important point is that you are unique. You must assess your own strengths and weaknesses, determine what techniques and ideas suit you best, and establish your own goals. Only in this way can you become the person you want to be. In the forthcoming chapters, we will outline some strategies you might find useful for overcoming common emotional hang-ups. Obviously, no one chapter says it all. The suggestions in each are intended to be incorporated into your total holistic health program.

A holistic approach to personality growth is challenging. There is no doubt about that. A growth program that touches many parts of your life cannot be simple, even though many ideas and techniques involved may be. Consequently, to get results, you have got to make a commitment. It should be clear by now that to get anything more than a few insights from this book you have to work on yourself. You also need determination. This doesn't mean a "wellness or bust" attitude, just a willingness to assess yourself honestly and stick with your plan for growth. You must give yourself time. Neither Rome nor holistic health was ever built in a day. Anyone who promises you instant results from a self-improvement program (whether it be fitness, weight reduction, sex therapy, or whatever) is either putting over a hoax or using a come-on. So be patient and threat yourself kindly. Finally, you have to be willing to expend some effort. More than two thousand years ago Euripides asked, "With slight effort, how should great results be achieved?" You can't expect great results from a holistic health program without effort.

Our culture has become so enamored with instant growth, effortless enlightenment, and automatic happiness that the realism of this book may be disappointing. Don't let it. What is clear is that you do have the power to become the person you want to be, if you choose to. Let's look at how you can.

15. How to Stop Making Yourself Miserable with Worry, Tension, or Anxiety

Worry and anxiety are the most widespread causes of emotional distress in our culture. According to a 1976 prescription audit by the Food and Drug Administration, the most prescribed drug in America is Valium, a tranquilizer for mild anxiety. Fourth on the list is Librium, Valium's leading competitor. The most widely used nonprescribed drug is aspirin, which relieves the physical symptoms of tension such as headache and backache. Obviously, if you worry or get anxious, you are not alone.

Before we go on, a word about the difference between anxiety and a healthy state of high arousal is in order. Actors usually get butterflies before going on stage. Athletes get psyched up before a competition. Effective speakers may feel excited before giving an important speech. This high-arousal state is physiologically akin to the anxiety that causes so much distress in everyday life, but there is an important distinction. While a high-arousal state energizes and mobilizes you for a peak effort, everyday anxiety paralyzes you and dissipates energy in useless fretting.

The Real Reasons Behind Worry and Anxiety

Why do you worry? The simplest answer is that there is a lot to worry about! The six o'clock news brings you the day's disasters. Inflation keeps driving prices up and it seems harder every month to keep pace. Our streets aren't safe during the day, much less at night. The energy crisis shows little sign of letting up. And there are still all the personal causes for worry. You can worry about your children, your health, your job, your marriage, your weight, a car accident, a plane crash, or your graying hair or deepening wrinkles. You can even worry about the weather. Will it be a nice weekend or will rain spoil the picnic?

Life is full of uncertainties. The only certainty is that all of us, including you, are going to grow old and die. Before you take all this too seriously and start worrying, ask yourself a simple question: Will any amount of worrying or anxiety change the future? Think about your favorite worries. Will worry prevent a car accident, keep your weight down, or help your health? The only thing worry can do is erode your health and hurry you toward your grave.

The first step in eliminating worry and anxiety from your life is understanding why you persist in such obviously self-defeating and self-destructive activity. Even though nervous tension is by and large unpleasant, it has its own psychological payoff. For example, by worrying, you can make yourself feel important. Though you may be immobilized and unable to do anything constructive about your problems, you can at least say to yourself, "I've got so much to worry about!" Furthermore, worry can help you avoid admitting that you choose to be immobilized because you don't want to risk failure, rejection, or loss. Worry and anxiety are also ways to prove how much you care for another person. You can tell yourself what a good mother or father you are because you worry about your children. Worry and anxiety can also get you sympathy from others. You can commiserate about your worries rather than take responsibility for your fulfillment.

The real reason behind your tension is simple: you use anxiety and worry to avoid the future, to prevent yourself from plunging ahead, enjoying yourself, and facing life's uncertainties. If you have a tension problem, you have chosen to be a worrier rather than a doer, to be anxious rather than fulfilled.

The Connection Between Anxiety and Worry

Anxiety is primarily a physiological condition; that is, it is a state of body rather than mind. Its physical components include an accelerated heart and breath rate, elevated muscular tension, perspiration, dry mouth, and high levels of stress hormones in the blood. This complex physiological condition results in that unpleasant and sometimes almost painful feeling of tension and apprehension that you call feeling anxious. Your feelings of irritability and immobility are rooted in the physical condition of your body. This explains why tranquilizers work. They lessen the physical substrata of anxiety and your anxious feelings subsequently subside.

Worry is primarily a mental and emotional condition. It is the obsessive rumination about possible negative events in the future. You single out some aspect of your life, and then you conjure up all the possible catastrophes that may occur. You vividly imagine these possible misfortunes and feel steadily worse.

The connection between worry and anxiety is simple. Without anxiety it is difficult to worry. Anxiety is fertile soil for worry; feeling good and self-confident destroys the seeds of worry. You'll find you just can't start worrying if you feel fully alive and self-confident. Worry, however, stokes the coals of anxiety. Should you be a bit anxious, all you need is a few images of future catastrophe and the fire of anxiety can start to blaze. With your steadily mounting anxiety, you feel progressively worse.

You probably know firsthand how hard it is to break the cycle of anxiety and worry. Though you tell yourself that your worries are foolish, you can't put them out of your mind. Anxiety mounts, and you worry even more. But if you can intervene directly to lessen your anxiety, your self-confidence and autonomy will be directly enhanced. You'll start to feel a glimmer of well-being even though you may still face problems that are cause for worry. This well-being will slow the racing of your mind. Your worry will subside and you'll regain control over your thoughts. You will, so to speak, come to your senses and see the absurdity of your worry. The time that you compressed in making the future so imminent will once again stretch out. You will see that you have ample time to solve your problems if you just stop worrying and get at it. Planning, doing, and enjoying will take the place of worrying.

Silencing Your Anxiety

Recent research has shown that the healing silence causes an immediate and dramatic reduction in anxiety. Exactly how it produces this effect is not yet fully understood. Reduction in stress hormones and muscle tension and changes in the electrical activity of the brain all undoubtedly play a part. In any case, it is clear that the healing silence works naturally and produces only positive effects.

Helen, a twenty-seven-year-old graduate student, sought help because anxiety was about to make her drop out of graduate school. She had been a perfectionist and a worrier all her life, and the pressures of her studies caused her to worry herself into a frenzy. She brooded constantly—What if I fail my comprehensives? What if I don't get an A on my next paper? What if I can't come up with a good dissertation topic? What if I get my degree and can't get a job? Despite her myriad worries, she plugged on, fighting headaches with aspirin and heartburn with antacids. But when she began crying uncontrollably one evening, she decided to get professional help.

Helen thought she needed tranquilizers and psychotherapy, but it was evident that she was basically a well-integrated and self-fulfilling person. Her doctor advised against tranquilizers because they would relieve her symptoms without helping her get at the roots of her tension. Instead he recommended the healing silence. Helen reluctantly agreed and expressed considerable doubt about its value. To no one's surprise but her own, it worked, and her headaches diminished dramatically in less than a month. She also enjoyed a burst of new self-confidence and began forging ahead with a new zest for her work.

Dan is an account executive with a large international brokerage firm. He is happily married and has three children. When he sought our help, he was forty-four. His chief complaint was a near addiction to Valium, which his doctor had prescribed for his nervous tension. The doctor had told him to take the Valium as needed, and after a year Dan found himself taking 40mg per day. His drug intake was helping less, and he didn't like what he saw as a growing drug dependency. He hoped a holistic approach to his tension might help him get the worry monkey off his back for good without pills.

The core of Dan's treatment program was the healing silence. He had heard about the TM program and was quite enthusiastic about trying it. We also helped him start exercising more regularly and suggested strategies to increase his efficiency and effectiveness in the use of his time. The net result was gratifying. Two months after he began treatment, we started lowering his Valium intake. Four months later he was off all medication, including his occasional sleeping pill. He had also decided that he was ready to give up smoking. Dan's enthusiasm and vitality grew so markedly that his wife commented that he had become a new man.

In numerous cases a holistic health program has caused a dramatic and lasting reduction in anxiety. The healing silence is important, but you have to cooperate with the changes taking place within. We draw on a large number of strategies to help our clients thoroughly eradicate their immobilizing worry and anxiety.

Eleven Strategies to End Worry and Anxiety

• Develop a healthy attitude about time. You live in the present; all your opportunities for planning, action, and enjoyment unfold in the now. Since the present moment is so important, be conscientious about how you use it. If you find yourself worrying, stop and ask yourself what you are trying to avoid. If you discover something specific, go ahead and attack it. If not, do something that is useful or gives you enjoyment. Recognize how foolish it is to kill time worrying when you could just as well enjoy it having fun!

• Don't accept hurry as a necessary part of your life. You can't increase your productivity or enjoyment by hurrying. On the contrary, if you persist in hurry and tension as a way of life, you're likely to miss life's greatest treasures in addition to destroying your health. You can't enjoy a sunset, smell a flower, or take a long walk in the woods if you are always in a rush. Don't be fooled into thinking you have to hurry because of pressures and responsibilities. The quality of your planning and action is ultimately more important than speed. William James got to the heart of the matter when he advised, "Beware of those absurd feelings of hurry and having no time, that breathlessness and tension, that anxiety of feature and that solicitude of results, that lack of inner harmony and ease."

• If you have got a problem, think it through once and for all. Worrying about it halfheartedly is a way to make yourself feel you are working on it while in fact you are just hoping it will solve itself.

• Be more active. Running, dance, yoga, hiking, swimming, and just simple walking are potent anti-anxiety agents. The combination of meditation and regular exercise is even more effective. Just be sure to start an exercise program you enjoy, and don't set unrealistic goals for improvement. Otherwise you might wind up worrying about your progress. That would indeed be foolish.

• If you have many things to do, make a list. One client, a manager of a retail store, complained of worry and tension headaches. When she described her anxiety, she explained that she constantly felt tense because she had so much to do. She had all her responsibilities at work plus those of running a home with three children. When asked how she kept track of her responsibilities, she said, "I just keep everything in my head." The source of her tension was obvious. No one can keep so many things on his or her mind at once. We advised her to make lists that included all she had to do at work and at home (including tasks like shopping and picking up the children at school). The lists helped her see which activities demanded immediate attention and which could be delayed. She never had to worry about forgetting a task because it was always there on her list until she did it. Within weeks after using this simple technique to establish daily priorities, her worry and tension dropped immensely. Once she took everything off her mind and put it on paper, she discovered she had much more time than she had thought.

• Tackle one task at a time. Give up trying to do two things at once, such as driving and dictating or watching TV and working. Dividing the mind is a cause of strain and tension.

• If you just cannot shake anxiety about some potential disaster (e.g., the possibility of a car accident when a loved one is driving home late), ask yourself three questions. What is the worst that can possibly happen? What is the likelihood that it will occur? Can my worry affect this potential disaster in any way? You'll soon see the futility of your anxiety and will turn your attention to some more productive and life-supporting activity. We call this turning your "what ifs" into "so what ifs."

• Stop trying to be superman or superwoman. You can't excel at everything you do. Trying to live up to an impossible ideal is a sure path to tension and anxiety; no one can be great at everything he or she does. So what if you're not a great dancer; you can still go dancing. What's wrong with being just an average tennis player; you can still enjoy it. Why not try sailing once or twice even though you don't plan to become an expert; it could still be fun. Stop worrying about how good you are at everything. To excel in today's world, you must become truly expert in one activity whether it be management, writing, tennis, cooking, scientific research, baseball, needlepoint, or politics. You will be much happier and much less tense if you apply your highest performance standards to that activity which you love best and settle for variety and lots of fun in your other activities.

• Give yourself and other people a break and go easy on criticism. Whenever your faultfinding does not lead to constructive change, you can be sure it is breeding tension that immobilizes and harms.

• Don't make every one of your interpersonal encounters a competition. If someone gets ahead of you on the highway, so what; you don't have to take it as a challenge and get tense. The same principle applies in getting on an elevator, in the supermarket, or on the sidewalk. This does not mean that you shouldn't stand up for your rights when it's important or that you should allow yourself to be pushed around. But it does mean that you should not become tense and anxious over trivial matters.

• Recognize the wisdom of accepting life's uncertainties and confusion. There are many aspects of your life over which you have little or no control. So why get worried or anxious? The far wiser course is to treat frustration like the weather: accept it and go on to other things.

Worry, anxiety, and tension are demons to be exorcised from your personality. They sap your energy and spoil your fun. With your innate potential for a fully satisfying life, there is no reason to let these demons have their way. You can silence them forever. It's up to you.

16. How to End Chronic Fatigue and Become a High-Energy Person

If you frequently find yourself short on energy or troubled by vague aches and pains, your problem could be chronic fatigue. Fatigue, especially when chronic, can be a frustrating condition. You lack energy to fulfill not just your responsibilities, but your aspirations as well. Your mind tends to become cloudy, your emotions raw, and your muscles tense and knotted. Your doctor may tell you that "there's nothing really wrong; just take it easy" and may recommend a tranquilizer, a mood elevator, or a stimulant. But you soon discover that these platitudes and prescriptions don't work.

Fatigue is one of the chief complaints of the 70 to 80 percent of people seeing their family doctors. In four out of five cases where fatigue is the overriding problem, the doctor can find no underlying illness. The result is frustration for patient and doctor. We are not implying that your doctor is incompetent or that you should not see him or her if you feel immobilizing fatigue. This symptom can be the chief sign of many serious illnesses such as infectious mononucleosis, an anemia, a kidney infection, or a variety of hormonal or chemical imbalances. Your doctor is adept at determining whether any of these disorders are present, and they must be ruled out before you attempt any other treatment for your problem. We are simply pointing out that conventional medicine is often unsuccessful in treating fatigue that does not stem from a diagnosable illness.

A New Approach

Holistic medicine begins with the assumption that you should feel great. If you don't, then you have a real health problem. If you complain of fatigue, a holistically oriented physician assumes that you have some kind of imbalance in your total physical-emotional-spiritual functioning that can be successfully treated.

Conventional medicine has identified a variety of nonillness-related factors in chronic fatigue, but these have not been incorporated in a coherent system of treatment. One reason for this shortcoming may be the tendency of conventional medical practitioners to disregard symptoms that do not have a clear organic origin. Despite this bias, the syndrome of chronic fatigue is so widespread that modern medicine has accumulated substantial though fragmented insights about it. The holistic approach has prompted the integration of these insights into an understanding of the signs, causes, and treatment of this major health problem.

The Signs of Chronic Fatigue

Fatigue has a wide range of mental and emotional effects. It is a generalized condition that can affect almost everything you do. Different people show fatigue in different ways, but the most common symptoms of chronic fatigue are:

—mental dullness, cloudiness, lack of alertness
—pouches and/or dark circles under the eyes
—pasty complexion
—poor muscle tone
—lack of spontaneity in gesture or speech
—increased fears, tensions, anxieties
—decreased ability to accept constructive criticism
—increased irritability, frequent temper outbursts
—impaired recent memory, lowered attention span
—decreased libido
—insomnia
—vague bodily aches and pains
—high caffeine (or other stimulant) consumption

If you are able to manage your life effectively but have been troubled by several of these symptoms over the last several months (or longer), you may well be suffering from chronic fatigue. Of course you can't be sure until your doctor has ruled out the possibility of some underlying illness.

One of the hallmarks of chronic fatigue is pill popping (stimulants, tranquilizers, and/or barbiturates) and high coffee, Coke, and tea consumption. How many cups of coffee do you need to get through the day? If you *need* any at all, you are probably suffering from fatigue. A daily intake of five or more cups means your fatigue is probably deep and chronic. This does not mean you are functioning ineffectively; coffee may allow you to get through your day and maintain a reasonably high level of performance. But don't fool yourself into believing you are functioning at your peak.

When chronic fatigue becomes extreme, pill popping is often the end stage before serious illness strikes. Chronic fatigue can so disorient your system that you need stimulants to get going in the morning and barbiturates to sleep at night. In between, a mild tranquilizer may be necessary to take the edge off your tension. If you are using pills in this way, you are flirting with disaster. Unless you do something about your fatigue, serious illness will strike sooner or later.

Causes

Non-illness-related chronic fatigue can have a wide range of causes, among them:

—excessive pressure at work or at home, especially time pressure
—stimulus overload—too many simultaneous responsibilities, demands, expectations, and activities
—insufficient sleep
—worry about family, especially medical and interpersonal problems
—inattention to daily rest-activity cycle—too much activity, and disregard of the body's natural rhythms
—too little physical activity, a sedentary life-style
—preconscious psychological conflicts, especially fear of failure
—monotonous, boring work
—chronic frustration at work, dissatisfaction with superiors, coworkers, and opportunities for advancement

—inadequate stimulation, especially lack of friends and social isolation
—emotional loss, especially of a loved one
—failure at work, in a marriage, of an investment, or at anything important to you

At first glance, it might appear that almost anything can cause chronic fatigue, but a closer examination of this list reveals a pattern. These apparently unrelated factors cluster around two opposite emotional poles. The first half of the list contains a variety of common experiences that cause overstimulation and excessive stress; the second half includes factors, primarily psychological, that produce physical-emotional inertia. It is also evident that the causes of chronic fatigue are not just biological, but social as well. Therefore, to understand chronic fatigue, we have got to consider it in a social context. Overcoming fatigue is not just a matter of reducing stimulation and getting rest or increasing excitement and activity. Your whole rest-activity cycle must be considered within a cultural framework.

A Social Disease

If you don't have an ample supply of energy, you are temporarily out of tune with the natural rhythms of your body and emotions. Regaining natural attunement is frequently difficult because cultural factors reinforce your lack of inner harmony.

One of the greatest cultural reinforcers of chronic fatigue is pressure toward excessive excitement. In fact, your problem may be that you are caught on what we call the *excitement treadmill,* and your body is now telling you to stop the punishment. Excitement is essential to the full enjoyment of living. A sports event, a love affair, a good book, or a great idea all generate high excitement. But excitement makes intense demands on your physical, emotional, and spiritual resources. And these demands mean stress, which depletes your energy reserves.

The pressure toward excitement in our culture has become so intense that the need for recuperation between periods of excitement has been forgotten. Many people go from a frenzied work environment to a hectic rush hour, only to arrive home and turn on an exciting TV program. Weekends are a time for sports, parties, movies, and TV. The result is a gradual erosion of bodily resources, a process which in turn increases your need for excitement to avoid feeling let down and exhausted. To keep yourself feeling "up," you've got to stay on the excitement treadmill. Eventually your system says "Enough," and you hit a period of chronic fatigue. If you then follow the cultural input that says "It's OK to take pills to cope," you may be in real trouble. To solve your energy problem and live a long, healthy life, you must learn to turn off this cultural bombardment and become attuned to your own needs and rhythms.

Another major cultural factor behind chronic fatigue is boring work and frustrating work environments. Boring, distasteful work causes psychological inertia, which blocks your natural flow of energy. It takes courage to change a job, and if your work has brought on chronic fatigue, courage is usually in short supply.

If the cause of your fatigue problem has a major social component, solving it won't be easy. However, it can be done.

Strategies for Becoming a High-Energy Person

• If you are taking pills and stimulants to cope with your problem, you have got to stop. Of course you should reduce prescribed medication only under your doctor's direction. On your own, however, you can cut back on your coffee, Coke, and tea intake. Only by cutting back on your consumption of stimulants, especially caffeine, will you re-establish your natural attunement and discover your full measure of natural inner energy. You should also cut back on sleeping medications in order to allow your body to re-establish a natural sleep cycle. Chapter 13 will help if you suffer temporary insomnia. To achieve positive wellness, your goal should be to cut out all sleeping medication and to limit your daily stimulant intake to one cup of coffee.

• Get off the excitement treadmill. Don't let advertising slogans and cultural expectations rule your life. The human nervous system is not designed for a constant diet of pressure, tension, speed, and excitement; it must have adequate rest to permit natural regeneration and recuperation. You won't be missing out on life by slowing down periodically to get adequate rest. In fact, the opposite will be true.

You will expand your capacity to enjoy and will discover quiet pleasures that you have probably long overlooked. In addition to your daily experience of the healing silence, we suggest that you take one morning each week just for yourself—to be alone, to read, to go for a long walk, or to enjoy whatever quiet pleasures you find nourishing to body, mind, and spirit. Once you start taking these few hours for yourself each week, you will never give them up.

• A camping trip in the woods for a weekend or a week can be very effective in re-establishing your natural attunement. The fresh air and contact with nature will help wash away fatigue. You will also find yourself rising early and going to bed with the sun. Camping is really a marvelous way to say goodbye to chronic fatigue.

• Take long walks, at least an hour a day, or start running regularly. Ironically exercise is necessary to overcome chronic fatigue. Whether the cause of your fatigue is stress or inertia, walking or running is helpful. It clears your mind and lifts your spirits. A half hour of any vigorous sport you enjoy will do.

• Take a hard look at how you feel about your work. If you aren't satisfied, draw up a list of ideas about how your job could become more satisfying and discuss your ideas with your boss. This discussion will show you clearly the future you have in your present position. Your boss will in all likelihood respect you for making your feelings and aspirations known. If you can't arrive at a satisfactory way to modify your current work, you should consider seeking employment elsewhere. You might contact an employment service to explore the job market in your area. A session with a vocational counselor may be a worthwhile investment. One of the best ways to locate a good vocational counselor is to call your local university's counseling or education department for a recommendation. In any case, proceed with caution and plan carefully because changing your place of employment or your occupation is a major endeavor.

• Your problem may be that you are not eating enough protein or getting enough vitamins and minerals. If your protein intake is inadequate, increasing it may cause a dramatic rise in your energy level. A vitamin and mineral supplement may also be helpful.

• If you have a serious problem at home, at work, or with yourself, face it and get help if you need it. Don't sit around hoping your problem will resolve itself. Constant almost unconscious worry about a problem may be the single most important cause of your fatigue. If you are afraid to tackle your difficulty, you need help. Your problem will probably seem much more manageable if you discuss it with a trusted friend or a mental health professional.

• If social isolation is part of your problem, you need to get out and meet people. The best way to do this is to join an organization that you might find interesting and enjoyable. You can join a health club or take an art or dance class. Outdoor groups such as the Sierra Club provide wonderful opportunities for enjoying (and conserving through political work) the wilderness. If you feel you are shy, don't worry about it. Just join an organization that interests you and become active in it. You'll be amazed at how your energy level increases and the many wonderful people you meet.

• The healing silence is helpful in reducing chronic fatigue. Whether your lack of energy stems from excessive stress or from physical-emotional inertia, the healing silence produces physiological changes that neutralize the block in your natural energy flow.

• In addition to the twice-daily experience of the healing silence, we frequently recommend weekend TM residence courses. These weekend programs provide an opportunity for additional meditation and complete rest. They are perhaps the best initial treatment for chronic fatigue. If you attend two or three of these weekends each year, you will in all likelihood find yourself overflowing with more energy and experiencing greater inner well-being than you ever have.

Remember that whatever the cause of your chronic fatigue, you can eliminate it. Abundant energy is natural to human life. With a carefully designed program to restore your natural attunement, you will soon say goodbye forever to chronic fatigue and become the high-energy person you were born to be.

17. Up from Depression

If you have been depressed or get depressed frequently, you are in good company. George Washington suffered physical signs of depression such as bowel trouble, sleeping difficulties, and inexplicable aches and pains. Abraham Lincoln was so brooding and withdrawn as a young man that his friends feared he might kill himself. Winston Churchill got depressed so often that he referred to his depressive tendency as his "black dog." Buzz Aldrin, chosen for the space program in part because of his emotional stability and ability to handle pressure, went through a long bout with depression shortly after his moon flight splashdown.

Mental health statistics indicate just how common depression actually is. The National Institute of Mental Health estimates that fifteen million Americans suffer a medically significant depression each year; of these only one and one-half million are in treatment at any one time. These statistics say nothing of the minor depressions that trouble almost everyone once in a while. Just like the common cold, depression strikes people of all ages, occupations, and socioeconomic positions.

All depressions are not the same; they vary considerably in duration and degree. What you call a "bout of the blues" may be a low-grade depression, the sadness of everyday life, that will pass on its own in a few weeks if you give yourself some extra tender, loving care, or it could be a debilitating loss of interest in everything or everyone, a severe depression that requires psychiatric treatment. In this chapter, we will discuss the full spectrum of depression but will emphasize what you can do to help yourself work through low-grade to moderate depressions.

Signs and Symptoms

The level of psychic pain varies with the degree of depression. If your depression is low-grade, you may be only vaguely aware that you feel unhappy. You may simply lack the energy and interest to enjoy everyday activities or you might just be more pessimistic than usual. On the other hand, with a severe depression, you may experience acute emotional pain. You may feel like bursting into tears, and do so frequently with no apparent reason. Irritability and fear may also trouble you.

While its symptoms vary, depression always impairs the ability to enjoy everyday living. The earliest sign of depression may be a vague feeling that you are losing your ability to enjoy yourself. Or you may lose interest in food or friends or find that spending time with the family no longer brings you any pleasure. If these feelings persist over a period of weeks, you are suffering from a low-grade depression. In the presence of this general inability to enjoy yourself, other symptoms indicative of low-grade to moderate depression are:

• A pessimistic, critical attitude. You may find that everyone and everything (including the weather) seem to make you uncomfortable. You have difficulty finding anything positive to say.

• Marked irritability. You may tend to get upset at the most trivial matters, such as a slow check-out line in the grocery store or an inability to find a parking space.

• Difficulty in making decisions. Again, the most trivial matters may cause trouble. Deciding what to wear, what to cook for dinner, or what to watch on TV may become an ordeal.

• Difficulty in concentrating. You may find that after reading a magazine article or listening to a news broadcast you cannot recall what you read or heard.

• Decrease in sexual vitality. You may not be interested in making love as often as usual, or you may even experience a temporary bout of sexual aversion or impotence. In some cases, promiscuity or a sudden affair may signal an inner struggle with depression.

If you start having difficulties with sleeping, especially awakening early, exhausted, and unable to go back to sleep, your depression is increasing. Inability to laugh and unprovoked crying spells also signal a deepening of your depression. Vague feelings of guilt and self-recrimination are also common at this stage.

It is not at all unusual to try to hide from your depression. Common masks of depression are compulsive eating, excessive drinking, overworking, adultery, temper outbursts, negative and critical behavior, compulsive gambling, headaches, dizziness, and physical illness.

If you lose interest in your appearance and personal hygiene, your depression has gone beyond the moderate stage and is becoming severe. If you feel sick, resigned and passive, if your muscles ache and you feel constantly exhausted and listless, and if thinking logically is difficult, your depression is severe. Guilt and regret may become your constant companions. You may feel oppressed by friends and family. Ability to function at work drops drastically at this point; you may not go to work at all. You may feel completely hopeless and despairing; you want to be left with your misery, and suicidal thoughts may become constant.

See your doctor if you have any symptoms of moderate or severe depression. The depressive cycle can be halted and reversed through proper medication and treatment. The most common warning signal of impending depression is early-morning awakening. If you are troubled by it, and you have the slightest belief that you may have some of the other major symptoms of depression, see your physician.

Good News About Treatment

You might be surprised to learn that over the last twenty years the medical literature has been filled with good news about depression. This illness, once among the most resistant to treatment, has finally yielded significantly to modern healing efforts. In fact the discovery of a wide variety of antidepressant drugs has made depression one of the most effectively treatable of emotional ills. No matter how depressed you may be or become, the odds are excellent that you can recover completely within a matter of months if you receive proper medical care.

All too often, however, depression is misdiagnosed or overlooked by family doctors. Equally problematic is the unwillingness of most people to face their depression and get help. Some people still feel there is a stigma attached to receiving medical treatment for depression. If you feel this way, you must be quite unaware of the modern medical understanding of depression and the psyche. In fact, depression may not be an indicator of deep psychological problems, neurosis, or anything of the sort. On the contrary, it may be primarily a physiological problem resulting from chemical imbalances. It is far more like a hypothyroid condition than a hang-up. In this light, anyone who puts up with a life of quiet desperation simply to avoid facing his depression and need for help is foolish indeed.

But if you periodically get "the blues" and you feel your depression is low-grade, there is much you can do on you own to help halt your depressive episodes when they occur and prevent future ones. A first step is understanding how depression starts.

The Biological Basis of Major Depression

Over the past twenty years, the medical understanding of depression has changed radically. No longer is depression regarded as an emotional illness with solely psychological origins. Instead, doctors now hypothesize that the roots of major depression are primarily physiological in nature. This new view of depression developed from research on antidepressant medications first introduced in the late 1950s.[114]

The basic findings of this research may be summarized rather simply. The nerves in your brain and body depend on two complementary processes to transmit nerve impulses. Within a single nerve cell, a nerve impulse travels by virtue of changing electrical potentials. Between separate nerve cells, however, the impulse transmission involves a chemical exchange. Nerve cells do not touch; between two nerve cells there is a gap called a *synapse*. To allow a nerve impulse to cross the synapse, the active nerve cell must discharge a chemical, called a neurotransmitter, into the synapse. This chemical crosses the gap and stimulates the adjoining nerve cell to transmit the impulse electrically to the next synapse. The whole process is elegant and simple.

A problem can arise, however, when the body uses up the chemical neurotransmitters too quickly without replenishing the supply. If this occurs, your whole system becomes sluggish. Your brain cannot function properly because it does not have the neurotransmitters necessary to maintain a lively communication among its billions of cells. This insufficiency of neurotransmitters appears to cause the common symptoms of depressive illness. Antidepressant drugs help the body maintain an ample supply of neurotransmitters and can facilitate the successful treatment of 70 to 80 percent of depressive episodes.

This does not mean that emotional and psychological factors play no role in the onset of depression. On the contrary, these discoveries shed some light on how emotional events in your daily life can precipitate a depressive episode. A common denominator in almost all depression is the loss of someone or something highly valued:

—the death of a spouse
—the breakup of a love relationship
—the death of a child
—the loss of a job
—rejection by someone you love or respect
—getting passed over for a promotion
—a failure at work or at school
—a major incapacitating illness

Any of these events may cause an emotional letdown marked by intense feelings of frustration and helplessness. If you happen to be fatigued, have a hereditary predisposition to depression, or have had a number of disappointments in quick succession, this letdown apparently has the power to cause an imbalance in your brain's supply of neurotransmitters. The result is depression.

Of course, depression does not have to begin with a clear-cut emotional loss or disappointment. The process can be much more gradual and subtle. The best example of this process is the mid-life depression that one study shows is likely to hit 80 percent of the population between the ages of thirty-four and forty-four.[199]

The mid-life depression starts when you begin to face the incongruity between the aspirations of your youth and your prospects for achievement as you enter mid-life. In confronting this incongruity you may suffer gnawing regrets about your choice of job, spouse, place to live, and career path. Feelings of entrapment are common.

You may feel weighed down by responsibility while your desires for self-expression and personal growth have yet to be fulfilled. Disappointment and self-recrimination may grow day by day until the symptoms of depression appear. Sleepless mornings, reduced productivity, self-recrimination, and inability to enjoy life may build to the point where you want to bolt and run.

How you cope with this mid-life depression has a major impact on your future sense of well-being and personal integration. A successful resolution results in enormous personal growth and a higher level of personality integration. You will enter mid-life and be enthusiastic about your prospects for further growth. An unsuccessful resolution may cause bitterness or drastic and perhaps inadvisable changes in your life. Future depressions will probably be infrequent if you handle this mid-life crisis successfully, but they will almost surely recur if you achieve an incomplete resolution to this crisis.

Silencing Depression

People who suffer from low-grade depression respond well to the healing silence of meditation.[26] They often notice a significant improvement in mood within a matter of weeks or months, as well as a long-term reduction in their tendency toward recurring emotional lows. In Chapter 7, Dorothy's case illustrated that the healing silence can also be a useful adjunct in the holistic treatment of severe depression. It should be noted, however, that a minority of individuals prone to severe depression may respond adversely to meditation. Several clinicians have reported that meditation has increased symptoms among depressed patients, and in some cases to the point of suicidal intention.[26,126] In view of these reports, we recommend that individuals prone to severe depression begin meditation only under psychiatric supervision.

Between low-grade and severe depression, there is a vast middle ground that we call moderate depression. The case of Susan S., a twenty-nine-year-old married woman and mother of one, will illustrate the impact of the healing silence along with psychiatric support but without medication on a moderate depression. Susan tells her story in her own words.

On the bus ride home from work one day, I happened to read an article in a magazine. I immediately became engrossed because it was about depressions and what to do about them. It seemed as though the article was written for me—I had spent Christmas lying on the living-room floor, too depressed to go to the bedroom or to lie in bed. My poor husband had spent Christmas Eve shopping for the tree and decorating it alone. On Christmas Day, when relatives called from the East Coast, I pretended to be at the store; I couldn't get myself to stop crying long enough to talk to anyone. Even my friends didn't hear from me for months. I was a mess. I lost twenty pounds in two months. I gagged upon waking and was nauseated all day. You can just imagine how "valuable" I was at work. The article I read explained how a depression of this sort was very serious. It explained that help was needed immediately upon the discovery that you were experiencing a major depression. So I sought professional help.

I felt pangs of paranoia and embarrassment when I first arrived at the psychiatrist's office. What if I saw someone I knew sitting in the waiting room? What if the doctor had me committed and didn't call my husband? What if he excused himself after meeting me, and returned with men in white coats and a straitjacket for me? I greeted the doctor and burst into hysterical tears. I gave him a two-page list of my feelings and physical ailments and continued sobbing while the doctor made his way through my "diary." I wonder now how he could have understood anything I said that day. I told him that my main reason for waiting so long to seek professional help was that I believed myself beyond help. I was so fearful that I couldn't be helped that suicide seemed like the only answer.

The following list of symptoms should give a feeling for what I was going through.

1. Cried constantly over things I couldn't pinpoint.
2. Had digestive tract problems.
3. Was nauseous all the time, with periods of gagging.
4. Food was very distasteful.
5. My stomach would get "butterflies" very often. I was constantly breaking out in sweat for no apparent reason.
6. Body and mind raced constantly. Thoughts were confused. Concentration nil.
7. I didn't smile or laugh; could not seem to find anything happy to think about.
8. My muscles twitched, making me fearful of cramps in my toes, etc.

The doctor was sensitive and calm. He immediately recognized my condition and explained that I had a stress problem. That I could not cope with it and that I had a lot of it inside me. He said I might need medication but wanted me first to try TM because I still wasn't having too many sleeping problems.

I was not convinced that my entire problem was stress, and felt that the doctor would find out later how insane I really was. And for the meditation part? I didn't want any hippie techniques, or a religion or whatever freaky thing I though it was. I told him this and he smiled and said that he had been practicing TM for nearly two years. When he explained some of the benefits that he had already received and was still receiving, I relaxed a little and started to listen . . . something I hadn't done in so long. After all, I was paying him a fortune an hour, and I had gone to him for help, and that was what he was offering me.

The next week, after painfully withdrawing $200 from a savings account we had so carefully guarded and had been building for years toward our first home, my husband and I began TM. We reasoned that $200 was useless toward a home or anything in life when I was in such a stupor. So, we went to the lectures. After the first one I stayed to talk to the speaker, telling her of my problems and hoping with all my heart that she would say that TM was exactly what I needed. But ironically, she said she hoped I wasn't expecting a great change in myself immediately—I would get better with each meditation as I released stress. The technique, she said, was cumulative. She didn't make any promises to me about being elated in six months, and I was let down.

When the day came to learn TM, I was nervous. I didn't want to go through with it, but with my husband's support, I did. What I couldn't believe was how different I felt after my first meditation. I was calmer than I had been in months. I was deeply rested, could think clearly, and found that I could tune in to others, something I had not been able to do in months because I was so caught up in my own problems. My elevated mood lasted about fifteen minutes; then my anxiety, tension, depression, and foggy thinking returned, but they were not quite as severe as before.

I continued to meditate twice a day and gradually began coming out of my depression. At times I felt discouraged and would remark to my husband, "I haven't come very far at all. I'm not improving." He would laugh and cite some "before and after" instances. That provided encouragement and I would be on my way again, feeling good. He could see my improvements, my happier moments, my clarity in thinking, my growth. I couldn't see any improvement, but it was happening. There were no big discoveries at first. Just a gradual release of stress and the emergence of the happiness I had in me all the time.

The last depression I had was a year ago after giving birth to our child. The "blues" didn't last long at all. Now that I can look back on two years of growth, I can see that I've come a long way. I am happy almost all the time, although there are times when I realize that I would prefer being somewhere else, and doing something else. But none of these thoughts changes the happy feeling that pervades regardless of the emotion I am experiencing.

I enjoy natural phenomena like sunsets, sunrises, rains, oceans, and many things in life most people take for granted. I don't need a radio or television blaring away when I'm home. I am not afraid to hear myself think. I am much more at peace with myself, and it keeps getting better. I like doing more things, and I am more interested in people. I am finding myself and beginning to know what things make me and my family happy. I have never been in tune with my feelings and the world before. This growth has fulfilled my desire for happiness. It has shown me the way to enjoy life, how to cope with life's ups and downs and how to take each day as it comes.

How Susan's Case Applies to You

Susan's case should encourage you about your ability to beat depression. To understand just how the healing silence can help, however, we have got to take a close look at Susan's healing and growth pattern.

First, it should be evident that inner silence is not an instant cure for depression. Your first experience of TM may produce a sharp improvement in your mood, and if you have been depressed for several weeks or more, the first half-hour after meditation may seem miraculous. You may have more energy, less anxiety, and greater emotional ease and mental clarity than you have had in a long time. You may feel as if a great burden has been lifted from your shoulders. All these feelings are natural, but you must recognize that the immediate effects of meditation wear off. You can't expect one meditation to end your depression forever. Your depressive feelings will return, though perhaps not as severely as before.

Second, long-term growth—emotional development that can end your recurring bouts with the blues—depends on the regular, cumulative effects of the healing silence. More than two years elapsed between Susan's depressive crisis and her victory over depression.

Third, if you are depressed, you will probably need the support of a friend, spouse, or physician to meditate regularly. Your depressive tendencies cause you to get discouraged easily. If you feel especially low one day, and haven't noticed any dramatic changes over a few weeks, you may want to skip meditation. Unless you have support from someone who can point out how you have grown, you may well stop meditating at the first low period you encounter. This need for support cannot be overemphasized if you plan to use the healing silence to overcome depression. Therefore, one of the components of your plan to beat depression must be a pact with a friend, spouse, or doctor to help you stay regular in your meditation program.

Finally, the healing silence alone cannot eliminate depression. You must develop an integrated program to deal with your depression physically, emotionally, and spiritually. There is much you can do for yourself to facilitate the healing process. One of the most important things to do, if you have a serious depression, is to follow your doctor's instructions and take medication as recommended.

Some Strategies for Overcoming Depression

Most depressions blow over by themselves within six to eight weeks if you give yourself some extra rest and let the natural healing process occur. The most important thing you can do is remind yourself to have hope. All is not darkness. There was once sunshine; there will be again. In addition, the following suggestions can be very helpful.

• Eliminate self-recrimination and regret. A technique called thought-stopping may work well. Whenever you start to ruminate about your mistakes or berate yourself as an ineffective, unattractive person, simply tell these thoughts to stop. They are worthless and untrue. You can silently or vocally yell, "Stop, go away, I won't have you in my head anymore." You will be surprised at how this simple exertion of your will gets rid of these destructive thoughts and lifts your mood.

• Recognize your depression as an opportunity for growth. Don't feel guilty, inadequate, or weak. Depressions are a natural part of living and do not indicate an underlying personality weakness. But they are a sign that you have been neglecting the most important person in your life—you. This low period is going to force you to start paying more attention to your needs, and as a result, you will grow into a much healthier, happier, and lively person.

• Accept your need for comforting. When you are depressed, you hurt, so you need some extra care. Tell your family and close friends that you feel low, and let them help you. They will want to give you the extra warmth, kindness, and attention you need at this time.

• Set up your own support system. These days you'll need the help of others. You can ask friends and family to help you meet some of your responsibilities if you are having difficulty meeting them alone. Oftentimes, companionship is all a depressed person requires to begin taking hold of his or her life again. Invite a friend to stay overnight, visit a relative for dinner, or spend an evening with your neighbors. Simple steps like these can make a world of difference.

• Ask your family to ease up on you. Failure to meet family expectations can exacerbate your feelings of worthlessness. You have a right to some time for healing and attending to your own needs.

• Communicate and ventilate. The worst thing you can do is stay home alone and brood about your misery. Discuss your depression with a close friend. You'll learn you are not the only one who gets depressed and will probably get some good suggestions about how to get yourself moving again.

• Treat yourself to what you enjoy most. Have a meal at a fine restaurant. Get a total beauty treatment at the finest salon you can afford. If you are an ice cream lover, go ahead and splurge; forget about calories for this one treat. Buy yourself a cashmere sweater or shawl, a suit, or a pair of fine shoes. Buy some fresh flowers. In short, indulge yourself.

• If you have been planning a vacation, now may be the time to take it, especially if your depression is mild.

• Surround yourself with life. Buy a plant, adopt a kitten or a puppy, set up a small aquarium, or just keep fresh fruit in a lovely bowl.

• Be a helper. Doing something for someone else is one of the best ways to stop feeling sorry for yourself. Volunteer to spend a few hours a week at a home for the elderly, become a Big Brother or a Big Sister, visit someone in the hospital, help a friend paint his or her apartment, volunteer in a hospital emergency room, help out at a local youth center, or do volunteer work for any charitable organization that you believe is worthwhile.

• Establish a schedule for your daily routine. If you start getting up, meditating, eating, and sleeping at roughly the same time every day, you will be surprised at how your brooding tends to lessen. Regularity is a tonic for the human biomachinery and helps your body restore its natural balance and attunement. This does not mean that you must become fanatical about your schedule; its purpose is simply to give your life a natural rhythm, especially during this period of distress.

• Rest and exercise. When depression disturbs your sleep cycle, you tend to feel tired during the day and to become sedentary. This worsens your condition. Moderate exercise will counteract this cycle and help you feel delightfully tired at bedtime. This physical fatigue will help you sleep through the night and wake up refreshed. The choice of exercise is up to you; walking, running, tennis, squash, swimming, and handball are all equally good.

• What you eat can make a difference. Extra protein will increase your energy, so eat more meat, fish, fowl, milk, seeds, soybeans, and whole grains. A vitamin B supplement, a vitamin C supplement, and a multivitamin supplement are also a good idea. Increased calcium (from a tablet or skim milk) and potassium (from a mineral supplement or potatoes, parsley, and bananas) are also recommended.

• If you are angry, express it safely. Depression is often a way to choke back anger that you are afraid to express. But by choking back the anger, you choke yourself. If you are angry at someone, go ahead and express your feelings appropriately. If you are enraged and can't get your anger under control, you can let some of it out viscerally. Try punching a pillow, hitting a punching bag, pounding on a piano, or just yelling at the top of your lungs (alone and with the windows closed, please). If your depression stems partly or wholly from repressed anger, you will note remarkable improvement when you let off some steam.

• Avoid making major decisions until you feel good again. Because depression clouds your judgment, you cannot expect to make important decisions wisely at this time. Effective decision making requires mental energy that you just don't have at the moment. If you try to make an important decision, you will probably find the whole process difficult and frustrating. You may even berate yourself for your apparent loss of ability. Recognize the nature of your condition and don't worsen it through the demands of decision making if you can avoid or postpone them.

• If your depression is the low-grade type that often accompanies entry into mid-life, you have got some special work to do. First, listen to your feelings; don't try to suppress them with more work, more sex, or more alcohol. Your depression is telling you that now is the time to take stock of where you have been and where you want to go. This is not an easy task. Coping with this transition period may take one or two years, but the outcome can be a deeply sustaining personal renewal. Second, face the issues in your life that are most troubling. You may be feeling trapped by family responsibility, discouraged about your career, angry about the loss of your idealism, or distraught about your inability to fulfill those desires most important to you. Satisfying resolutions to these issues can be found, and you now have the maturity to do it. A new joy in your family, a renewed confidence in your work, an optimistic outlook, and a sense of personal liberation are within your reach. Finally, be bold. Just by exploring these issues within yourself, your depression will begin to lift. As you get closer to discovering new directions that are right for you, you will note a spontaneous surge of energy and enthusiasm for life. This is the initial stage of your renewal. Have confidence in yourself and your insights. Act, change, grow. The future is yours to enjoy.

18. Improving Your Sexual Attunement

For the past decade, the media have propagated the idea that a great sexual revolution is taking place, that everybody is enjoying sex, and that the key to sexual fulfillment is knowledge of sophisticated technique. While it is no doubt true that a significant change in sexual attitudes is under way, it also appears that the sexual revolution has been oversold. People are talking more openly about sex and may be engaging in it more freely, but not everyone is enjoying it. In fact, the majority of Americans today feel some dissatisfaction with their sex lives and want to improve. The liberalization of attitudes about sexuality is in part helping people admit this fact to themselves and their sexual partners.

You may be among the majority who would like to improve their sex lives. If so, the first thing you should know is how much company you actually have. In one survey, 98 percent of men and women reported some anxiety about their sex lives.[20] Dr. William Masters estimates that sexual problems are so widespread that nearly half of all marriages are troubled by them. Recognizing a problem is the first step toward solving it; so if you have admitted that you want to improve your sex life, you are already well on the way.

In one very important sense, there is a great irony about sexual problems. On the one hand, sexual anxieties can cause great distress and worry; on the other, few psychological problems respond so well to treatment and are so easy to resolve. Unfortunately, shame and embarrassment all too often cause people to avoid seeking help. The first step in improving your sex life is recognizing how relatively easy it is to do! Sex therapy clinics have a very high rate of success, often over 90 percent. We are going to present some of the principles and techniques taught in these clinics to help resolve the most common sexual anxieties and problems. Enhancing your sexual satisfaction is an important part of a holistic health program.

What is your concern? You may be bothered by simple fears and self-doubt that block your full enjoyment and make you feel inhibited. Or you may have a specific sexual problem, such as the inability to climax or climaxing too soon. Because sexuality in its true sense is not just confined to the bedroom, your problem may be broader. You may need to develop your capacity to enjoy the sensual dimension of everyday life. You might also feel that you live too much through your head and not enough through your heart and body. In any case, the likelihood is that you will benefit significantly from a holistic program.

Common Sexual Problems and Their Origins

Healthy sexuality evolves through a natural developmental process that begins with the child's curiosity about his sex organs. A period of intense concern about sexual identity almost inevitably occurs during adolescence. Few people are exempt from the need during young adulthood to abandon their efforts to prove themselves and discover the natural rhythms that lead to sexual fulfillment. Further stages in the development of a fully vibrant sexual identity involve the discovery of the relation between sexuality and love, and the willingness to assume responsibility inherent in that relationship. Experimentation, play, and personality growth under stress-free conditions all tend to coalesce into a healthy adult sexual identity.

The fact is that few people enjoy an upbringing conducive to fully healthy sexual development. Some people internalize negative feelings such as guilt, shame, and anger that impede their sexual functioning along with their total personality development. Due to social pressures about sexual achievement, almost everyone harbors some performance anxieties that may interfere with fully satisfying sexual functioning. Finally, misinformation and ignorance about sexuality still cause debilitating worries for large numbers of people. These in fact are the most common sexual problems: anxieties about performance, inhibiting feelings such as guilt and shame, and belief in debilitating sexual myths.

Over the past decade medical thinking about sexual problems has

changed significantly.[152] It was once thought that all sexual disturbances originated in deep, unconscious psychological disturbances
such as castration fears, unresolved Oedipal conflicts, and real or fan-
tasized sexual trauma during childhood. Psychiatrists assumed that
treatment required long reconstructive psychotherapy. With the
work of Masters and Johnson, the error in this thinking has become
apparent. In the vast majority of cases, sexual difficulties are rooted
in far simpler terrain.

The two principal obstacles to vibrant sexual functioning are performance fears and spectator roles. Anxiety inhibits normal sexual
functioning in men and women alike. If you doubt your ability to
function well or fear you may be unable to satisfy your partner, your
fears become self-fulfilling. Through fear you become anxious and
physiologically inhibit your natural sexual capacity. Similarly, if you
hold back from abandonment to sensual, sexual pleasure (i.e., remain
a spectator who watches your every move), you inhibit your capacity
for enjoyment. The result again is self-fulfilling. By holding back,
you confirm your worst fears. Either you fail to become aroused or
you find your partner responding slowly.

These common causes of sexual dysfunction are exacerbated by
emphasis on achievement. Many men and a growing number of
women have internalized a sense of competition regarding their ability to satisfy their partners, and as a result either consciously or un-
consciously fear not performing up to standard. The tendency to
measure sexual success in terms of "how long" or "how many"
strongly reinforces this approach to sexuality. This competitive attitude requires that you divide yourself into the sexual performer and
the nonparticipating judge. As a result, you put half of your energies
into enjoyment and the other half into self-criticism and anxiety.

While simple anxieties are the primary causes of most sexual problems, sex therapists define sexual dysfunctions very specifically. In
clinical terms, sexual dysfunction is a disturbance in arousal (vasocongestion) and/or climax (orgastic release) during sex play or intercourse. There basically are six dysfunctions, three each for men and
women.

The three dysfunctions of women are:

1. Vaginismus—The muscles surrounding the vaginal entrance
   contract spasmodically when an attempt at penetration oc-

curs. Entry of the penis into the vagina is thus painful for the woman or altogether impossible.

2. Aversion—Despite adequate sexual stimulation, small vessels in the genital area fail to fill with blood and lubrication does not occur. This condition was once known by the misnomer frigidity. Research has shown that warm, sensitive, responsive women can suffer from aversion; consequently, the term "frigidity" is no longer thought to be accurate to describe the condition.

3. Orgastic Dysfunction—Though arousal with its symptoms of vasocongestion and lubrication may occur, the woman may have difficulty releasing the orgastic reflex through clitoral stimulation, coitus, or both.

Male dysfunctions are:

1. Impotence—Despite sexual stimulation of the penis and testes, vasocongestion leading to erection of the penis does not occur.

2. Premature Ejaculation—Though erection occurs normally, the individual has difficulty controlling his orgastic reflex. Ejaculation occurs within minutes or seconds after intromission of the phallus into the vagina.

3. Retarded Ejaculation—Erection occurs normally, but the individual has difficulty releasing the orgastic reflex even though he may receive a great deal of stimulation either manually or through coitus.

Despite cultural reinforcement of competitive sexual attitudes, most sexual dysfunctions are not hard to cure. They respond well to treatment because they result from mild problems such as superficial insecurities, tension due to poor communication, anxiety resulting from misconceptions about human sexuality, or temporary causes such as fatigue, worries, or pressure at work. Of course, in some cases, the roots of sexual dysfunction run deeper. Crippling guilt, debilitating shame, and venomous hostility may underlie marked personality as well as sexual disturbance. Of all people with sexual problems, however, this group composes a small minority.

More significant but more often forgotten is another cause of sexual dysfunction—organic illness. It is estimated that as much as 15 percent of all sexual dysfunctions have a physical or metabolic origin.[110] Some of the common illnesses that disrupt sexual functioning are diabetes, multiple sclerosis, and thyroid dysfunction. In addition, some medications such as reserpine and quanethidine (antihypertensive drugs) and Mellaril (a major tranquilizer) can disrupt sexual arousal. These physical causes of sexual dysfunction deserve special mention because they are too often overlooked, resulting in unnecessarily prolonged suffering and wasted time. Prior to any therapy for sexual dysfunction, a thorough medical exam is essential.

The most heartening conclusion of current research on sexual dysfunction is that most sexual problems can be easily solved. If you have anxieties due to misconceptions or ignorance about technique, or if your problems are rooted in simple insecurities, you can probably benefit substantially from self-help. By simple insecurities we mean fear of failure, inadequate performance, rejection, or difficulty letting go and enjoying sexual abandon. Your principal need is a healthy ambiance, an atmosphere of mutual disinhibition and trust, during sex play and coitus. This ambiance can help you lose your fears and discover your natural sexual power. Security, openness, comfort, and a mature partner whom you can trust are the elements for the ambiance you need. This atmosphere along with a better understanding of human sexuality can help your sexuality to blossom.

A Physiological Review

Our purpose here is to explain the physiological high points of sexual functioning in order to help you see how performance fears and spectator roles block your natural sexual capability and what you can do to change. We will also review several of the most common, anxiety-producing sexual myths.

Dr. William Masters has repeatedly pointed out that fully vital sexual health unfolds automatically as a person learns to let go and be natural. At the 1975 American Psychiatric Association convention he explained: "Sex is a natural function. Our difficulties in the late 1950s were that we were making tremendous efforts and putting a lot of energy in trying to teach men to have an erection and women to respond sexually. No wonder we didn't have much success in our treatment . . . There is no way we can teach a man to have an erection . . . if [sex] is a natural function, then we don't need to teach anything; we only need to remove the stumbling blocks."

Human sexuality is one of the most delicately balanced natural functions of your body. It depends upon the smooth interplay between the parasympathetic (relaxing and energy-restoring) and sympathetic (stimulating and energy-expending) branches of your autonomic (involuntary) nervous system. What makes this interplay so easily subject to disruption is the power of each branch to inhibit the other's functioning and the sensitivity of the entire system to emotional states.

Paradoxically, the initial stages of sexual arousal—erection and vaginal lubrication—depend primarily on the predominance of parasympathetic activity. In everyday terms, this means that sexual arousal requires a relatively rested, relaxed state of mind and body. If you try too hard or feel tense during foreplay, your sympathetic system is mobilized, often to the point where parasympathetic activity, along with the biological capacity for sexual arousal, becomes inhibited. Once this occurs, you have lost touch with the natural rhythms of sexual enjoyment, and your experience is certain to be unsatisfying unless you stop and regain your lost attunement.

A completely fulfilling sexual experience requires a smooth shift from parasympathetic dominance during arousal to sympathetic dominance at climax. If you respect your physical and emotional rhythms, this whole process will work easily, automatically, and with delightful pleasures. The key to mutually fulfilling sex is to begin with an ample period of relaxed sex play. With adequate understanding about arousal techniques, this period of sex play can guarantee optimum sexual fulfillment. It can dispel the superficial fears and anxieties that cause sexual problems and can heighten the tenderness and sharing so crucial to fully satisfying sex. By learning to let sexual arousal build at its own pace, you take pressure off yourself and your partner, and free yourself to enjoy full sexual abandon. Play, delight, trust, and pleasure are the key elements in this process.

A healthy ambiance during sex play is impossible, however, if you are burdened by any of the common myths about sexuality.

For example, there is the myth of the vaginal orgasm. Anxiety and worry about orgasm are basic building blocks of orgasmic dysfunction. The Freudian distinction between the so-called mature vaginal orgasm as opposed to the immature clitoral one has long been cause for distress among women. Recent sex research has shown that all the searching for the grand vaginal orgasm is for naught. There is only one kind of female orgasm and it involves both the clitoris and the vagina. During arousal, which requires stimulation of the clitoris, vasocongestion occurs in the vagina, clitoris, and breasts. At climax, muscles around the vagina contract at .8-second intervals and a surge of pleasure occurs. The intensity of pleasure can vary from that of a purely localized feeling around the clitoris and vagina to a rush of pleasure filling the entire body. A variation in the intensity from time to time is perfectly natural. Striving for a grand orgasm, however, is a mistake, because striving contributes to anxiety that blocks natural abandon. And the key to orgasmic delight is the capacity to abandon yourself to the natural rhythms of arousal and climax.

Another myth that causes unnecessary worry is that about penile size. Numerous studies have shown that depth of penetration is not a key to female arousal. The inner two-thirds of the vagina is devoid of nerve endings and is relatively insensitive. Therefore, the small differences in size among erect penises is not significant. Furthermore, research shows that the difference in size among smaller and larger flaccid penises is frequently minimized in the erect state. The smaller flaccid penis undergoes a greater degree of enlargement relative to its initial size than does the larger flaccid penis. In any case, the vagina accommodates itself to the penis, whether large or small. The most important element in arousing a woman is providing adequate stimulation to the clitoris. For this reason, many women find shallow penetration more exciting; it can allow for greater clitoral stimulation.

Despite recently liberated sexual attitudes, myths about the dangers of masturbation still abound. Many men and women still believe that self-stimulation is immature, neurotic, degrading, and harmful. In fact, none of these is true. Self-stimulation is normal, natural, and healthy. It won't cause physical damage or make you neurotic. On the contrary, some recent research indicates that it may be a prerequisite to fully healthy, sexual functioning.[20,110] There appears to be a direct correlation between frequency of adolescent masturbation and adult sexual responsiveness among men and women. Through self-stimulation, you become sensitive to your own rhythms of arousal and climax, and can better communicate what arouses you to your partner. Masturbation with your partner can increase warmth, trust, and communication. For men and women it can be helpful in resolving orgastic dysfunctions and developing orgastic control. It should not be thought less desirable than coitus. Self-stimulation is simply one among many forms of healthy sexual activity, and it has the special value of providing the full cycle of arousal and climax without the performance pressure that sometimes accompanies coitus.

The myth of ever-ready male functioning is one of the most disturbing for men. The most common cause of impotence is fear that an earlier temporary bout of impotence will be repeated. This fear stems from the belief that the penis should work like a machine—on command. During adolescence, men become accustomed to arousal at the slightest provocation. By their late twenties, however, the storms of hormonal changes have long since subsided and their arousal capacity becomes much more sensitive to such everyday factors as fatigue, alcohol, and the pressures of work. Failure to become aroused when you're very tired or pressured should not be cause for shame or concern, and you needn't worry that a temporary bout of erectile dysfunction will be repeated as long as you get rest. You have to learn that you're not a machine and your virility depends on a balanced life including adequate rest and recreation.

Perhaps the most disturbing myth for women is that failure to reach orgasm during coitus indicates an abnormality. Some women feel guilty because they achieve orgasm easily and regularly through self-stimulation but infrequently during coitus. Others feel guilty because they achieve much more pleasurable orgasms through self-stimulation than coitus. The simple truth is that these reports indicate the norm rather than the exception. Most women do achieve more satisfying orgasm through self-stimulation and do not achieve orgasm regularly through coitus. These findings do not indicate poor sexual responsiveness among women but simply that coitus does not provide most women with adequate clitoral stimulation to reach orgasm. Despite the psychologically arousing and satisfying nature of coitus, the thrusting phallus does not provide the best possible mechanical stimulation of the clitoris. The traction of the thrusting phallus against the clitoral hood and the pressure of the male pubic bone around the clitoral area are simply not enough for most women to reach orgasm. This fact suggests that more direct stimulation is appropriate before, after, or during coitus.

Because our culture has only recently begun to regard sex as a natural function, numerous other myths about male and female sexual functioning still abound. There are myths about "frigidity," oral sex, venereal disease, coitus during menstruation and pregnancy, to mention just a few of the subjects still clouded in misunderstanding. If you do not feel comfortable about any phase of your own sexuality, educating yourself by reading several leading books on human sexuality can be very helpful. In particular, we recommend Masters and Johnson's *Human Sexual Response*, Alex Comfort's *The Joy of Sex*, and Helen Singer Kaplan's *The Illustrated Manual of Sex Therapy*.

Ways to Enhance Your Sexual Pleasuring

In treating thousands of people with sexual dysfunctions, modern sex therapists have compiled many techniques useful in overcoming specific dysfunctions as well as generally heightening sexual experience. Few of these techniques are actually new. Men and women have been using them for hundreds if not thousands of years. The most valuable contribution of modern sex therapy is the lifting of veils of myth and ignorance that have deterred people from exploring these ways of enhancing sexual satisfaction.

Our point in presenting these techniques is not to make you feel pressured to improve your sexual ability. Too many sex manuals inadvertently heighten performance anxiety in this way. When reviewing the following techniques, try to think of them as possibilities for you to explore when the time feels right rather than as technical maneuvers to solve specific problems. All these techniques are used in sex therapy, but you can achieve best results by treating them simply as new ways to enhance your pleasure and have fun.

• Slow down, take your time, and cherish your lover. This is the single most important piece of advice we can give. A symphony does not open with a crescendo, and you can't make a symphony of your lovemaking if you rush to climax. Slowing down is important because it allows you to tune in to the rhythms of your own and your partner's arousal. By slowing down, you can also take time to explore new sensual erotic techniques that can heighten your pleasure.

• Try some old-fashioned romanticism. With the explicit sex in literature and film, many old-fashioned erotic techniques are forgotten. Remember the passion of your teen-age kisses, or the first time your lover took off your clothes? Subtle, delicate kisses will always remain a wonderful turn-on, as will slowly, artfully disrobing your mate. A slow, sexy strip is another technique that rarely fails to arouse a lover's passion, and almost every woman knows how to disrobe in a highly erotic fashion. Even if she is wearing only a negligee, taking it off can be a wonderfully erotic step. Don't be shy or ashamed. Go with your imagination and enjoy your fantasies. You may be surprised at how aroused you and your partner can get even before you are both nude.

• Take plenty of time to delight in giving each other pleasures. A basic prescription in sex therapy is for a couple to take off all their clothes and then take turns nuzzling, kissing, and playing with each other. The couple is specifically instructed to engage in so-called pleasuring without proceeding on to intercourse no matter how aroused they may become. This technique is very helpful in diminishing anxiety about performance as well as encouraging abandon to sensual experience.

What do you do during pleasuring? Anything to give your partner pleasure except having intercourse. Don't think that pleasuring means you must immediately turn to the nipples, clitoris, or penis. Try a feather-light stroking with your fingertips up the underside of the arm. Or light kisses on the nape of the neck, between the breasts, along the stomach and each inner thigh. Take plenty of time before you finally directly stimulate penis, vagina, or clitoris. Sometimes, your lover may prefer a firm touch, but again your caresses can explore buttocks, thighs, or anywhere before you finally tease penis or clitoris. The key is to use your imagination and enjoy.

• Be sensitive to what arouses your mate and communicate what arouses you. He or she may find slow, light touching most arousing or prefer firm stroking of muscle. Common turn-offs are a hasty jump to coitus, and a demanding attitude. In any case, you have to learn specifically what you and your mate find most erotic. And you can't expect to do this without direct communication. Don't be afraid of simple direct statements such as: "I like it when you . . ." "It turns me on when you let me . . ." "I really enjoy when you . . . my clitoris." "I'd like it if you'd . . . more." It is also helpful if you communicate your feelings. If you feel anxious during pleasuring, tell your partner "I get uptight when you . . ." Expressing your feelings will deepen your trust and help lessen anxiety. Communication helps take the pressure out of lovemaking and opens unexpected possibilities for enjoyment because you learn new ways of arousing and satisfying each other. Intercourse becomes one delightful part of your lovemaking and not its only element.

• Experiment with sexual fantasy. Dreams are an important part of living. They expand your vision of what life can be. So too with sexual fantasies. There is absolutely no reason to feel guilty or inhibited about your fantasies no matter how wild or "forbidden" you may believe they are. In fact, sex therapists frequently prescribe fantasy to help overcome many dysfunctions. Sexual fantasy can be very helpful in reducing anxiety and nurturing arousal. It can also help dispel boredom and monotony. You and your mate can use it as a stepping stone to exploring sexual adventures that can enhance your love life. Finally, sexual fantasy can be used to develop communication and trust. By sharing your fantasies with your partner, you can mutually disinhibit each other. You can provide a warm, safe environment where anxieties that may surface can dissolve in love and pleasure.

Don't worry about how wild your fantasies may be, and don't be judgmental about them. Fantasies of group sex, incest, homosexual acts, exhibitionist acts, seduction, rape, and sexually initiating an adolescent are all normal. You needn't feel ashamed or guilty about them. There is a world of difference between fantasy and behavior. On the other hand, many fully normal, healthy, and sexy people do not fantasize, so don't worry if you don't either.

If you would like to develop your ability to fantasize, try the following steps.

1. Begin simply. The easiest fantasies to create are new and interesting places to make love. How about a beach in the early morning, in a swimming pool at midday, or in a meadow during late afternoon. Don't hesitate to get wild. How about under a table in a posh restaurant, in the back seat of a commuter train, or in a taxicab.

2. Next you could try fantasizing sex with a variety of partners. You might dream up a dark Latin or a blond Scandinavian. You can envision two lovers at the same time fulfilling your wildest desires. Your fantasies might go further to include people whom you know, such as your neighbor, a co-worker, or your boss. Don't worry; fantasies

needn't be acted out, and you needn't fear losing your good judgment about the appropriateness of doing so.

3. Once your fantasies begin to erupt in rich detail, let yourself go. Don't slam the door on any of your fantasies because of guilt or inhibition. One of the most important values of fantasy is its effect in helping you lessen your anxiety. So enjoy. If you feel inclined, go ahead and stimulate yourself while you fantasize. You will gain richness, heighten your pleasure, and enhance the value of your fantasy.

4. When you feel comfortable with your fantasies, try sharing some of them with your partner. Be cautious here. Unless you both feel very secure, you might run into difficulty (e.g., with a fantasy about a co-worker or a neighbor). Jealousy may raise its head. If you go slowly and take care to provide each other with ample support, however, sharing your fantasies can deepen your love and open a great adventure. You may decide to live out some mutually appealing ones.

• Enjoy erotica. While a considerable portion of today's erotic literature and film is boring and some downright distasteful, selective viewing and reading can be worthwhile. Like sexual fantasy, pleasing erotica can enhance your capacity for arousal and heighten your sexual responsiveness. Attitudes about the X rating have changed so markedly over the past decade that you needn't worry that erotic films can be found only in sleazy neighborhoods. By choosing wisely, and going to an erotic film with your mate (e.g., *Emmanuelle, Deep Throat, Bilitis*), you can break down inhibitions and learn what turns each other on.

• Massage can be wonderfully erotic and useful in reducing anxiety. You need a warm, quiet setting, soft lighting, scented oil (warmed by candle heat or a coffee warmer), a firm mattress, soft pillows or carpet, and lots of time. Use plenty of oil and touch continuously in a regular, easy rhythm. Use the full surface of your hands. You may use different strokes—circling, pressing, kneading, rotating, shaking, lifting, pulling—for different parts of the body. Don't neglect any body parts. The head, hands, legs, and feet are too often neglected. A soft hairbrush, shampooing the scalp, a rolling pin on the back and legs, a vibrator (or two, one in each hand), and an alcohol rub can add delightful effects. Above all, an atmosphere of safety and trust is essential. Never criticize or tease your partner about being tense, ticklish, or guarded. The purpose of this exercise is to help tension and anxieties fade. Intuition is the best guide to good massage, but a book such as *The Art of Sensual Massage* may also help.

• Masturbation alone and with your partner can be very helpful in enhancing your sexual pleasure and skill. To some people, the word "masturbation" generates feelings of disgust, but these are usually individuals with a low level of sexual responsiveness and a high level of anxiety. Surveys indicate that masturbation is a normal, valuable part of healthy sexual functioning, and the most highly sexually responsive people feel very comfortable with it. Guilt and shame about masturbation, on the other hand, can be quite disruptive. Sex therapists do not view masturbation as an immature or adolescent avenue to sexual satisfaction. On the contrary, they see it as another, highly reliable method that can be very useful in developing sexual responsiveness and orgastic control.

• Exercising musculature in your pelvis and groin can also enhance sexual responsiveness by improving blood flow and sensitivity. Sex therapists often recommend the pubococcygeus muscle exercise for women. These muscles surround your vagina and you use them to stem the flow of urine. To tone them up, you should contract them (imagine you are stopping the urinary flow) for a few minutes several times a day for a month. You can do this while cooking, watching television, driving, or during almost any routine activity. For men also, pelvic tension can be a problem. One exercise you might try in order to loosen up is to sit on a chair and contract one buttock at a time. Try this ten times a day for several weeks and you may notice significant heightening of orgasmic intensity.

• Don't be afraid to experiment with a variety of techniques for direct genital stimulation. One of the most arousing techniques for a male is for his mate to lubricate the penis with petroleum jelly and then use manual stimulation. Sex therapists report this technique highly effective with men suffering from temporary erectile dysfunction. During this technique, the man should not focus on his penis. He shouldn't look to see whether he is getting an erection or how hard it may be. Instead, he should displace his anxiety with lush fantasy. Among the most effective pleasure-enhancing aids for women is the vibrator. Sex therapists report that it is often effective in stimulating highly unresponsive women to orgasm. By increasing the frequency of your orgasms with a vibrator, you can also enhance your orgasmic potential during coitus. Don't be embarrassed or ashamed about adding a mechanical dimension to your sex life. Even fully orgasmic women report that vibrators expand their pleasure. Select your vibrator with care. The phallically shaped, battery-operated type are not recommended because they do not provide sufficient stimulation. Almost any electric massager, widely available in drugstores, will work well.

• Oral sex is an avenue for giving and receiving delightful pleasures. Developing your skill in satisfying your partner orally can be helpful in reducing anxiety about intercourse. Once you know that you can satisfy him or her orally, pressure to perform through coitus diminishes drastically. The result is a two-fold enhancement of your sexual experience. You develop a new way to give and receive pleasure, and you free yourself to enjoy coitus without anxiety. Skillful oral sex requires practice and communication. You must take your time and your partner must tell you what he or she likes just as you must tell him/her. Because some people have an initial aversion to the idea of oral sex, you should never try to force it on your partner. Go slowly, share your fantasy, practice good hygiene, be tender, and initial barriers will disappear.

• Two techniques have proved helpful for men to increase their orgastic control. One technique is called Seeman's maneuver. Once you achieve a good erection, you ask your partner to squeeze your penis just below the glans (head). This will not hurt, but your erection will partially diminish. When it returns, you will have enhanced your staying power. You can also use this technique to advantage during coitus. When you feel the early signs of impending orgasm, withdraw and ask your partner to squeeze you until your erection partially abates. Don't worry, it will return and you will be able to resume with better control. The second technique is known as stop-start. Several seconds prior to ejaculation, the male experiences pleasurable contractions. If you stop thrusting when you feel them, you can postpone ejaculation. When you stop, you should concentrate on your feelings. Don't get lost in fantasy or you may lose control. Breathe deeply and relax. The pressure for orgasm will lessen. After a few minutes, you can slowly resume thrusting. A cooperative partner is essential for developing orgastic control. You must be sensitive to each other's signs of impending orgasm. Describe what happens and how you feel. Initial success will build confidence and control.

Mastering the stop-start technique is the key to developing your potential for multiorgasms. Men, like women, can have one orgasm after another. The key is for the male to retard ejaculation. By concentrating on your sensations immediately prior to orgasm, you can experience a minor orgasm without ejaculation. You can enjoy these minor orgasms as frequently as one per minute. The net result is a slow building of pleasure until you finally decide to give in to a grand finale. If you try to make a competition of this process by keeping score, you are bound to be disappointed. You won't achieve multiorgasms through striving. What you need is a very close relationship with your partner physically, emotionally, and spiritually. You must be able to trust her completely.

• A very valuable technique for women is called the bridge maneuver. If you can easily masturbate to orgasm, this technique can help you achieve orgasm regularly during coitus. Most women need more clitoral stimulation to achieve orgasm than is usually provided by a thrusting phallus. What you do is "bridge" your need for additional stimulation during coitus by providing it manually. When your partner enters your vagina, you both make sure to continue stimulating your clitoris as directly as possible. Either you do it with your hand, he does it with his, or for a titanic experience, you might try a vibrator. Don't be put off by how this technique may sound. It is not cheating. Most couples find it effective and liberating. Performance anxieties drop sharply and regular practice of the bridge may sufficiently enhance your orgasmic potential so as to make the bridge no longer necessary.

• There is one technique we recommend that is just beginning to gain recognition. Start running every day. What could running have to do with sex? Everything. Evidence is mounting that running or daily vigorous exercise has a very dramatic effect on capacity for full sexual abandon and enjoyment. Certainly it will reduce anxiety and improve your physical self-image. These effects alone are bound to enhance sexual attunement. Some runners go so far as to say that you really haven't lived until you have taken a jogger to bed, especially if that jogger is you.

• By far the most important element for fulfilling sex is love. You can achieve purely physical satisfaction with a stranger, but love opens the doors for tenderness and sharing that can make sexual experience divine. The more fully you and your partner can be in touch with each other's feelings, the better will be your sexual experience. A compulsive search for bigger and better orgasms alone will only produce flashes of excitement followed by boredom and irritation. The key to developing your full sexual potential lies not just in learning new techniques but in unfolding your full capacity for love. When sex play flows on a strong current of love, you may discover what many cultures have recognized for thousands of years. Sexual sharing can become a sublime sacrament.

High-Level Sexual Attunement

The foundation of normal sexual functioning and high levels of sexual satisfaction is a relaxed, rested mind and body. Sex therapists have recently rediscovered this principle, but it has actually been known for thousands of years. It appears in the oldest texts on sexual health such as the *Kama Sutra.*

A principal obstacle in sex therapy is the client's tendency, usually in response to anxiety or fear, to control or manipulate his experience. This effort heightens activity of the sympathetic nervous system and blocks parasympathetic functioning critical to arousal. Because the client usually knows that he or she needs to stop trying, a therapist's instruction to "take it easy, stop trying so hard" can be irritating.

Healing silence produces deep and lasting relaxation. Beyond that, it increases sensitivity to a natural, uncontrived, and unhurried progression of experience. Through the experience of deepening inner silence, you discover how feelings of security and pleasure can grow without the slightest effort to control or manipulate your mind, body, or emotions. By making this experience a part of your everyday life, you learn to accept the natural and become more comfortable with letting your experiences unfold according to their own rhythms. Sooner or later, this learning carries over to your sexual experiences, and you achieve a major improvement in your sexual attunement without even having tried to do so.

Some couples have also reported that inner silence enhances the natural beauty and joy of lovemaking. We frequently hear couples with no symptoms of sexual dysfunction complain that they sometimes feel lonely, distant, or let down after coitus and that they want to get more out of their experience. Many factors such as inadequate trust, mild but unspoken fears, or simple fatigue may underlie this disappointment. The essential problem, however, is an inability to let go completely at the height of orgasm and allow the body's natural sexual reflexes to generate an ecstatic merging of ego boundaries. When inhibitions of whatever origin cause lovemaking to end in a tightening of ego boundaries, disappointment will result. The healing silence lessens the likelihood of this occurrence by increasing trust and inner well-being. Through the regular experience of the healing silence over a period of years, a couple eventually achieves a peak of sexual attunement where they can enjoy complete abandon to the flow of sexual experience. Leaving all the controls in the hands of nature, they achieve ecstatic merging in an intimacy of indescribable tenderness and beauty. In this way, deepening inner silence can ultimately transform lovemaking in its totality from an almost machinelike preoccupation with foreplay and climax into a graceful, ecstatic, and almost sacred sharing.

The value of the healing silence for improving psychosexual attunement is most graphically illustrated with case histories. It should be noted that we do not consider the healing silence a sex therapy per se.

Carol

Carol was a twenty-two-year-old salesclerk who had been married for two and a half years before she sought help for her "frigidity" (sexual aversion). The product of a very moralistic upbringing, she was a virgin when she married. From her wedding night onward, she had difficulties in her conjugal relations. She grew progressively more dissatisfied with her inability to experience sexual satisfaction, and in her second year of marriage began to suffer from dyspareunia (painful sexual intercourse). When her sexual difficulties led to a marital crisis, she went to her gynecologist for assistance. His examination did not reveal a physical problem so he referred her to our center for further evaluation.

After an initial session with Carol and a second session with her and her husband, it was clear that she had substantial guilt and fear about her sexuality. She needed psychotherapy along with considerable patience and support from her husband. We recommended conjoint sexual counseling and the healing silence, not specifically to solve their sexual difficulties but for its general benefits. Carol and her husband made the healing silence a part of their daily lives, but had time for only three psychotherapy sessions before a job reassignment forced them to move to another city. When they moved, we referred them to a well-recognized sex therapy clinic in their new city, but for financial reasons they never followed through. Ten months later, however, they completed a follow-up questionnaire as part of our clinical research program. In addition, a follow-up interview became possible when, eighteen months after Carol's first session, she and her husband visited San Diego.

Follow-up revealed that during the first four months of regularly experiencing the healing silence, Carol showed only slight improvement in her sexual dysfunction. Toward the end of her first year, however, she began to notice a growth of ease and a progressive decline in her sexual fears and dyspareunia. She became much less anxious about achieving coital satisfaction and found herself enjoying foreplay as never before. Within six months after noticing initial improvement in her sexual responsiveness, her dyspareunia subsided completely. About her growth, she commented:

> Since I have been meditating, my whole experience of lovemaking has dramatically changed. It's no longer a painful duty and has become deeply satisfying. I've discovered that it's right and good for me to enjoy the pleasures of my body. This may not seem important, but I was raised to believe that sex is filthy and degrading. I've also become a much more sensual person! I'm more in touch with my physical self and I'm really learning what it means to delight in everyday living. Sex is now a joyful part of my married life, but beyond that, I have grown as a person, and this has been important to me and helped my marriage.

Carol and her husband became closer to each other through the healing silence. They reported that the natural ease which they discovered within themselves blossomed into a more loving give-and-take in all aspects of their relationship. They have fewer arguments, and now feel confident about raising a family.

Carol had been a chronically tense and self-deprecating individual with many unresolved childhood feelings of shame and guilt. When sexual impulses arose, she apparently repressed them, producing a concentration of tension in her pelvis and preventing her enjoyment of what she had always been told was degrading. The experience of inner silence eventually broke this cycle of tension and guilt by promoting a generalized reduction in her anxiety and muscular tension. It also gradually allowed her to discover that sexual pleasures are natural and in no way degrading or shameful. Improved communication between Carol and her husband undoubtedly helped her feel the safety necessary to begin discovering the joyful cascade of pleasures that accompany fully healthy sex play.

Richard

Another client, Richard, a thirty-four-year-old real estate salesman, had suffered from chronic anxiety and premature ejaculation ever since the beginning of his coital life at twenty-three. Ejaculation generally occurred immediately before or within thirty seconds after intromission. Three years earlier, he had about twenty sessions with a psychoanalytically oriented psychotherapist but found the probing type of approach uncomfortable. He stopped therapy because he felt that his self-confidence was further deteriorating and his anxiety increasing as he learned about his "fears of beind devoured by his mother." At one point, he began avoiding women altogether and secretly feared becoming homosexual.

Richard sought our help at the suggestion of a meditating friend who was aware that we offered a holistic treatment program. After a referral to a urologist revealed no organic disease, we started Richard on a psychotherapy program that involved ten intensive sessions during the first two months and six more follow-up visits over the next year. In these sessions Richard worked on developing emotional freedom and correcting his misunderstandings about sex. To promote his overall self-improvement, we recommended the healing silence. He agreed and seemed particularly pleased that he could make use of it on his own. He was also intrigued by the possibility that it might help improve his work as well as his personal and sexual life.

Within several weeks after starting to experience the healing silence regularly, he noticed his fears diminishing, and several months later he began to date again. His homosexual anxieties subsided, and he grew in confidence. Finally, he met a woman whom he grew to trust enough to try once again a sexual relationship. To his great satisfaction he discovered that his premature ejaculation had disappeared. He reported, "I no longer feel like I've got to be a sexual athlete. . . . I trust myself now and I've realized through my own experience how easy and natural it is to have a meaningful sexual relationship."

When Richard first sought our help, he was a self-preoccupied individual who had great difficulty identifying with others. Though he had many acquaintances, he admitted having no close friends to whom he could confide his feelings. He was also overweight and moderately anxious. The deepening experience of inner silence helped him with his anxiety and overweight, but more importantly, it enhanced his self-esteem and basic trust. It allowed him to start reaching out to others. He grew from a "phallically preoccupied male" totally absorbed in achievement and performance into a mature adult capable of enjoying the pleasure of emotional intimacy and responding to others' needs.

The Professional Approach

If you try some of the techniques we recommend but feel your progress is slow, then you might consider sex therapy. The two principal medical approaches to treating sexual dysfunction are Masters and Johnson's dual sex team therapy and conventional psychotherapy.* These methods may be used together or separately, depending on the individual case.

Psychiatrists emphasize personality growth in helping people resolve sexual dysfunctions because certain healthy personality characteristics almost preclude sexual difficulties. If you can be freely in touch with your own feelings and fully express them to others without inhibition and doubt, if you can be naturally receptive to other

* To locate a trained sex therapist, you can contact your local university medical center or county medical society. Masters-and-Johnson-trained teams are widely available and your county medical society should be able to recommend one to you because one member of the team must be a physician. If your county medical society is not helpful, you can also write Masters and Johnson at their St. Louis institute for information about where you can get help.

people's feelings and capable of responding to them with empathy, warmth, and trust, and if you can enjoy the sensations of your body without fear or guilt, then healthy and rewarding sexuality will come naturally and automatically. The psychotherapeutic approach produces good results about 70 percent of the time and has the added benefit of developing not just psychosexual attunement but the whole personality. It can, however, take many months to produce significant effects.

Behavior therapists and Masters-and-Johnson-trained sex therapists treat cases of sexual dysfunction by reducing generalized anxiety and performance fears that accompany increasing sexual arousal. To achieve this end, they usually prescribe a careful program involving relaxation exercises and graded sexual assignments. For example, a client will practice a relaxation exercise until he learns to relax various muscles in his body. At this point, he will then begin engaging in the least anxiety-provoking sexual act, perhaps kissing. If the client begins to feel anxious while kissing, he will stop, practice the relaxation exercise until anxiety lessens, then go back to kissing. Once the client masters his first assignment without anxiety, he will go on to a second assignment, perhaps hugging, and a third, perhaps petting, and will eventually work on reducing anxiety associated with coitus. This approach, which requires a skilled therapist and an understanding partner, produces good results about 85 percent of the time, and often within a matter of weeks.

The likelihood of good results from sex therapy depends on three factors—the nature of the dysfunction, the depth of psychological conflict, and the quality of the couples' relationship. The three most common dysfunctions—premature ejaculation, vaginismus, and female orgastic problems—respond extremely well. Impotence and retarded ejaculation often require longer, more intensive treatment, and the totally unresponsive woman may need extensive psychotherapy along with sex therapy to achieve results. If the fears and anxieties surrounding the dysfunction are superficial, if the person's self-esteem is sound, and if feelings of guilt, shame, and hostility are mild, the likelihood of a rapid response to sex therapy is great. The more deeply rooted a person's fears and the more intense his or her guilt or hostility, the more slowly can sex therapy proceed. Finally, sex therapy requires a good relationship between the couple. The more understanding, warmth, and trust, the better are the results.

Any hostility between the couple may preclude the possibility of sex therapy altogether. All factors considered, there is great reason to be optimistic about the likelihood of good results through sex therapy.

Whether or not you pursue therapy, you are likely to be surprised with how a holistic health program improves your sex life. The combination of exercise, meditation, regular sleep, good nutrition, and reduced anxiety cannot help making you feel better about yourself physically and sexually. Glowing health naturally leads to fulfilling sex. For this reason, a holistic health program is a great way to improve your sexual attunement.

19. Alcohol's Silent Substitute

How much is too much? Where does light social drinking end and excessive alcohol consumption begin? While we are not teatotalers or prohibitionists, we feel obliged to emphasize that excessive alcohol consumption has become one of the major health hazards of modern living. In view of the potentially damaging effects of excessive drinking over a ten-, twenty-, or thirty-year period, it pays to become aware of your drinking pattern now.

Through the study of thousands of cases, medical researchers have established criteria to distinguish different kinds of drinkers. You are a heavy drinker if you:

—have at least one drink daily and three drinks per day five times per week
—have one drink per day and four drinks at least three times per week
—have six or seven drinks several times per month

You are a moderate drinker if you:

—drink almost every day and have at least one but usually two drinks
—have three or four drinks once or twice a week
—drink several times per month and have three or four but sometimes five or six cocktails

You are a light drinker if you:

—have not more than one drink several days a week
—have no more than three drinks several days per month

How much do you drink? Don't be embarrassed if you're not sure; many people aren't. One of the best ways to assess your drinking is to keep an alcohol intake diary. For the next three weeks, jot down in a notebook the number of drinks you have each day and when you have them. Don't increase or decrease your drinking simply because you are logging it. If you want a drink, have it. If you want to get "tight," go ahead. Your goal at this point is not to change your drinking pattern but to discover it.

Now you know how much you drink; the next step is to determine if your drinking pattern has changed over the last several years. Try to recall how often and how much you drank two, five, and ten years ago. Write down your best estimates. Don't be surprised if your alcohol consumption has increased over the years. Your body may have become accustomed to alcohol, and you may now need more than you did to produce the effects you desire.

If you are a moderate or heavy drinker, or if your alcohol consumption is steadily increasing over the years, then you should take heed of the threat that your drinking pattern may be posing to your health and longevity. While some research shows that light drinkers are healthier and live longer than nondrinkers, additional research also indicates that you needn't be an alcoholic for your drinking pattern to endanger your health and well-being.

Risks

Alcohol has become such an integral part of our culture that few people are aware of how their drinking affects their health. The harmful effects of excessive alcohol consumption go far beyond hangovers, social embarrassment, and reduced productivity. Even moderate alcohol consumption may erode your health and take years off your life. Are you aware of the following facts about the health risks of alcohol?

• A heavy drinker at age thirty has a life expectancy about eight years shorter than a thirty-year-old nondrinker or light drinker.

• Even moderate consumption of alcohol can cause toxic effects in your liver.

• Moderate to heavy alcohol consumption can contribute to permanent, though gradual, impairment of neurological functioning through destruction of brain cells. The result can be a measureable and permanent reduction in intellectual acuity, emotional balance, and mind-body coordination.

• Alcohol consumption and smoking are cited as the principal causes of oral cancer.

• Among the most serious health risks of alcohol is injury or death in a traffic accident. More than half of all traffic fatalities, or at least twenty-five thousand per year, involve an intoxicated driver. The vast majority of these "drunken drivers" are not alcoholics but social drinkers who have had a bit too much at a party. No matter how well you think you can hold your liquor, even one drink is enough to impair your driving ability and significantly raise your risk of an accident.

• Heavy alcohol consumption not only causes liver disease, but also contributes to digestive disorders such as ulcers, inflammation of the pancreas, and heart disease.

• Even light alcohol consumption is dangerous if you have any one of the following conditions: high blood pressure, severe atherosclerosis, varicose veins, liver disease, gout, diabetes, kidney disease, prostate trouble, or an acute infection. It can also be lethal when taken in combination with sleeping medicines and antihistamines.

• Alcohol is not the harmless drug that many people think it is. Your risk of negative health consequences from alcohol is low only if you are a light drinker. It should be evident that you would be wise to consider cutting down on your alcohol consumption if you are a moderate drinker and/or if your drinking has increased over the years. By examining your drinking pattern to discover why you drink, you may find additional reasons to cut down.

Why Do You Drink?

You probably tell yourself that you drink because you enjoy it. Undoubtedly you do, but a closer look at your drinking pattern may reveal some more subtle reasons, among them—

—to relax at the end of a hectic day
—to reduce anxiety, especially in a social setting
—to pick yourself up when you feel sad

—to cope with loneliness
—to reduce inhibitions and fears
—to mask sexual difficulties and frustrations
—to escape from problems at work or at home
—to make yourself feel powerful or important

If any of these reasons underlie your drinking pattern, alcohol has become an integral part of your coping style. Several times a week you probably say to yourself, "I could use a drink." While alcohol may help you cope, it won't satisfy your underlying psychological needs. It may pick you up for an hour or two when you feel blue, but it won't help you become a happy person. On the contrary, because alcohol is a depressant, not a stimulant, any underlying depression may worsen. Alcohol may help you mask sexual fears, but it won't enable you to become the sensual person you want to be. It may reduce your inhibitions at a party, but it won't help you become a congenial, attractive, self-actualized, and genuinely self-confident individual.

The only healthy reason to drink is for occasional celebration, fun, and enjoyment. Any other reason means your drinking has a hidden psychological payoff. If fun alone is your reason for drinking, you are probably a light drinker. You never say, "I need a drink," because you never do. On the other hand, if you drink to cope, you are probably a moderate or heavy drinker because you need alcohol to maintain your emotional equilibrium. If your need for alcohol becomes strong enough, alcoholism ensues.

No matter how much you drink, a major factor behind your drinking is likely to be cultural pressure. Business lunches, parties, and even small get-togethers with friends have become occasions for drinking. "Let's have a drink" has become a ubiquitous phrase. National drinking patterns reflect this cultural dependency on alcohol. For example, the annual per capita consumption of alcoholic beverages in the United States increased by the following percentages from 1950 to 1971: hard liquor, 92 percent; wine, 44 percent; and beer, 14 percent.[59] The number of people who drink has also increased. In 1940, studies show that 38 percent of women and 64 percent of men were drinking regularly (i.e., an ounce of hard liquor or its equivalent daily); by 1970, the figures had jumped to 60 percent for women and 77 percent for men. In addition, alcohol consumption is starting at an earlier age. One study indicated that in 1950 only 27 percent of high-school students had consumed an alcoholic beverage by age fourteen. In 1974, this figure was up to 55 percent.

Silencing the Need for Alcohol

At this point you may say, "OK, drinking may be harmful to me in the long run, but it provides a lot of enjoyment that I don't want to give up now. Maybe it's not the best way to cope, but it works for me."

You have every right to make this statement and stick to it. Unless you develop a serious alcohol addiction or frequently drive after drinking, the deleterious effects of your alcohol intake will be gradual. And if you try to reduce your alcohol consumption by willpower alone, the resulting strain and frustration may be more harmful than the alcohol. There is, however, a natural way to reduce your alcohol intake. You can gradually silence your need for alcohol from within and let your decreasing desire for alcohol guide an almost unconscious reduction in your drinking.

There is good evidence that the healing silence contributes to reduced alcohol consumption. Psychiatrist Mohammed Shafii asked 216 students at the University of Michigan, Ann Arbor, about their drinking patterns. One hundred and twenty-six of these students had practiced the TM program for three to forty months.[195] Shafii's results showed that roughly 30 percent of the meditators reduced their consumption of beer, wine, and hard liquor within the first three months of the TM program. Though 87 percent of the meditators reported consuming alcoholic beverages prior to starting the TM technique, 60 percent of those meditating for two or more years reported discontinuing all drinking. This study is especially important because it shows a decrease in alcohol consumption in students at an age when drinking usually increases.

At our center we have found the healing silence to be very helpful for the moderate to heavy drinker. For example, Ellen was a thirty-three-year-old housewife who had a family history of alcoholism and depression. After the birth of her children, she began drinking to cope with her feelings of loneliness, entrapment, and depression. Soon she found herself drinking frequently during the day, and at her husband's insistence she sought help. After six months of the TM program along with counseling and life enrichment classes, her life took a new turn. She stopped drinking, got her children into a day care program, and went back to work. What makes her case worthy of note is her insight into how inner silence reduced her need for alcohol. "I drank," she said, "to dull the deep empty feeling that kept tearing at me. Nothing really helped but getting drunk, but that was obviously no solution. What the TM program did was, for me, something sacred. I started feeling complete again, like I had something to give. I saw that my life held possibilities for happiness that I had never recognized."

In another case, a forty-three-year-old executive came to our center for court-ordered treatment after his arrest on a drunk driving charge. A light drinker in college, he had increased his alcohol consumption with each small step up the corporate ladder, until he had finally become dependent on alcohol as a tranquilizer. Whenever he got tense—in the face of a rough decision, when his department fell behind in meeting production quotas, before an important party—he turned to liquor. Drinking gave him transient relief from his anxiety, but he feared that he was becoming an alcoholic. We recommended the healing silence and put him on a mild tranquilizer. Within two months he was off his medication but quite regular in his meditation. Four months later he had stopped drinking completely because he "didn't need it." "What surprised me," he said, "was that I started noticing how a drink clouded my mind and actually hindered my ability to enjoy myself. I didn't stop drinking because I had to. I didn't need it, and I guess I lost my taste for it."

Teen-age alcohol abuse, one of the fastest-rising drug abuse problems in America, is very difficult to treat. Often hiding deep feelings of inadequacy and insecurity, the teen-age alcohol abuser is usually unable to ask for help and unwilling to listen to counseling. For this reason, the unique contribution of the healing silence is welcomed by physicians and parents as well as the adolescent. Regular practice of the TM technique will increase self-esteem and promote emotional maturity.

Allan, a seventeen-year-old, was drinking a six-pack of beer five or six times a week in addition to experimenting with other drugs. The reasons behind Allan's drug abuse were complex; his relation with his father was poor and he felt an excessively strong rivalry with his brother. During the course of treatment, he needed constant encouragement to meditate regularly, and after four months of counseling and follow-up, he began cutting down on his drinking. Over the next year, he matured considerably. His brashness gave way to an honest self-confidence that allowed him to start setting personal goals and developing friendships. It is impossible to determine the relative contributions of the healing silence and of psychotherapy in Allan's emotional development; they played significant and complementary roles. But the importance of the healing silence was evident in a statement he made six months after starting the program. "TM is great," he said. "My boozing days are over."

In addition to reducing psychological need, the healing silence contributes to reduced alcohol consumption by increasing sensitivity to alcohol's toxic effects. Meditators often notice within a period of months or years that because they feel relaxed, full of vitality, and free to express their feelings, alcohol no longer provides much pleasure. In fact, it may produce effects such as dizziness, headache, emotional insensitivity, and cloudy thinking that reduce enjoyment and optimum functioning. As long as you need alcohol to cope, relax, or let go and have fun, its toxic effects seem small compared to its psychological benefits. When this need is absent, however, you will discover that drinking to a point of even moderate intoxication is unpleasant.

Strategies to Help Yourself Ease Off Alcohol

The healing silence will reduce your need for alcohol, but it is only part of a holistic program to reduce drinking. The following strategies will also help.

• The best substitute for alcohol is exercise. When you want a drink badly and a nonalcoholic one just won't do, go swimming, play tennis, or just go for a brisk walk. Above all, don't just sit around the house worrying about your problems. Get out and enjoy yourself. (See Chapter 10.)

• Set a limit to the number of drinks you will have in any one day. If you are a moderate drinker, set your limit at two. If you are a light drinker, set it at one. Remember that this limit is a maximum and not a goal. After several months, reduce the limit and keep reducing it gradually until you are drinking no more than three cocktails or beers a week.

. Allow yourself to drink only at certain times. No drinking before five is an old rule you might try. You will soon find that your business lunches are much more productive if you don't drink at them.

. Decide never to have a drink before meditating when you come home in the evening. You will find that after meditation, you just won't feel the need for those two martinis before dinner.

. Try a change of pace. Instead of ordering your usual Scotch and water, try a tonic water with lime. It will seem quite tame, but with your increasing natural attunement through the healing silence, you may soon grow to prefer it, even at parties.

. Experiment with other nonalcoholic drinks at home. Fresh fruit and vegetable juices can be true taste treats. They also make a perfect "cocktail" to have between meditation and dinner.

• Don't feel you have to take a drink every time one is offered. Remember that saying no often inspires more respect than saying yes.

• Drink only when you enjoy it, not out of boredom, frustration, or worry. When you feel you would like to have a drink, reflect for a moment about your motivation. If you feel you "need it," then drinking is a mask for some deeper emotional need. Instead of pouring a drink, see what you can do to discover your real need and fulfill it in an active way. You may just be tired, and a walk will be enough to refresh you.

• When you do have a drink, sip it very slowly. You want to enjoy yourself, not get drunk. And by drinking slowly, you will drink less.

• Resolve never to get drunk. You need willpower for this one, but it is very important in allowing the gradual reduction in your physiological and psychological need for excessive alcohol intake. There is a corollary to this resolution: never drink on an empty stomach. You get drunk too easily and the alcohol hits your system too hard when you drink without food.

• If you drink, don't drive. If you disregard this basic rule of wise drinking, you are foolhardy indeed.

• Reward yourself after you notice a reduction in your alcohol intake. You will be saving a good sum of money, so go out and spend it on something you have wanted to do or to have. Anything that makes you happy will be fine.

Heavy Drinker or Alcoholic?

Up to this point, we have focused on how the moderate to heavy drinker can reduce his alcohol intake. This level of excessive alcohol consumption is amenable to reduction through a self-help approach. If you are more than a heavy drinker, however, then we would be doing you a great disservice to recommend self-help. The problems of the alcohol-dependent person are qualitatively and quantitatively different from those of the heavy drinker.

Alcohol addiction varies in degree. You can be seriously alcohol dependent and still not show the signs of acute alcoholism. Nevertheless, the health risks of alcohol dependency are very great, especially because it usually leads to alcoholism. The signs of alcohol dependency are easy to recognize. The alcohol-dependent person drinks at least as much as the heavy drinker but in addition:

—suffers marked distress when deprived of alcohol
—seeks opportunities to drink (e.g., at lunch, midafternoon, the cocktail hour, after dinner)
—has difficulty enjoying himself or herself without alcohol
—displays emotional outbursts of anger, despair, or sadness when drinking
—shows deterioration of performance at work and at home
—usually keeps a bottle handy
—may carry a flask
—frequently has alcohol on his or her breath

The boundary between alcohol dependency and alcoholism is not a sharp one. Additional signs that indicate chronic alcoholism include:

—a marked change in appearance, slovenly dress, red puffy eyes and face
—binging, bouts of drunkenness lasting two days or more
—blackouts, drinking to the point of losing consciousness
—deterioration of memory
—early-morning drinking
—frequent drunkenness
—drinking alone, deceitfully

—denying drinking or drunkenness
—highly anxious when deprived of alcohol
—physical signs such as tremors, profuse sweating, vomiting
—emotional signs such as boastfulness, uncontrollable crying,
    rage, or despair
—irresponsible behavior at work or with personal finances

Alcoholism and alcohol dependency are insidious. Few heavy
drinkers realize when they are crossing the boundary of alcohol dependency. In the struggle to cope with financial setbacks, failures,
loneliness, poor self-esteem, and other emotional problems, they fail
to see how they grow to rely on alcohol to blunt their distress.

While heavy drinking often begins early in life, alcoholism usually
does not. The prime age for the onset of alcoholism is between thirty
and sixty, a period when the ideals of youth often crash on the hard
rocks of the real world. The key to beating alcoholism, as with most
other illnesses, is early diagnosis and treatment.

If you have any doubt whatsoever about whether you are alcohol
dependent or an alcoholic, you should assume the worst. The most
serious obstacle in the treatment of alcoholism is the alcohol-dependent person's denial of his or her drinking problem. Alcohol dependency is not difficult to recognize, and we can't emphasize that doubt
about the safety of your drinking pattern means you are drinking too
much and should take serious steps to change.

You should undertake the following steps immediately if you believe you may be alcohol dependent.

1. Admit without equivocation that you have a serious drinking
   problem. Don't argue about it with yourself or anyone else.
2. Face the fact that you suffer from a *serious* and *progressive*
   disease. It *will get worse* unless you do something about it
   now.
3. Recognize that you can't treat yourself. The self-help approach of this book is not appropriate for your condition. You
   need professional care.
4. Visit your family doctor and ask for help. He may treat you
   himself or send you to a specialist. In any case, follow his
   advice. If you don't have a family doctor, then call your

county medical society and ask it to recommend a physician who treats alcoholism.

5. If necessary, be willing to take a leave of absence from work for intensive treatment in a therapeutic milieu. This leave of absence could be among the wisest decisions you make to assure your successful future.

6. Renounce all forms of alcohol for as long as you live. Once you have acquired an alcohol addiction, you will always have a potential for readdiction. Once you have managed to quit drinking, you risk returning to serious alcohol dependency if you ever again take even one sip.

7. Try Alcoholics Anonymous. The support provided by this group has proved invaluable to thousands of people with alcohol problems. You may not like every aspect of the program at first, but don't be put off. In time, you may appreciate it all. Once you beat your problem, consider devoting time to helping others do likewise. Whatever time you spend will bring enormous rewards.

Remember, if you have an alcohol problem, you have nothing to be ashamed of. Because our culture pushes alcohol at every opportunity, this disease is naturally rampant. At least fifteen million people share your problem. The fact that millions have also beaten it is cause for hope. Alcoholism can be treated effectively. A better, healthier, more satisfying life can be yours if you take steps to get help.

Healing the Alcoholic

A discussion of the healing silence and excessive drinking would be incomplete without considering in brief its value in the treatment of chronic alcoholism. With a number of these patients, we have found the TM program very helpful in concert with psychotherapy, Alcoholics Anonymous, and when appropriate, support from a clergyman.

A fifty-six-year-old widow, Betty was admitted to the hospital in an extremely agitated state. She complained of severe back pain that had begun after she had fallen while drunk. She was fearful, anxious, and depressed. For three months prior to her admission, she had been drinking very heavily, and her fall precipitated an emotional breakdown. Psychiatric evaluation revealed that she had a history of chronic alcoholism. Lately, she had begun drinking as soon as she got up in the morning and had often drunk to the point of losing consciousness. Her back injury turned out to be a fracture that required hospitalization for a month.

While hospitalized, she began psychotherapy and medication to relieve her depression, and she continued in treatment after her discharge. Though her depression began to lift, her tendency to drink excessively was still strong. It took several months for her to recognize that she was an alcoholic and should do something to help herself. After much encouragement, she began attending Alcoholics Anonymous meetings. She heard about the TM program at this time but was encouraged to remain sober for a month before learning the technique. Two months later, she finally went four weeks without a drink and took the TM course with the hope that it would help her handle her anxiety. She noticed little change during the first few weeks of TM practice, but eventually found herself less anxious; so she decided to continue meditating. Over the next six months, with daily meditations, twice weekly AA meetings, regular church attendance, and monthly counseling sessions, she began to blossom. Her depression lifted completely and she made new friends at TM lectures and AA meetings. Free from incapacitating anxiety, she also started volunteering her time and services and expressed more optimism about her life. A four-year follow-up showed her still sober and an active member of her community. Again, the role of the healing silence in her improvement cannot be isolated from the other elements in her treatment, but it clearly added to a reduction in her psychological needs for alcohol and to an overall growth in her self-esteem and happiness.

20. How to Choose a Therapy and a Therapist

So far we have emphasized how you can improve your emotional health on your own. Over a period of years the healing silence will raise your emotional wellness to a very high level. A holistic self-improvement program incorporating some of the strategies we have detailed will enhance this whole process. Nevertheless, you might benefit from therapy. It may be especially helpful in dealing with any personality weakness that remains troublesome after intensive self-help.

There is nothing mysterious about psychotherapy, and the therapist certainly cannot perform magic. He or she will not solve your problem but will help you discover how to solve it yourself. A psychotherapist is essentially a person who has specialized in helping others discover how to solve their emotional problems and learn interpersonal skills they did not assimilate while growing up. If your therapist is a psychiatrist, he or she can also prescribe medication as necessary. Actually, a psychotherapist can serve as a good friend who is acutely insightful and willing to try very hard to help you solve any emotional problem you might have.

Keeping in mind that a psychotherapist, no matter how brilliant, can only assist you in discovering how to solve your problems but cannot solve them for you, let's assume that you have decided to seek psychotherapeutic help. You are faced with an array of therapeutic approaches, many apparently conflicting in theory and practice. How do you know which therapy to choose and which therapist is best for you?

According to a recent survey by the National Institute of Mental Health, more than 130 different psychotherapies are now being practiced. Psychiatrist Harold Greenwald writes, "Psychotherapy has recently undergone such a vast proliferation that it is almost impossible for even the most nimble of researchers in the field to keep up with the almost infinite variety of new approaches and new techniques." (182, p. 13) Dr. Joel Elkes, a pioneer in the use of psychotropic medication and professor emeritus at Johns Hopkins School of Medicine, likes to quip about psychotherapy, "If you understand the situation, you are not fully informed."

Since you must make a decision despite this confusion, you should take the time to make the most intelligent choice you can. Despite the disagreement about what works and what doesn't, there are some guidelines you can use.

The Psychotherapy Supermarket

The current state of affairs in psychology is reminiscent of an ancient Sufi story about a man who brought an elephant for exhibition at a fair but kept it in a dark room. Because the visitors to the exhibition could not see the elephant, they felt it with their hands. One wise man entered the darkness, felt the elephant's trunk, and proclaimed it like a downspout. Another touched the elephant's ear and thought it like a fan. The third felt its legs and thought them like pillars. Once outside the darkened room, the three wise men proceeded to argue for hours about the shape of an elephant.

In their efforts to understand the human psyche, psychotherapists have developed many, often conflicting theories and practices. The efficacy of each psychotherapy with some clients, however, suggests that each is at least partially valid. Here you have the essential truth about all the therapies: they all work to some degree. Does this mean that you can choose any therapy and be sure you will benefit? No, it's not that simple. Current research indicates that each therapy works best for a particular type of person and is most suitable for particular personality problems.[118] As a result, the current trend in training psychotherapists is to prepare the student for an eclectic practice in which he or she will use a wide range of therapies. He or she will then select the so-called "therapy of choice" for your unique personality and problem.

While the psychotherapist with an eclectic approach can relieve you of some of the burden of choosing a therapy, you would still be wise to do some homework. You might have difficulty finding an eclectically oriented therapist, or you might decide that one approach appears so perfectly suited to your needs that you want to see an expert in that therapy.

The dominant therapeutic approach today is still psychoanalytically oriented psychotherapy and psychoanalysis.[172] In this approach, you work through your conflicts by exploring their origins with the therapist. Because this approach is insight-oriented, it is best suited to intellectual, psychologically minded people.[118] It is most useful for freeing yourself from the legacies of childhood dependency, frustration, and unacknowledged hurt. Increased ego strength, self-understanding, self-acceptance, self-esteem, and autonomy are its primary results. Over the past two decades, however, this technique has been sharply criticized as being too lengthy and costly. More recently, critics have assailed its other limitations. Psychoanalyst Robert J. Lifton summarized this criticism when he wrote that this approach fails to recognize "the human hunger and potential for an evolutionary leap." (133, p. 9) In their preoccupation with conflict and neurosis, psychoanalysts on the whole have overlooked those powerful unconscious forces that press us all toward self-renewal and growth. As a result, psychoanalysis has been pessimistic about the human potential for happiness and what we have called *wellness*. However, this situation is changing. Many contemporary psychoanalysts are showing interest in a holistic framework that ranges from biological psychiatry to the work of C. G. Jung. You can find analysts who will help you resolve hidden conflicts as well as tap your potential for achieving high levels of wellness.

Another major approach is called behavior therapy.[239] This is often the therapy of choice for resolving inhibitions, phobias, and sexual dysfunctions and for increasing self-assertiveness. Because this method is simple and involves no intellectual probing of the psyche, it works well for a wide spectrum of people. The therapist employs one or more teaching techniques that help you learn new behaviors to replace old, maladapative ones. One of the techniques is called *operant conditioning* and involves the reward of the new behavior and punishment of the old. For example, if you want to quit smoking, the behavior therapist will help you devise a plan to reward yourself every time you resist a cigarette and punish yourself if you light up. In another technique, *role-modeling*, the therapist models the new behavior (e.g., to develop assertiveness, the behavior might be asking your boss for a raise); you practice the demonstrated behavior until you feel comfortable with it. With a third technique, *systematic desensitization,* the therapist takes you through a step-by-step process to relieve specific fears or inhibitions.

The specificity of behavior-therapy makes it a useful complement to a holistic health program. While the healing silence promotes overall development, a few sessions of behavior therapy may be useful to resolve a specific inhibition or weakness.

The third principal psychotherapeutic approach is that of the humanistic school, which encompasses a wide range of therapies.[118] These therapies emphasize self-actualization and aim primarily at developing emotional freedom and interpersonal skills. Gestalt therapy is one of the better-known humanistic methods.[175] It helps you discover and absorb "lost" parts of yourself that you have denied or failed to develop. For example, if you are shy, you may discover that you don't use your eyes and heart to see and feel others. When this unused ability becomes an active part of your present personality, your shyness may disappear. Encounter and sensitivity groups of all kinds constitute another important part of the humanistic approach.[242] While these groups have been criticized as harmful to some participants, investigation has revealed that "casualties" result only in groups with poorly trained leaders. To find a competent group leader, consult your local psychiatric or psychological society, or write the American Group Psychotherapy Association in New York City. It is now clear that these groups can be very helpful in learning how others perceive you and in improving your interpersonal skills.

There is a wide variety of other therapies, though most fall into one of these three major categories. A few prominent methods deserve mention.

• Transactional analysis is an insight-oriented therapy that helps you understand why you behave the way you do with others. It offers an excellent simplification of complex psychological concepts, and can be very useful in developing emotional maturity.[88]

• Bioenergetic therapy focuses on relieving chronic muscular tension and enhancing your capacity for pleasure. It involves physical exercises as well as manipulations of your body by the therapist. Analytic insight into the psychological components of your tension is also involved.[136]

• Primal therapy aims at helping you get emotionally in touch with the repressed hurts of childhood. When you allow these hurts to surface, they presumably dissolve, and you become a more integrated authentic person.[100]

• Reality therapy helps you accept yourself, assume responsibility for your own happiness, and take steps toward fulfilling your needs and desires. It is a talk therapy but involves no analytic probing of your psyche. The discussions with the therapists focus on current, real problems and what to do about them.[78]

• Marital therapy involves husband and wife participating in therapy sessions sometimes together and sometimes apart. It is useful in resolving tensions in a marriage and helping both partners become more autonomous, self-fulfilling people.[118]

• Family therapy is useful when one or more members of a family have an emotional problem that is causing turmoil. The whole family sees the therapist together, and each member is likely to get a new perspective on his or her place within the family.[118]

Choosing a therapy is not a task that you should take lightly. The only way to do it wisely is to learn about the various therapies and decide which one seems best for you. You might find it useful to read one of the current guides to psychotherapy such as Dr. Joel Kovel's *A Complete Guide to Therapy.* After this survey, you may then want to read the principal work by the chief exponent of the therapy you like best. Nearly all the modern therapies have been well summarized in one volume, usually available in an inexpensive edition. Obviously, choosing a therapy takes time, but considering the stakes, it is time well spent.

The Therapist Is the Key

It might seem paradoxical to follow a review of the psychotherapy supermarket with detailed recommendations about choosing a therapist rather than a therapy. However, research indicates clearly that your therapist's personality rather than his or her theoretical persuasion is the critical factor in determining whether or not you will benefit from therapy. Psychologists Charles Truax and Kevin Mitchell point out on the basis of their research and that of others:

> Basically the personality of the therapist is more important than his techniques. Conversely, however, techniques that are specific to certain kinds of patients and psychotherapy goals can be quite potent in the hands of a therapist who is inherently helpful, and who offers a high ideal of empathic understanding, warmth, genuineness, potency, immediacy, and who can confront his clients in a constructive manner. (221, p. 343)

Carl Rogers was one of the first to assert the importance of the therapist's personality to effective psychotherapy.[180] Among the most critical personality characteristics, he cited empathy (the ability to "stand in another person's shoes"), unconditional positive regard (the ability to remain warm and supportive no matter what the client might say or do), and authenticity (the ability to express real feelings and insights that reflect a deep understanding of the client's problems). Similarly, Truax and Mitchell conclude that the important characteristics are genuineness, non-possessive warmth, and accurate empathy. Summarizing these personality factors, they write:

> The essence of non-possessive warmth is to preserve the client's self-respect as a person and a human being and to provide a trusting, safe atmosphere; the purpose of genuineness is to provide an honest, non-defensive relationship that allows us to point to unpleasant truths about the relationship and about the client rather than to hide behind a facade; accurate empathetic understanding serves as the work of the therapeutic relationship. (221, p. 322)

How to Choose a Therapist

In light of these findings, the importance of choosing a therapist carefully cannot be overemphasized. Ironically, you might be inclined to spend more time buying a car than looking for the right therapist. Before beginning treatment, you should, we believe, visit several therapists with the intention of determining which would be most suitable. It can also be helpful if a family member or close friend goes along on these initial visits to provide additional input

THERAPIST-SELECTION QUESTIONNAIRE*

Directions: Answer each question by circling a number from 0 to 4, where 0 means *not at all* and 4 means *very much*. When you have finished, add up the numbers for a total score which you can use to compare therapists.

1) I feel comfortable with the therapist (T).   0   1   2   3   4

2) T seems comfortable with me.   0   1   2   3   4

3) T is casual and informal rather than stiff and formal.   0   1   2   3   4

4) T does not treat me as if I am sick, defective, and about to fall apart.   0   1   2   3   4

5) T is flexible and open to new ideas rather than pursuing one point of view.   0   1   2   3   4

6) T has a good sense of humor and a pleasant disposition.   0   1   2   3   4

7) T is willing to tell me how s(he) feels about me.   0   1   2   3   4

8) T admits limitations and does not pretend to know things s(he) doesn't know.   0   1   2   3   4

9) T is very willing to acknowledge being wrong and apologizes for making errors or for being inconsiderate, instead of justifying this kind of behavior.   0   1   2   3   4

10) T answers direct questions rather than simply asking me what I think.   0   1   2   3   4

11) T reveals things about herself or himself either spontaneously or in response to my inquiries (but not by bragging and talking incessantly and irrelevantly).   0   1   2   3   4

12) T encourages the feeling that I am as good as s(he) is.   0   1   2   3   4

13) T acts as if s(he) is my consultant rather than the manager of my life.   0   1   2   3   4

14) T encourages differences of opinion rather than telling me that I am resisting if I disagree with him or her.   0   1   2   3   4

15) T is interested in seeing people who share my life (or is at least willing to do so). This would include family, friends, lovers, work associates, or any other significant people in my environment.   0   1   2   3   4

16) The things that T says make sense to me.   0   1   2   3   4

17) In general, my contacts with T lead to my feeling more hopeful and having higher self-esteem.   0   1   2   3   4

* Copyright© by Arnold Lazarus, Ph.D., and Allen Fay, M.D. Used by permission.

for your final decision. Drs. Arnold Lazarus and Allen Fay have developed a simple Therapist-Selection Questionnaire that might be used to rate each therapist. You can use this questionnaire to help identify a therapist with whom you can work best. Fill out the questionnaire immediately after your initial visit with each therapist. A score of 58–68 indicates the potential for an excellent working relationship, 48–58 a good relationship, 38–48 an adequate one, and below 38 inadequate. (See questionnaire.)

In the initial interview the therapist should be willing to explain his or her approach to treatment, including his assessment of your problem(s), treatment goals, and techniques. It is also reasonable to ask for an estimate of how long treatment will take in order to achieve specific therapeutic goals such as the alleviation of particular symptoms. Depending on the therapist's orientation (analytic, behavioral, humanistic, and so on), these estimates may vary significantly. Though most therapists embrace one theoretical orientation as the basis of their general therapeutic approach, you should be cautious if the therapist shows no openness to other approaches. "The ideal psychiatrist," asserts Dr. Arnold J. Mandell, chairman of the department of psychiatry, UCSD Medical School, "is one who has the entire spectrum of therapeutic modalities at his fingertips, and who uses his intelligence, sensitivity and awareness to choose the modality that is most appropriate for a patient."[141]

PART V

Spirit: The Forgotten Dimension of Health

And I have felt
A presence that disturbs me with joy
Of elevated thought: a sense sublime
Of something far more deeply interfused
Whose dwelling is the light of setting suns
And the round ocean and the living air,
And the blue sky, and in the mind of man:
A motion and a spirit, that impels
All thinking things, all objects of all thought
And rolls through all things.

—WILLIAM WORDSWORTH

We shall not cease from exploration
And the end of all our exploring
Will be to arrive where we started
And know the place for the first time.

—T. S. ELIOT

21. Your Spiritual Crisis and Growth

At some time in your life you are almost certain to undergo a spiritual crisis. Its core will be a deep, gnawing doubt about the life direction you have chosen and the value of following it through. None of the beliefs or principles by which you have ordered your world and established your place in it will be immune from question. Your faith in the value of love, success, money, religion, marriage, or work will be severely shaken. You may even fear an imminent nervous breakdown. Along with this relentless, probing doubt, you may be buffeted by emotional and physical turmoil that can disrupt your marriage, work, health, self-esteem, and relationships with those nearest to you.

Spiritual crises may occur at any time, but they are most likely during periods of major life change. Typical events that precipitate spiritual turmoil are:

—going away to college
—graduation from college
—marriage
—separation/divorce
—pregnancy/birth of first child
—major professional success or failure
—major change in financial status
—death of a family member or friend
—serious personal illness or injury
—loss of job/career change
—children leaving home
—retirement

243

These events and others like them force you to reappraise your answers to fundamental questions. What do you want from life? What do you value? What do you find most satisfying and meaningful? What are your real abilities? Your happiness and well-being for years to come depend on whether or not you find answers commensurate with your real needs and abilities.

Descriptions of spiritual crises may sound mysterious and frightening. If you don't understand the spiritual dimension of your personality and aren't prepared to cope with your spiritual needs, a spiritual crisis can be terrifying. Like all crises that accompany transitions from one life stage to another, however, a spiritual crisis is not just a dislocation, but also an opportunity for personal growth.

The spiritual dimension of your personality is the basis of your total satisfaction or dissatisfaction with living. Spiritual health generates a sense of personal fulfillment, a sense of peace with yourself and the world. It may also l' ad to a sense of unity with the cosmos or a personal closeness to God. The greatest reward of spiritual growth is the discovery that you have the power to be a self-fulfilling person despite all life's vicissitudes. Rather than continue looking for a key to happiness outside yourself, you discover that the source of your fulfillment is within. Doubts about meaning and purpose of your life find resolution in an honest appraisal of your real talents and prospects for achievement. You develop an increased capacity to be alone, come to grips with the issue of death, and ultimately achieve peace with yourself.

While the rewards of spiritual growth are great, the path can be rough. We don't have to turn to the lives of saints to make this discovery; our own lives show it clearly. A crisis of the spirit forces you to face very difficult issues. You may have to surrender the psychological security of programming your life to meet the wishes of parents or employers or the cultural expectations that you have internalized. You may also have to stop pushing aside ultimate issues such as the inevitablity of your own death and how long you have left to fulfill your creative desires or to leave your mark on the world. But by letting go of your programmed security and taking the time for self-examination that your spirit requires, you stand to make a great discovery: your deepest needs and the personal power to fulfill them.

Only in the last ten years have psychologists begun to recognize how common spiritual crises actually are. Although Jung boldly introduced the issue of spiritual growth to modern medicine more than fifty years ago, he was rebuked by his colleagues.[104] Later Erik Erikson asserted that the human life cycle involves eight distinct stages, each with its attendant difficulties and potentiality for a developmental crisis.[52] Today, the importance of spiritual growth to health has begun receiving recognition in part through the study of adult life crises.[199]

Despite increased recognition and study of spiritual crises, it is still a difficult condition to diagnose. The physical and/or emotional symptoms can be so intense that you and your doctor may well be led to believe that you have some underlying illness, such as anxiety neurosis, acute depression, or even one of a variety of physical illnesses (until tests prove otherwise). This failure to recognize a spiritual crisis naturally prolongs it. You may get involved in one treatment program after another in hopes of curing your symptoms, but your symptoms will not abate because tranquilizers, antidepressants, and conventional psychotherapy do not solve the underlying problem. In frustration you might try travel, more work, or affairs, only to find yourself exhausted and still in turmoil. Until you finally begin recognizing the spiritual nature of your crisis and take steps to meet your deepest needs, this turmoil will continue.

To further complicate diagnosis, a spiritual crisis resembles in many ways a serious psychoneurosis or borderline schizophrenic state. However, several important factors differentiate a spiritual crisis from an ordinary neurosis or a preschizophrenic episode. First, the unconscious stirrings of a spiritual crisis are distinctly progressive, while those of ordinary neurosis are clearly regressive. For example, the person in a spiritual crisis seeks a greater participation in life, while the neurotic shows avoidance behaviors and seeks to withdraw. Second, the person in a spiritual crisis does not resort to manipulative, deceitful ways of avoiding responsibility, whereas the neurotic may try to seek refuge in illness or invalidism in hopes of lessening the pressures of work or family life. Third, though people in spiritual turmoil may show anxiety, depression, and wide mood shifts, they usually exhibit a reasonably high level of emotional maturity and are both willing and able to express their feelings. In contrast, the neurotic almost always shows clear evidence of emotional immaturity, such as inability to express feelings easily or appropriately. Finally, the personal history of the person undergoing a spiritual crisis reveals symptoms emerging out of a vague discontent, while the neurotic's personal history is often characterized by poor adaptation in childhood and adolescence.

The Origins and Dynamics of a Spiritual Crisis

The origin of a spiritual crisis is lack of personal meaning and fulfillment. It is that simple. Once you gain a measure of success in your struggle for achievement and financial independence, the need for an underlying sense of integrity, satisfaction, and wide horizons of happiness becomes critical to your health. Jung put the matter plainly when he wrote:

> To be normal is a splendid ideal for the unsuccessful, for all those who have not yet found an adaptation. But for people who have more ability than the average, for whom it was never hard . . . to accomplish their share of the world's work—for them, restriction to the normal signifies the bed of Procrustes, unbearable boredom, infernal sterility, and hopelessness. (106, p. 95)

Prior to achieving an initial level of adult security and independence, a rich spiritual dimension to the personality can be a great asset, but its need does not usually emerge as critical. During the twenties and early thirties, the formative struggles to find a mate, a career path, and a degree of financial independence often displace spiritual needs. For this reason, most people enter mid-life poor in understanding of their spirituality and consequently get caught by surprise when these powerful forces finally press into consciousness.

Although a spiritual crisis can occur anytime after childhood, we now know that it is especially likely between the ages of twenty-eight and forty-five. Few people indeed will reach fifty without going through some measure of spiritual turmoil. Those who manage to avoid it may not be either the most healthy or the most fortunate.

Current research indicates that a spiritual crisis during mid-life may be a necessary step toward discovery of inner creative resources that can bring renewal to the second half of your life.[199] Through a successful resolution of a spiritual crisis, you can give up hidden childhood legacies of fear and dependency that block the full blossoming of self-reliance and self-actualization. In many cases, this process may involve a major life adjustment, such as the breakup of a stifling marriage, resignation from an unsatisfying job, and the beginning of a new career. While initially trying and sometimes painful, these steps away from the past lead to a future of increased personal fulfillment and enhanced joy in living.

A spiritual crisis usually assumes a focus around one of several major issues. One of the most common is a lack of authenticity, which is a lack of congruence between thoughts, feelings, and actions. The inauthentic person feels/thinks one thing and says/does another. He has a private inner world that does not correspond to his public façade. When a major event such as a failure at work dents that façade, hidden feelings may press for expression. If they get to the surface, a spiritual crisis is likely to ensue. To resolve a spiritual crisis of authenticity, you must accept your inner world fully so that you can give honest expression to your deepest feelings.

Early in life many people internalize standards, goals, and aspirations that are not consonant with their real needs and abilities. These parental and societal expectations, which often take the form of shoulds and should nots, can become a heavy burden to carry because they breed guilt, shame, and indecision if you cannot live up to them. When the load becomes too great, a spiritual crisis can result. This crisis presents an opportunity to throw off these false demands and give the real you full rein. Instead of struggling to meet self-imposed demands of others, you can begin generating your own cycle of aspiration and success. In this process, you may raise or lower your internalized standards and expectations. The important point, however, is that in the arena of your mind you enter center stage. You become the judge of what aspirations you should try to achieve.

There are other common focuses for spiritual crises. A feeling of self-recrimination for having failed to make a meaningful contribution to social betterment is especially common among thirty-five-year-old men and women who ten years earlier were highly committed social activists. Few twenty-five-year-olds realize that the unbending idealism of their twenties will almost inevitably give way to realism and compromises in their thirties. When the thirties finally arrive, this gap between ideals and compromises can become fertile ground for spiritual doubt. Today, this focus for spiritual upheaval is just as likely for the business-school graduate determined to make a large corporation more receptive to consumer issues as for the social worker trying to revitalize and upgrade an urban ghetto.

One of the most common issues of spiritual crises is an inability to come to terms with aging and death. In our youth-oriented culture, aging and death have become taboo. As a result, it has become commonplace to fight the signs of aging with face-lifts, hair transplants, breast lifts, and long stays at health spas. Inexorably, however, the years pass and aging generates in many a panic that they are running out of time. Among the most common ways for both men and women to cope with this anxiety is to bed one new partner after another. This may stave off anxiety for a while, but eventually the spiritual issues surface, and the individual must ask what level of real fulfillment he or she has experienced.

Whatever the focus of a particular person's crisis, the dynamic is essentially the same. For some months or even years prior to the major upheaval, doubts and anxieties about the purpose and value of living begin to emerge. These remain relatively mild until an event such as a business failure, illness, or death in the family occurs and shatters youthful feelings of invincibility and immortality. Abruptly, questions like "What have I accomplished?" or "What am I getting out of life?" or "Where am I headed?" become major concerns. Doubt and self-recrimination may grow to the point of causing significant emotional and physical distress.

Among the physical and emotional consequences that may be precipitated by a severe spiritual crisis are physical illness, depression, anxiety, and self-destructive behavior such as drug abuse and alcoholism.

Tom, a Spiritual Crisis up Close

A spiritual crisis is most likely for women around age thirty-five and for men about age forty, but this timetable varies widely. Tom, a successful, married architect, faced the abyss of his first spiritual crisis at age thirty-three.

Tom was a classic super-achiever. Soon after earning his degree in architecture, he joined a leading firm. Through a combination of outstanding work and aggressive drive, he became the firm's youngest full partner. He bought a new home, started collecting primitive art, and tried to keep up his reading, but soon found little time for it. While he enjoyed travel and sports cars, his increased work load also forced him to spend less and less time with these hobbies. He began spending his after-work hours entertaining prospective clients. Fortunately for him, Cynthia, his wife, was intelligent and capable, and provided the support structure he needed to make his rapid career ascent. When he called late in the day to announce that he was bringing a client home for dinner, or when he couldn't take Cynthia to the concert as he had promised, or when he came home late and exhausted, Cynthia understood.

In terms of modern cultural standards, Tom had made it, and he knew it. He had a lovely wife and home, a well above average income, and a bright future in his chosen profession. Within two years after becoming a partner, however, his sense of security and well-being began to vanish. In its place arose a powerful gut feeling that he was missing out on life, and that his responsibilities were slowly choking him.

What followed for Tom was a plaguing sense of panic. Little analysis was necessary for him to see that he had committed himself to a life-style that required an enormous expenditure of his time and energy at work. The mortgage, clothes, parties, the cars, and eventually the education of the children he hoped to have all had to be paid for, and he needed a lot of money to do it. He was already making enough and would make more, but he was finding less and less time to do those things that mattered most.

"I began to face the futility of my life," he said. "I worked hard to provide my wife with a high standard of living, but never saw her; I owned a sports car, but could never work on it; I liked to travel, but didn't have time for vacations. In college and graduate school, I buckled down to get top grades, thinking that I'd be in control of my life when I got my degree with honors. I got a top job, but then had to put my nose to the grindstone again to make partner. I made it, but had less control over my own time and destiny than ever. I had to be totally committed to the firm in order to support the life-style I had established."

Tom fought his growing despair by trying to make more time to have fun. He took weekend vacations with his wife, went to parties frequently, and even experimented with marijuana. To his dismay, he soon discovered that these efforts yielded only fleeting enjoyments that reinforced his deep-seated feelings of futility and purposelessness. He hadn't yet realized that his efforts to have fun were merely extensions of his adolescent desire for kicks, while his real search was for meaning and lasting satisfactions. He was still looking for fulfillment outside himself in the reflection of something he did rather than within his own sense of personal autonomy. He was still trying to find fulfillment according to someone else's expectations rather than his own. Consequently, all his efforts to "get more out of life" resulted only in more strain and anxiety.

Soon his persistent inner turmoil began producing physical and emotional symptoms. He stopped sleeping well and became restless, fatigued, and depressed. He also noted a slight pain in his chest, which he interpreted as an early sign of the coronary artery disease that he thought would eventually kill him. He even feared that his psychological defenses were crumbling and that he might become psychotic. When he went to his family doctor, he learned that the pain in his chest was caused by a pulled muscle and that his other symptoms were "apparently no more than a case of nerves." His doctor prescribed Valium as needed for anxiety and a sleeping pill as needed for insomnia. Tom took the pills but his condition worsened.

Tom began to show signs of what would normally be interpreted as a worsening depression. He started losing interest in his personal and professional affairs, and felt that he was losing his capacity to enjoy life. He became preoccupied with questions about the purpose of life, the meaning of his own despair, and the likelihood of his own death cutting his life short before he had a chance to discover what living was really all about.

When he tried to share his concerns with Cynthia, she became anxious and communication broke down. She had great difficulty appreciating his existential doubt because she was younger, presently fulfilled in her work, and not yet ready for her own spiritual crisis. Tom began to feel that Cynthia did not understand him and could not always be relied upon after all. He felt let down and angry. She felt hurt and worried. When Tom finally blurted out that he felt trapped by the house, his work, and his commitment to Cynthia, a full-scale marital crisis ensued.

By the time Tom came to us for help, he was convinced that he was having a nervous breakdown. He described himself as trapped in a box with his inner self pounding the walls. With relatively little insight into what was happening to him, he entertained ideas ranging from quitting his job to leaving his marriage and even taking his own life. His decision-making and reasoning abilities were clearly impaired. The prospect of failing to fulfill his commitment to his wife filled him with guilt and remorse.

After examining and interviewing him, it was clear to us that his problem was primarily spiritual. We recommended meditation, and Tom decided to take the TM course with his wife. Within several weeks after completing the course, he began noticing a reduction of symptoms. His insomnia cleared and his anxiety lessened. With the easing of his inner psychic pressure, he no longer felt trapped and began recognizing his power to give his life whatever direction he chose. Because of the reduction in his anxiety and depressive feelings, his reasoning ability and productivity soon returned to normal. He also stopped blaming his wife for his distress and began to rediscover how much he loved her and how much she had helped him.

Several months after starting the TM program, Tom began to reassess his desires and goals. He recognized that a principal source of his dissatisfaction was his job; he felt that the firm stifled creativity and innovation. For the first time in his life, he decided to take a major risk, and he formed his own architectural firm. Before resigning from his firm, he used his accumulated vacation time for an eight-week trip to Europe, where he studied the latest European developments in design. When he returned, he went ahead full steam with his own firm. He realized that he would have to take a substantial cut in income for a few years, but he and his wife agreed they were making the right move. He also agreed with his wife to spend more time together.

Tom's case illustrates clearly that spiritual development is not easy, but it also shows how much the healing silence can help. Two years later, his firm was well established, and he had discovered a new enthusiasm for living. His marriage was stronger than ever and based on a much deeper level of respect and appreciation. They now feel ready to have children. He literally radiated energy and well-being. It was quite evident that the rewards of spiritual growth were worth his efforts for spiritual development.

Silence and Spiritual Growth

The cultivation of inner silence has long been recognized as a cornerstone of spiritual growth. Meditation, after all, has been passed down for thousands of years not primarily as a means to better health but rather to achieve the heights of spiritual development. Recent scientific research on the effects of meditation suggests that the direct experience of the healing silence is the most potent means to promote your own spiritual growth.

Deep in meditation, you are very likely to achieve what may be the core spiritual experience. Your mind will settle down to such a profound inner silence that you will gain a state of expanded awareness and recognize your innermost self as distinct from your body, mind, and feelings. This experience is deeply satisfying and produces lasting positive effects.

This experience has been esteemed in almost every culture. In the West, we are advised to "seek the Kingdom of Heaven within." In the East, the great spiritual masters explain the immense value of achieving *samadhi* or *satori*. The cornerstone of ancient Greek wisdom was the simple statement, "Know thyself." Humanistic psychologists express this same idea today in their discussions of the importance of self-actualization.

This experience is the goal of all meditation techniques. We have found, however, that some techniques result in this experience more easily and effectively than others. The TM technique appears to be particularly effective. Maharishi Mahesh Yogi gives a description of how this experience unfolds in meditation:

> Proceeding toward the subtler layers . . . within the mind, we experience a tender field of feeling. Deep within the tenderness of feeling we experience the "myness" of feeling. We say, "I feel like this," "I feel," "I feel *my* feelings." So the I in the seat of all my myness is more tenderly located within the feeling. Deep within the *I* is a more tender level . . . which is *I-ness*. The *I-ness* is almost the abstract value of individual existence, intelligence. And deep within, that individual *I-ness* is boundless—the unmanifest, non-changing, immortal, eternal reality. (140, VIII)

In other words, meditation allows you to experience *the core of your own self-consciousness, a silent boundless field of pure awareness.*

The value of this experience may not be immediately apparent to spiritual development as we have defined it. Its import becomes clear, however, when it is viewed in light of its scientifically substantiated effects.

First and foremost, this experience will increase your sense of personal autonomy and heighten your feeling of personal power. It will help you recognize the independence of your innermost self from all the pressures and problems of everyday living. In this way, it will provide you with an immutable experience of personal freedom to give your life direction according to your needs rather than the demands of others. It will also provide a lasting sense of inner well-being independent of what you may be doing or where you may be. This inner stability enables you at any time to stand back from your everyday involvements and assess your life clearly and with a broad perspective.

There is also substantial evidence that this experience enhances wholeness by integrating conflicting functions and forces in the psyche. For example, neurophysiologists have known for some time that the two hemispheres of your brain are responsible for very different types of thinking.[204] Your dominant hemisphere (left in a right-handed person) specializes in analytic rational thinking, especially verbal and mathematical functions. Your nondominant brain half is the locus of synthetic, intuitive, and imaginative thought. There is clear evidence that this core spiritual experience increases coherence of electrical activity between the two brain hemispheres.[10,11,12,132] This finding provides a physiological clue to explain how the healing silence develops and harmonizes the analytic and intuitive dimensions of the mind.[169]

Another age-old conflict apparently resolved through the growth of inner silence is that between reason and emotion. Your feelings and primitive drives such as hunger, thirst, and sex are rooted in evolutionarily "old" neurological structures deep within your brain. Surrounding these structures is the evolutionarily "new" cortex that imbues you with the power to reason. Some scientists speculate that the human propensity for strife and self-destruction has its roots in poor coordination between these two brain structures. There is evidence that the healing silence increases coherence of electrical activity between the "old" and "new" parts of the brain, and this physiological finding may explain the increased harmony between reason and emotion, "will" and "want," that we have observed in our clients. Compulsions and cravings, even in mild form, gradually lose their power. At the same time, authenticity grows. In light of our observations and those reported by other psychotherapists, you may expect the healing silence to increase you ability to recognize your deepest feelings and express them appropriately.

One more dimension of wholeness that grows with inner silence is the integration of what philosophers and theologians have long recognized as the conflict between spirit and flesh. In the modern psychiatrist's office, this conflict shows up in two principal character types. On the one hand, there is the person so caught up in his super-ego values of work, discipline, and achievement that he fails to enjoy life. Always concerned about what he has to do or has not done, he lives in the future at the expense of enjoying the present. At home with his family, he still thinks about work. Though he can afford vacations, he takes them infrequently because he has so much to do. On the other hand, there is the hedonistic individual whose life is a muddle. Typically a young adult with problems at work or with school, this person seeks only to gratify his desires with the least effort, which often means that parents must foot the bill. While he may appear outwardly self-satisfied and nonchalant, he often harbors deep feelings of self-doubt and self-contempt.

The healing silence restores balance to this polarity by strengthening both the spiritual and sensual dimensions of the personality. On the one hand, you begin to discover that the innermost foundation of your personality is the self, unbounded and eternal. On the other hand, you grow in your appreciation of your body as a vehicle for participation in the full joy of living. You learn from experience that the full expression of the spirit depends upon the full development and natural enjoyment of your body, and that the enjoyment of your sensuality is vastly enriched through the development of your spirit. Purposefulness and playfulness, responsibility and pleasure, work and family life, become fully integrated in the growing wholeness of your personality.

You may expect a wide range of other conflicting tendencies in your personality to find resolution with growing inner silence. Selfishness and selflessness, dynamism and restfulness, and strength and compassion are but a few examples.

Professional Help

The healing silence generates a profound experience of inner fulfillment. A person undergoing a spiritual crisis is desperately seeking this feeling of inner wholeness and satisfaction. Once it is experienced, the clouds of crisis begin to be burned away by the glow of inner fulfillment. For growth to continue and this fulfillment to become lasting, the healing silence is not enough. The real work of individuation must begin. Needs must be reassessed and a life course recharted to fulfill those needs. The healing silence helps generate the strength for this task, but guidance from a professional may also be useful.

Should you seek professional guidance in navigating your spiritual crisis, you need to find a counselor with some special skills. Above all, your counselor must be sensitive to the issues and dynamics of spiritual growth as well as those of ordinary emotional illness. You might inquire whether your potential counselor is familiar with the work of Assagioli and Jung, two of the modern pioneers in the psychological exploration of spiritual growth.[6,106] If he or she is not familiar with this work, then you are probably talking to the wrong person. Your potential counselor is likely to view your turmoil as an ordinary emotional illness rather than a spiritual crisis.

The appropriate treatment for a person embroiled in a spiritual crisis is different from that for an emotional illness. The person in a spiritual crisis needs help in expanding his emotional and intellectual horizons to allow his deepest spiritual needs a proper place in his personality. He also needs guidance in realizing his innate power to fulfill those needs. The neurotic, on the other hand, must be assisted in eliminating fears, inhibitions, and dependency and in developing a mature ego appreciative of self and others. In some cases, a spiritual crisis may unearth neurotic fears and inhibitions. If so, the therapist must encourage spiritual growth while also assisting the person in resolving specific neurotic symptoms.

The counselor you seek need not be a psychiatrist or psychologist. Your priest, rabbi, or minister may be very helpful, especially if he or she has been trained in pastoral counseling. A well-trained pastoral counselor will not encourage you to repress your inner turmoil by adopting a set of prefabricated beliefs. Instead, he will help you bring your feelings to the surface and discover your deepest needs. The pastoral counselor has the advantage of personal familiarity with a long tradition of religious activities that millions of people have found helpful for spiritual growth. He or she can assist you in Bible study and learning how to pray. These traditional activities may lead you to a renewed faith in God, or at least some transcendental ordering principle in the universe. Ultimately, this faith leads to a renewed faith in yourself. To locate a pastoral counselor, contact your local church, synagogue, or hospital.

If you feel the need for help during a spiritual crisis, don't hesitate to seek it. Spiritual upheaval from time to time is a natural part of living, and you shouldn't feel ashamed because you have deep doubts about the purpose and direction of your life. Also, you shouldn't fear coming to grips with your doubts head-on. Your world won't fall apart if you admit that you are not happy and can't quite pinpoint why. Only by making this admission can you begin the work that will lead to personal renewal and greater happiness. If you try to resist the upheaval when a spiritual crisis occurs, you are likely to cause yourself prolonged suffering.

While counseling can help you work through a spiritual crisis, don't expect your counselor to do the hard work for you. We all tend to look to others when we are faced with difficult decisions. We sometimes feel we'd like others to make them. If a counselor tries to make your decisions for you, he or she is not helping you resolve your crisis. One of the most important steps in resolving a spiritual crisis is learning to take full responsibility for important decisions about your future. There is no substitute for the long, hard self-examination necessary to make these decisions wisely.

Further Suggestions

Achieving the core spiritual experience is relatively easy, but maintaining spiritual growth is not. Beyond making the healing silence a part of your life and perhaps seeking professional counseling, there are some other strategies that may help you.

• Face and accept the reality of your own death as an imminent possibility. Paradoxically, recognition of your mortality can be an enormously liberating experience. When you realize how short and fragile your life is, you also awaken to your responsibility to savor every minute of it. You recognize the foolishness of wasting your time in worry, blaming, unsatisfying work, a bad marriage, unnecessary illness, or any one of the hundreds of ways that people kill time. Confronting and then accepting your own mortality is the best possible antidote to the bad habit of killing time.

• Accept the responsibility for your own happiness. You—not your spouse, your parents, your friends, or your lovers—must determine your deepest needs and fulfill them. The task is wholly yours, and it is not easy. So many of your life decisions have been programmed by society and family that unearthing what you really want from life requires considerable time and effort. You may be tempted to keep postponing this task, putting up with vague discontent and unhappiness while you follow the life path laid out for you by others. In the short run, this may appear to be a safe decision, but in fact you are risking your happiness and satisfaction. You are choosing a life of unfulfilled desires. The far wiser choice is to begin the work of individuation. The needs you discover may be at odds with your programming and what you have always considered safe. You can expect a degree of anxiety about your discoveries. But, by recognizing your deepest needs and taking responsibility for meeting them, you give yourself a chance to own the greatest treasure in life—lasting inner fulfillment.

• Develop balance and harmony. More than two thousand years ago, Aristotle wrote that wisdom lies in following the golden mean. And if you want to live a full, healthy, satisfying life, you must discover a golden mean of balance and harmony. The importance of balance extends to every part of your life: your rest-activity cycle, your diet, your work and recreation, your emotional sphere, and so on. Balance in your personal relations means that you respect the opinions of others and don't always insist on having things your way. There are at least two sides to every issue, and if you look for the truth rather than reinforcement of your own opinions, you will not only save yourself frustration, but also gain in wisdom.

• Face your weaknesses and grow. You can't let parts of your personality remain undeveloped. It's easy to excuse your weaknesses by pointing out your strengths. If you are insensitive, you can say that you are basically an analytic person. Or if you are unassertive, you can point out your compassion for others. But these excuses are no substitute for the satisfaction you could achieve by developing the weaker parts of your personality and growing into a fully integrated person.

• Spend time alone. Spiritual growth is almost impossible if you never give yourself a chance to explore your own thoughts and feelings in private. The expectations, beliefs, and criticisms of others are a major obstacle to your own personal development, and this obstacle is at its strongest when you are with others. If you rarely spend much time alone, then your initial efforts to do so may result in a significant level of anxiety. Put that anxiety to work in a constructive task that expresses your innermost feelings. You could write poetry, paint, take pictures, or go for a walk in the woods. Almost any activity other than sitting in front of the tube will help you get in touch with your real needs. Once you make a habit of spending time alone, you will treasure solitude because you will have discovered how nourishing it is to your soul. You will also realize that you can find fulfillment only within yourself. You can never find fulfillment in someone else; you can only share it with them once you have found it within.

• Read about spiritual growth. Whether you prefer the Bible or Walt Whitman, you can learn much by studying what others have written about spiritual development. At the very least you will gain the reassurance that others have shared your experience, and that spiritual crises are a universal part of human experience. You may also find the insights of others useful in formulating your own understanding of the meaning and purpose of your life.

• Strengthen your religious ties. Bible study classes and religious retreats can provide an atmosphere and a community for exploration of spiritual questions. You might also learn to pray, if you do not already pray regularly. It has been said and we have seen that prayer can sometimes work miracles in medical cases that were seemingly hopeless.[137] Certainly, during a spiritual crisis, prayer can be a great comfort and a source of strength.

• Don't be hesitant to ponder the big unanswered questions of life. For example, take time one evening to drive out into the country on a clear night and look at the sky. Ask yourself where it all came from, how it keeps going, whether there is a divine design. Or take a walk by the ocean and let yourself muse about the purpose of life, or whether it has a purpose at all. Beware of cynicism. These questions can provoke anxiety if you consider them honestly, and cynicism is a common defense. Be open to the possibility that these questions may indeed have real answers that you can discover. Your goal should not be to find some absolute answer that you can proclaim as a new religion, but simply to develop a personal philosophy of life that will sustain you as you work toward your own personal fulfillment.

You may believe that you don't have a philosophy of life now and you won't need one in the future. If so, you re mistaken. You do have a set of beliefs about death, God, the purpose of your life, and how you should interact with others. These beliefs can be termed your philosophy, and they have a major impact on what you do and how you live. You should consciously take part in the development of your philosophy of life. Like Socrates, you should realize that "the unexamined life is not worth living."

• Finally, beware of the belief that you will ever reach a plateau of development where you can stop growing. The joy of living is through growth and change. So accept the ever-rolling waves of change as opportunities for delight and satisfaction.

22. The Social Impact of Your Spiritual Growth

In this age of advanced technology and mammoth institutions, many people believe that they can have no effect on the course of social development. By discussing large social problems (crime, health care, poverty, etc.) in terms of institutions rather than individuals, academicians, legislators, and the news media reinforce this attitude. Responsibility for many important elements of our lives now lies with professionals. Doctors are supposed to keep us healthy, police to prevent crime, economists to make the economy prosper, and so on. The sheer immensity of modern institutions has set in motion social forces beyond individual control, but you can have a far greater influence on social trends than you have come to believe.

The historian Arnold Toynbee believed that the turning within on the part of a small segment of a population during a period of crisis was not a retreat from the troubles of the time, but a step toward new solutions.[217] Many social observers believe that modern industrial society is now in a period of crisis. Library shelves are full of books written by eminent scholars who assert that the solutions or lack thereof to the social problems of the next several decades (e.g., nuclear weapons, energy, poverty) will determine the course of history for a long time to come. It is also widely acknowledged that people have begun turning within. In 1974 one study conducted by Andrew Greeley and William McCready at the University of Chicago indicated that 40 percent of all American adults could recall at least one spiritual awakening. This was double the number reported by a 1962 Gallup poll. Perhaps the best example of the current revival of interest in spiritual growth is the millions of Americans who meditate. This turning inward to experience the healing silence may have significant social effects. By exploring these potential effects, you may

261

be surprised to learn what impact your own spiritual growth can have on others.

The Healing Person

The key to understanding the social effects of the healing silence lies in recent scientific research on the qualities of what has been called the *healing person*. Numerous scientific evaluations of the effects of psychotherapy indicate that in a given group of emotionally distressed individuals, a significant number (more than 30 percent) will improve without professional therapy.[18] Until recently these cases were considered "spontaneous remissions," and the phenomenon was ignored. But a number of researchers were not satisfied with this vague concept and began to explore it. The results of their studies are striking. Contrary to previous belief, the investigators found that these cases of improvement were not in fact spontaneous; the distressed individuals had in fact received a substantial amount of "therapeutic" help and guidance, not from therapists but from friends, family members, or clergymen who had no psychotherapeutic training yet exhibited the qualities of the healing person.

Psychologist Allen Bergin argues that a related process is at work in the occasional emergence of an exceptionally effective person out of highly pathological family surroundings.[18] He cites the case of a young college graduate who came from a highly disturbed home in which every family member except himself had been hospitalized for severe mental illness. Nevertheless, he graduated with honors from a renowned university, had starred on the football team, and was unusually popular. When Bergin and his research team explored this young man's past, they discovered that he had had a close relationship with a neighborhood family and spent many hours with them. The mother of this family was this young man's guide, counselor, and chief source of love; she helped many other neighborhood children as well. Clearly, this woman's level of wholeness and integration had a very powerful effect on those around her.

Research indicates that a person's level of wholeness significantly affects others in a normal interpersonal setting. Psychologists Jeffrey Shapiro and Therese Voog found that college students whose roommates demonstrated high levels of understanding warmth and genuineness achieved higher grades than those whose roommates showed lower levels of psychological integration.[198] The roommates' levels of psychological integration were a more accurate predictor of freshman achievement than academic ability as measured by standard aptitude tests. In a review of this and several other similar studies, psychologists Charles Truax and Kevin Mitchell conclude:

> If the untrained or minimally trained individual has a naturally high level of accurate empathy, non-possessive warmth, genuineness, and other interpersonal skills, then it seems likely, from the present vantage point, that individuals who spend time with him will be as helped, if not more helped, than if they were receiving formal psychotherapy from a trained professional. (221, p. 327).

David, a Beacon of Wellness

David came to us with the chief complaint of chronic low back pain. In completing the Holistic Health Survey, he also indicated that he had recently been straining at work and had become quite dissatisfied with his job because he saw no further opportunity for advancement. He smoked a pack of cigarettes per day and usually had two martinis before dinner in order to unwind. His physical exam revealed a significantly elevated blood pressure and muscular tension in his lower back.

In his initial inverview, however, it became clear that the tension in his life was not only localized in his back and arteries. At home, his wife had begun suffering from the "empty nest" syndrome after their youngest son had gone off to college. She needed her husband's companionship and understanding in her efforts to find new outlets for her creativity, but he was struggling with his own problems and his dissatisfaction at work. As a result, her demands added to his tension. Unable to sleep well or relax easily, he was becoming an increasingly abrasive person, especially at work, where he had on several occasions angrily chewed out his secretary and staff for mistakes that he later felt were quite minor. He also recounted an incident where he had exploded on the tennis court when his opponent, a colleague at work, made a bad call. He felt deeply troubled that he was becoming a tense, abrasive person.

After reviewing David's test results—all of which proved unremarkable—we started him on a multifaceted treatment program aimed at reducing his generalized tension. To control his blood pressure, we put him on medication and a salt-restricted diet. For his chronic back pain, we prescribed a program of massage, biofeedback, and exercise. Finally, we suggested that he begin the TM program to improve his level of psychological well-being and promote his overall growth of wholeness.

After three months of this regime, he showed some improvement. He had achieved sufficient relief from his chronic back pain to discontinue the biofeedback and massage, but he continued his exercises at home. Though he noted few benefits from the TM program, he did mention a moderate easing of inner tension. The medication and salt-restricted diet were working well in controlling his blood pressure. He continued to improve over the next three months, and we decided to begin decreasing his medication. While he still was not overly enthusiastic about meditation, he reported that several colleagues at work and his wife had commented on changes in him. In fact, his wife was sufficiently impressed to begin the TM program on her own.

One year after his initial visit, David's progress was substantial. His low back pain had completely subsided, and though he continued on a salt-restricted diet, he no longer required medication to reduce his blood pressure. After having attended a TM residence course where he had the opportunity to experience the concentrated benefits of the healing silence, he had grown much more positive about the TM program. To his surprise, he had quit smoking; he also reported that his alcohol consumption had dropped to fewer than four drinks per week. Particularly important to our current discussion were his changes at work and at home.

The tension at home had eased considerably; he and his wife were spending more time together, not at the expense of his work, but because he began finding more time in his busy schedule. At work, he began working more easily with his staff than he had in years. He began feeling not only able to handle the pressures of his job but better able to assert his creativity and leadership qualities that had earned him his previous promotions.

The effects of the growing wholeness in David's life were obvious; much less so, though equally important, were its effects on those around him. Like most people, David did not recognize prior to his treatment at our health center how much he created his own environment. Though a dynamic person, capable of taking initiative, he had gotten caught up in blaming others—his wife, his secretary, his colleagues at work—for his problems when, in fact, many of his difficulties had their origins in his inability to handle trying situations with equanimity, understanding, and sustained positivity. Growing in wholeness, however, he began to radiate qualities of well-being rather than tension. As a result, he elicited cooperation and commitment rather than anger and resentment from his staff; he helped his wife get training for a new career in real estate; and he also renewed his long-neglected role as a father. He became active in the Red Cross and accepted the presidency of his synagogue. In short, he became a much more helping person.

The Social Effects of Silence

Stress and well-being are both highly contagious. If we could put a radioisotope on stress, we could see it pass from one individual to another. For example, if a person leaves home in the morning upset or with a chip on his or her shoulder, that inner tension colors every interaction with others throughout the day. Boss, co-workers, subordinates, even the grocery clerk feel that tension, react to it, and to some degree pass it on to others. In the same way, feelings of optimism and well-being spread from one person to another; a cheerful person uplifts the spirits of whomever he or she meets just as the distressed person distresses others. In human psychological transactions positive and negative feelings are self-reinforcing.

In promoting the growth of wholeness, the healing silence increases emotional ease and well-being and develops the qualities of the healing person. One can imagine that simply by increasing the number of helping people in a given population, a whole range of social problems that have their roots in individual emotional distress (crime, drug abuse, mental illness, and so on) might decrease in intensity. These healing individuals would presumably provide the guidance or emotional nurture necessary to help distressed individuals find solutions to their problems. Equally important, the general increase in well-being among meditators would presumably reinforce well-being in others. The healing silence, experienced by even a small number of people, would function like a catalyst for the growth of optimism and well-being throughout the population. In providing a climate for better interpersonal relations, this collective decrease in tension would presumably contribute to improved functioning of social institutions.

Admittedly, these are speculations. We do not mean to imply that the experience of inner silence alone will heal all the problems that beset modern societies. Of course, the healing silence will not magically create jobs or lead to the discovery of new energy sources to resolve the world's energy problems or resolve all the psychopathology that fuels the problems of crime and drug abuse. But we are suggesting that the healing silence could contribute to the solution of many social problems in three important ways. First, it may increase the number of "helping people" in a society. Second, it may lower the collective tension level in a society by enhancing individual well-being and happiness. Finally, by developing individual creative intelligence and lessening the waste of time and energy in interpersonal strife, it may increase individual capacity for creative, productive thinking and action. "It is through the inward development of the personality," wrote Arnold Toynbee, "that individual human beings are able to perform those creative acts . . . that cause the growth of human society."

23. Health and Happiness

What are the physical, emotional, and spiritual qualities of a person at the height of positive wellness? A final look may enhance your appreciation of your own potential for health and inspire you to re-read this book. Once through isn't enough to improve your total well-being. If a chapter applies to you, you can't expect to get much out of it unless you go back, study it, and adapt its principles to your every-day living. If several chapters fit your needs, you should reread Chapter 7 and carefully design your own holistic health program.

Positive wellness may seem like an impossible goal. Nevertheless, many people enjoy the natural expression of their full potential for health. You can't distinguish these people by race, sex, occupation, or age. If you look closely, however, you can recognize them by their exceptional vitality. Others have achieved positive wellness, and so can you. By now you should at least realize that dramatically improv-ing your health needn't be a painful struggle. It can be done, and even enjoyably.

Wellness and Your Physical Being

One of the foremost characteristics of the fully well person is a high level of fitness. Such a person glows with a radiance of physical well-being. The eyes are bright, the posture erect, the stride firm, and the body trim and fit. This outer radiance is a reflection of an inner zest for living. The well person enjoys the physical, sensual dimension of being.

A peak of wellness means a high level of energy. The well person usually needs less sleep than other people, but almost never feels an energy slump during the day. Should the well individual require a surge of energy to complete an important task on schedule, the energy is there. While well people will not choose to push themselves to exhausting extremes, they can go without sleep and show relatively few effects. They can stay up for thirty-six hours with little trouble at all. On the other hand, a cornerstone of the well individual's sustained energy level is a balanced rest-activity cycle. During particularly difficult work, these people will take brief breaks to refresh themselves physically and psychologically. In addition, because well individuals are free from anxiety and worry, they don't waste their energy in fruitless physical or mental activity. Free from boredom, they don't squander their energy in time-killing activities. Wherever they might be, they find opportunities for expressing their creative potential.

Well people are free from the everyday aches and pains that send most people running to the medicine cabinet for aspirins, antacids, and laxatives. Of course, an especially hard set of tennis may cause some soreness, or a gastronomic excess may result in distress, but these are rare occurrences. And when these healthy people fall prey to a headache, indigestion, or constipation, they don't go around talking about their troubles. They have confidence in their physical ability to cure minor distress and go on enjoying themselves. Well people simply don't allow minor aches and pains to stand in their way of enjoying everyday living.

These people show remarkably high resistance to disease. They seem to be deeply attuned to their physical needs, limits, and sensitivities. Consequently, they rarely get colds. And when the flu season comes around, they are the ones whom the flu bug doesn't bite. This doesn't mean that these individuals are hothouse flowers. They don't sit home during the winter with the thermostat up to 76°. They are active, dynamic individuals who generally love to be outdoors. Despite their high levels of resistance, well individuals are never foolhardy about their health. They may not like going to doctors, but should a troublesome and persistent symptom arise, they get medical attention early. They also have checkups from time to time.

These people delight in their active orientation to living. They play vigorous sports, but they also love to go for walks and take them regularly. If you try to talk to them about what is on the tube, you will have a difficult time. They can imagine few worse punishments than having to sit night after night in front of TV. Fitness is a natural part of their lives because they don't always look for the easy way to perform simple tasks. They prefer the stairs to an elevator for one to two flights, and they often park their cars several blocks from their destinations just to get some exercise. In short, they love to be active and involved.

Well individuals are physically powerful, though they may or may not be highly muscular. The source of their power is their physical attunement. They maintain a peak of muscle tone and a minimum of muscle tension. They also reflect a high level of mind-body coordination. These factors enable them to react much more quickly than other people. If they are athletic, this trait becomes especially apparent in fast-paced sports such as tennis or handball. Of course, wellness does not automatically give you exceptional physical strength and is no substitute for training. However, the well person has the physical power to enjoy a large measure of physical self-confidence.

A final physical hallmark of a well person is a natural ease and grace in activity. Movements are fluid and free from strain. There is no trace of shame, awkwardness, or lack of physical confidence. While not necessarily reflecting a fashion-model ideal of beauty, well people delight in the physical dimension of their beings and genuinely like their bodies. This delight renders each well person beautiful in his or her own unique way.

Wellness and Your Mental-Emotional Being

The emotional hallmark of positive wellness is an unshakable base-line happiness. This powerful inner contentment provides an emotional anchor that gives the well person a natural stability in the face of success and failure. Individuals at the peak of wellness recognize that unexpected setbacks are part of life. Just as a child expresses a spontaneous bubbling of happiness, these exceptionally healthy individuals radiate their inner well-being. They are friendly and unself-conscious about their enjoyment of everyday living. No matter where these people find themselves, they never waste time wishing that their circumstances were different. Rather than foolishly waste the present, they simply make the best of their circumstances and derive whatever joy they can. This is all but impossible for people without a high level of base-line happiness; people without a locus of inner contentment have difficulty being happy no matter where they are.

People at the peak of wellness are free from worry and anxiety. They know that no amount of worrying or anxious fretting will change the future. Only planning and action can make a difference. Healthy people know that they cannot control all the aspects of any undertaking. Even a short drive to the store can be interrupted by a flat tire. With so many ways for plans to go wrong, healthy people know that worry is foolish. So they choose to be optimistic rather than worried, careful rather than anxious, and confident rather than fearful.

These people are also free from depression. While disappointments may trigger a bout with the blues for others, people at the peak of wellness somehow have the ability to take them in stride without losing a step. They are able to enjoy their everyday lives no matter what unexpected events may come their way. One of their greatest assets is their ability to live fully in the present. Should an unhappy event befall them, they don't start ruminating about the past, what they could have done or should have done. They accept their lives without self-delusion or self-punishment because they know that doing so is the only way to happiness, and ultimately success. Above all, they never make the mistake of pinning all their hopes for happiness on anyone or anything. They assiduously avoid the trap of believing that they will be happy if they get a promotion, meet the right lover, win the lottery, write a best seller, inherit some money, or get a degree. These wise individuals know that the only source of happiness is within.

Spontaneity is another important quality of peak wellness. Through deep contact with inner silence, healthy individuals have healed the traumas and stresses they suffered while growing up. Consequently, they are free from the hang-ups, fears, and inhibitions that bother most people. They are aware of their deep feelings and let them flow freely without fear. They never worry about appearing foolish or unsophisticated because their self-esteem is high and they are naturally sensitive to others' feelings as well as their own. Pent-up feelings do not cloud their relations with others. As a result, they quite easily achieve intimacy. In contrast, psychological game playing is completely foreign to their way of relating. They do not need defensive behavior, and don't build themselves up by putting others down.

These people are insightful about themselves and others. They know how their personalities work and why. They also easily see through people who try to be manipulative. These exceptionally happy individuals may seem so friendly and genuine as to be naive, but don't let this natural, unpretentious warmth fool you. Their clarity of mind is acute and their timing precise. One of their emotional assets is an almost complete freedom from inner tension that so often clouds the thinking of others. As a result, they find it easy to focus their full attention on a trying problem until a solution finally emerges.

It is almost impossible to shake the self-confidence of one of these unique people. Their self-esteem is high, and they don't feel obligated to prove themselves at every turn, or at any turn, for that matter. Consequently, they never waste time in useless bickering or debating. While they enjoy discussions, they don't feel they have to force others to accept their point of view. These exceptionally healthy individuals don't see their interpersonal relationships as contests and never feel the need for one-upmanship. If they meet an ardent interpersonal power player, they are likely to dismiss the interaction as a waste of time. This unwillingness to engage in useless psychological combat is not a sign of weakness. In fact, their self-confidence gives well individuals all the power they need to intimidate others should the situation demand.

Healthy people accept complete responsibility for their health and happiness. These people are mature. They are emotionally grown up and have forgiven others (parents, grandparents, siblings, teachers) for early hurts. As a result, they have given up blaming as a way of coping with frustration or misfortune. Instead, they take full responsibility when their plans work out as well as when things go wrong. By assuming this responsibility, they free themselves from pent-up anger and resentment. If there is no one to blame, there is also no one to resent or get angry with. These people realize that anger, in all but the rarest of occasions, is destructive and just a heated way to blame. They understand that no amount of blaming can bring a moment of happiness.

Wellness and Your Spiritual Being

Well people have a firm sense of self. In fact, the well person's experience of self is so strong that it might best be termed invincible. For this reason, these highly integrated individuals are completely free from feelings of spiritual asphyxiation. They never feel trapped by their spouses, jobs, children, parents, or financial responsibilities because they don't define themselves, their essential being, in terms of the boundaries of everyday living. Instead they are continually nourished by an uninterrupted flow of creative intelligence from the core of their being. As a result, they can never feel trapped by life. They have unlimited confidence in their capacity to accept responsibilities of their own choosing and break boundaries that become constricting.

These highly developed individuals are aggressively interested in their own growth. They are always ready for new experiences and want to learn more about life at every opportunity. Boredom is alien to them because they don't wait for new experiences; they actively seek the new and interesting. They will engage anyone—the doctor, the florist, the garage mechanic—in conversation if they can learn something new. Unlike most people who look for security in the status quo, these individuals realize that the only real security is in their continued development and in the progress of humanity as a whole. They know that they will never reach a plateau of perfection where the need for growth vanishes. Well people find renewal in change and see it as fundamental to their enjoyment of living. Therefore, they read, study, listen, and remain ever on the lookout for new experiences that can enrich their souls and teach them more about life.

While well people are generous with their love, they don't get involved in one intimate relationship after another. They see a long string of love relationships as a sign of immaturity and a tendency toward dependency. They are not looking for a surrogate Mommy or Daddy, and don't want to play that role themselves. They want those they love to be autonomous and self-fulfilling, to enjoy an independent fullness of life that can be shared. An ample measure of privacy is one of their greatest treasures. They like to be alone just as much as they like to be with others, and they will go to great lengths to protect their privacy. For dependent people solitude can be terrifying, because to them it means loneliness. But for healthy people solitude is a source of strength and satisfaction. They are never lonely because they have discovered their ability to commune with the power and vastness of creation.

In contrast to their autonomy, they are also humble. They have a deep respect for the mysteries of creation and never forget that their own fragile lives depend on a harmony of forces far beyond their imagination, much less their control. They are also humble in their relations with others. They don't show off and never try to impress others with their erudition or achievements. They just don't know how to be snobbish because false feelings of superiority are not part of their personalities. Though they may not be orthodox in their religious outlook, they have a deep respect for the order and beauty of the universe.

Authenticity is another one of their spiritual hallmarks. They are not pretentious and never feel the need to seem what they are not. They are honest; they regard lying as a means of self-deception that ultimately undermines their own opportunities for happiness. On the other hand, they never use honesty as a weapon. Should expressing a sentiment truthfully result only in hurting someone else's feelings, they may well withhold that opinion. Another important dimension of their authenticity is self-acceptance. They don't indulge in self-hate, nor do they complain about their physical endowments. Whether they are tall or short, athletic or unathletic, brilliant or of average intelligence, they accept themselves fully and completely. Rather than wish they were otherwise, they look for their strengths and develop themselves from there.

They also have a healthy sense for the tragicomic nature of life. They have a strong sense of humor and laugh easily. Of equal importance is their capacity for compassion and tenderness.

They have a sustaining sense of purpose and meaning. Whatever their work, they find it satisfying and see themselves contributing to the welfare of humanity. They identify themselves first as responsible members of the human race and only secondarily as belonging to a particular group, community, religion, or nation. While they have high ideals, they are not naive idealists. They don't have much use for pipe dreams; they prefer a realistic approach that leads to real contributions to human betterment. They enjoy helping others and look for opportunities to do so. They might be regarded by some as corny or old-fashioned. But healthy people are not concerned with what others think of their behavior or beliefs.

Finally, healthy people appreciate every aspect of life. What to others has become mundane always remains new and fresh to them. Everywhere they look, they see the fullness of life and enjoy a unique attunement with the rhythms of the world. While they especially relish forests, mountains, clear lakes, the ocean, and the desert, they also enjoy the city. They can find a skyscraper just as inspiring as a sequoia. Because they find it so easy to enjoy themselves, they don't have to chase after entertainment. They aren't particularly interested in bars, night clubs, and discotheques, although they can enjoy these too when the occasion arises. If you talk to one of these happy people about appreciating the world, you will soon discover that they have a very special reverence for life. To them, the earth is a wonderful garden. These people are enthusiastic about life and savor every phase, every aspect, every pleasure, and every pain. They genuinely delight in the fullness of living.

Throughout this book, we have had one goal—to help you begin making use of your full capacity for wellness and become a fully vital and vibrant individual. If you have recognized your potential to improve, you are already well on the way to the peak of wellness. All you need do now is design a step-by-step plan to raise your level of wellness, then follow through. Remember that enjoyment of living rather than speed of results must be your goal. There is joy in taking full responsibility for your health and happiness.

Appendix I
Holistic Health Survey *

This detailed survey of all aspects of your health (mind, body, environment, relations, spirit) has been designed to serve a twofold purpose. It will not only gather health history but will also help you raise your health awareness. It will provide the staff of the Age of Enlightenment Center for Holistic Health with a comprehensive picture of your total health status. And it will provide *you* and us with information to guide your program for further growth and development.

In completing the survey, keep in mind the eight basic principles of holistic health:

1. Health requires an integration of mind, body, and spirit.
2. Positive wellness rather than the mere absence of symptoms must be the goal of health care.
3. Everyday living habits are the basis of health.
4. The individual must affirm personal responsibility for his or her health.
5. Illness provides an opportunity for growth.
6. Environmental factors play a major role in individual health.
7. All modalities of healing, ancient as well as modern, deserve careful scientific exploration and should be used where appropriate.
8. Your inner capacity for health is the foundation for achieving positive wellness.

INSTRUCTIONS: Please check each statement that is true for you.

* This is a sampling of five out of twelve sections from the complete survey used by the Center for Holistic Health, San Diego, California.

Rest

The body needs rest so that it can normalize the effects of stress and fatigue accumulated during the day. Rest is the basis of activity. The more profound the level of rest, the greater the potential for dynamic, productive activity.

___ Take more than twenty minutes to fall asleep at night.
___ Wake up several times in the night to urinate.
___ Wake up several times in the night for other reasons:
   ___ Worries.
   ___ Eating just before bedtime.
   ___ Dreams or nightmares.
   ___ Uncomfortable bed, cramped quarters.
___ Take time for extra rest when sick.
___ Frequently feel "hyper," body or mind going too fast.
___ Awake feeling rested, refreshed.
___ Are aware of your earliest signs of fatigue.
___ (Attention wandering, agitation, headache, eyes tired, sore shoulders or lower back, etc.). What are they?

_____

_____

___ Practice a meditation or relaxation exercise.
What technique?

_____

How often? _____

Exercise

Exercise is a vital part of achieving optimal health. Your unused muscles receive less blood flow, and therefore less nutrients and oxygen. The heart and the respiratory system are prime beneficiaries of a sensible exercise program. Physical activities increase the work capacity of the heart and lungs and allow for their more effortless, efficient function at resting levels. Exercise also breaks up excess muscular tension, a noted depletor of your energy and vitality.

__ My daily activity involves:
  __ Little physical effort (sitting most of the time, pushing a pencil, etc.).
  __ Moderate physical effort (gardening, factory work, raising small children, etc.).
  __ Strenuous physical effort (construction, farming, lifting and loading, etc.).
  __ Bike riding or taking long walks.
  __ Jogging __ miles __ times per week.
__ Enjoy exercise.
__ View exercise as a chore.
__ Know not to strain but to gradually increase my amount of exercise.
__ Exercise outdoors whenever possible to get the benefits of sunshine and fresh air.
__ Recover quickly and easily from vigorous physical activity.
__ Perform yoga asanas or some stretching exercise 10–15 minutes __ times per week (such postural exercise prevents stiffening of joints and musculoskeletal degeneration).

Environmental Care

Home safety, conservation of our natural resources, and ecological awareness must become daily life habits for you and for succeeding generations to enjoy optimal health.

__ Are careful to avoid safety hazards around the home (electrical circuit overloading, combustible materials).
__ Keep medicines and cleaning agents out of the possible reach of children.
__ Keep the number of the fire department, police, family physician, and poison center posted near the telephone.
__ Have a warm, happy home environment.
__ Recognize every family member as a growing, evolving being.
__ Avoid chemical deodorants that clog up pores and prevent normal cooling through the excretion of moisture.
__ Read labels of skin preparations you purchase (soaps, shampoos,

creams) to avoid the destruction of important skin oils and natural helpful bacteria by "antibacterial" chemicals or the plugging of pores by heavy synthetic creams or oils.

__ Regularly brush your teeth __ once or __ twice daily.

__ Avoid "brightener" toothpastes that use abrasives which wear out tooth enamel.

__ Use low-phosphate detergents.

__ Avoid synthetic clothes because synthetic fibers do not allow air to circulate through them, causing overheating, perspiration, and an imbalance of skin bacteria.

__ Buy clothes of at least 50% natural fiber (cotton, wool, or silk).

__ Change clothes when you come home from work to give yourself a psychological "change of pace," a new mind-set.

__ Walk barefoot periodically to strengthen the feet and let them "breathe."

__ Avoid smoke-filled rooms, toxic fumes, etc.

__ Avoid excess noise pollution.

__ Turn off lights and appliances when not needed.

__ Automobile gets better than 20 miles per gallon.

__ Keep thermostat below 70° during winter.

__ Recycle cans, paper, clothing, books, organic waste.

__ Avoid littering.

__ Go camping or hiking __ times yearly.

Nutrition

__ Generally eat in a slow, relaxed manner (this allows blood to flow from the muscles to the digestive system).

__ Generally too busy to eat slowly.

__ Have indigestion (gas, pain, bloating) for 1–2 hours after eating.

__ Use antacids or laxatives frequently.

__ Eat candy or other sweets for quick "pick-me-ups."

__ Eat an uncooked fruit or vegetable at least once a day.

__ Have more than two cups of coffee per day.

__ Read the labels on foods you buy.

    __ Avoid refined or processed foods.

    __ Avoid foods with sugar added.

    __ Avoid preservatives or artificial coloring.

___ Drink no more than one soft drink per week.
___ Have fewer than four alcoholic drinks or beers per week.
___ Add little salt to your food.
___ Are frequently dieting.
___ Don't eat unless hungry (your body will tell you when it needs food).
___ Have a good appetite.
___ Maintain your weight within ten pounds of your ideal weight.
___ Feel the quality of food you eat is significant to your well-being.

Psychosocial Well-being

___ Am happy most of the time.
___ Nervous with strangers.
___ Difficulty making decisions.
___ Worry a lot.
___ Get angry easily.
___ Annoyed by little things.
___ Sexual problems.
___ Difficulties at work.
___ Considered suicide.
___ Desire psychiatric help.
___ Can say "no" without feeling guilty.
___ Enjoy complimenting other people.
___ Feel okay about crying, expressing anger, feeling joyful or sad.
___ Am afraid of criticism.
___ Laugh easily and frequently.
___ Have at least two close friends with whom to share deeply personal concerns.
___ Dread the future.
___ Excited about the next ten years of life.
___ Actively support some community activity or charitable cause.
___ Vote regularly.
___ Attend church services regularly.
___ Would call the police if you saw a crime being committed.
___ Never drink when driving.
___ Buckle up your seat belts.
___ Drive with caution and stay within five miles of the speed limit.

Appendix II
Simple Recommendations for Reducing Cholesterol and Fat Consumption

	Enjoy	*Avoid*
Meat	Lean meat (choose lean cuts; before cooking trim visible fat)	Lamb, pork, ham, fatty meat (frankfurters, bacon, sausage, mutton, spareribs, luncheon meats)
Poultry	Chicken, turkey	Duck, goose
Fish	Trout, bluefish, cod, flounder, salmon, mackerel, whitefish, haddock, halibut, herring	Shrimp, shellfish
Eggs	Egg whites	Egg yolks
Nuts	Almonds, pignolias, cashews, English walnuts, seeds (sunflower and pumpkin)	Peanuts, macadamia nuts, black walnuts
Beans	Dried beans: lentils, split peas, and lima, pinto, kidney, red, white, calico, and navy beans; chickpeas, soybeans	
Vegetables	All vegetables: raw, steamed, or baked	
Fruit	All fruits except . . .	Olives and avocados (occasionally in moderation)
Breads	White, wheat, rye, pumpernickel, oatmeal, corn, matzo, pretzels, tortillas, homemade pancakes, biscuits, and muffins	All commercially prepared rolls, muffins, biscuits, doughnuts, and bread made with sugar, shortening, and dried eggs
Pasta	All pasta without eggs	Egg noodles

21	Grains	Barley, bran, oats, rice, rye	
22	Cereals	Corn meal, wheat, farina, hot cereals	Dry or hot cereals prepared with sugar and shortening
23		*Enjoy*	*Avoid*
24	Dairy	Low-fat and skim milk; dry skim milk fortified with vitamins A and D; products made from low-fat or skim milk, such as buttermilk, yogurt; canned evaporated milk, cheese (creamed, cottage, uncreamed, hooped, mozzarella, farmer, and sapsago)	Whole milk and whole milk products, such as canned whole milk, yogurt, butter, cream, cheese, ice cream, sour cream
25	Fats, Oils	Polyunsaturated margarine and mayonnaise, salad oil, polyunsaturated oil such as corn, cottonseed, safflower, sesame, soybean, and sunflower	Any meat fats, shortening, and hydrogenated margarine
26	Beverages	Vegetable and fruit juices made without sugar, herb teas, tea and coffee in moderation, beer and wine in moderation	Juices prepared with sugar
27	Desserts, Snacks, Condiments	Dried and fresh fruit; crackers and breads made without sugar and shortening; nuts and seeds	Bakery goods, candy, puddings, canned fruit with sugar, gelatin desserts

Acknowledgments

Holistic medicine is growing rapidly because many people are contributing to its development. This book reflects the thinking of many leaders in the holistic health field, and we thank all from whom we have drawn ideas and inspiration, especially Nedra Belloc, M.D., Lester Breslow, M.D., Robert Brook, M.D., Rick Carlson, J.D., James Fadiman, Ph.D., Jerome Frank, M.D., Victor Fuchs, Ph.D., David Harris, John Knowles, M.D., Stanley Krippner, Ph.D., Elisabeth Kubler-Ross, M.D., George Leonard, Evarts Loomis, M.D., Thomas McKeown, M.D., Walter McNerney, Kenneth Pelletier, Ph.D., Jonas Salk, M.D., Hans Selye, M.D., Mohammed Shafii, M.D., John Travis, M.D., and Ernest Wynder, M.D.

We also wish to thank Maharishi Mahesh Yogi for his untiring effort to dispel misunderstanding about meditation and make the TM technique available to all.

Without the staff at the Center for Holistic Health in San Diego, California, we could not have written this book. For their dedication and excellence in patient care we thank Dr. Clifford and Carol Ward, Dr. Stuart and Joan Rothenberg, Dr. Michael and Kathryn Vesselago, Dr. John and Penny Farrow, Dr. Helene Aronson, Dr. Tai-Nan Wang, Rita McDonagh, Barbara Ross, and Della Grayson.

Others who have helped us are Ali and Sybil Rubottom, Dr. Bruce and Nacy Wales, Dr. David Simon, Dr. Nelson Leone, Marianne Huening, Ken Weiner, Mike and Donna Fletcher, Connie Dawson, Liz Locati, and Kris Rickards. We thank Florence Gottleib, Hermine Meinhard, and Claudia Moore for their secretarial assistance.

Finally, we thank Cherylyn Davis for her inspiration and support.

Bibliography

1   Akishige, Y. "A Historical Survey of the Psychological Studies in Zen," *Kyushu Psychological Studies*, Akishige (ed.). Bulletin of the Faculty of Literature of Nyushu University, Number 77, Nyushu University, Fukuska, Japan, 1968, pp. 1–56.
2   Anand, B. K., G. S. Chhina, and B. Singh. "Some Aspects of Electroencephalographic Studies in Yogis," *Altered States of Consciousness*, C. T. Tart (ed.). New York, John Wiley and Sons, 1969, pp. 503–506.
3   Anand, B. K., G. S. Chhina, and B. Singh. "Studies on Sri Ramanand Yogi During His Stay in an Airtight Box." *The Indian Journal of Medical Research*, Vol. 49, No. 1, 1961, pp. 82–89.
4   Aronson, H. D. "The Applications of the Science of Creative Intelligence to Transactional Analysis and Other Treatment Modalities." Proceedings of The First International Conference on Psychology and the Science of Creative Intelligence, Fairfield, Iowa, November 28–30, 1975.
5   Aserinsky, E., and N. Kleitman. "Regularly Occurring Periods of Eye Motility and Concomitant Phenomena During Sleep." *Science*, Vol. 118, 1953, pp. 273–274.
6   Assagioli, R. *Psychosynthesis.* New York, Hobbs, Dorman, 1965.
7   Bagchi, B. K., and M. A. Wenger. "Electrophysiological Correlates of Some Yogi Exercises." *Electroencephalography and Clinical Neurophysiology*, Vol. 9, Supplement 7, 1957, pp. 132–149.
8   Bagchi, B. K., and M. A., Wenger. "Simultaneous EEG and Other Recordings During Some Yogic Practices." *Electroencephalography and Clinical Neurophysiology*, Vol. 10, 1958, p. 1963.
9   Balint, M. "The Three Areas of the Mind." *International Journal of Psychoanalysis*, Vol. 39, 1958, pp. 328–340.
10 Banquet, J. P. "EEG and Meditation." *Electroencephalography and Clinical Neurophysiology*, Vol. 33, 1972, p. 454.
11 Banquet, J. P. "Spectral Analysis of the EEG in Meditation." *Electroencephalography and Clinical Neurophysiology*, Vol. 35, 1973, pp. 143–151.
12 Banquet, J. P., and M. Sailhan. "Quantified EEG Spectral Analysis of Sleep and Transcendental Meditation." Proceedings of the Second European Congress on Sleep Research, Rome, Italy, April 10, 1974. Also in *Scientific Research on the Transcendental Meditation Program:*

Collected Papers, Vol. I, D. W. Orme-Johnson and J. T. Farrow (eds.). West Germany, MERU Press, 1976, pp. 182–186.
13 Belloc, N., L. Breslow, and J. Hochstim. "Measurement of Physical Health in a General Population Survey." *American Journal of Epidemiology*, Vol. 93, No. 1, 1970, pp. 328–336.
14 Belloc, N. B. "Relationship of Health Practices and Mortality." *Preventive Medicine*, Vol. 2, 1973, pp. 67–81.
14a Belloc, N. B., and L. Breslow. "Relationship of Physical Health Status and Health Practices." *Preventive Medicine*, Vol. 1, No. 3, August 1972, pp. 409–421.
15 Benson, H. *The Relaxation Response*. New York, William Morrow, 1975.
16 Benson, H., and R. K. Wallace. "Decreased Blood Pressure in Hypertensive Subjects Who Practiced Meditation." *Circulation*, Supplement II to Vols. 45 and 46, 1972, p. 516.
17 Benson, H., and R. K. Wallace. "Decreased Drug Abuse with Transcendental Meditation: A Study of 1,862 Subjects," *Drug Abuse: Proceedings of the International Conference*, C. J. D. Zarafonetis (ed.). Philadelphia, Lea and Febiger, 1972, pp. 369–376.
18 Bergin, A. E. "The Evaluation of Therapeutic Outcomes," *Handbook of Psychotherapy and Behavior Change: An Empirical Analysis*, A. E. Bergin and S. L. Garfield (eds.). New York, John Wiley and Sons, 1971, pp. 217–270.
19 Berkman, P. "Measurement of Mental Health in a General Population Survey." *American Journal of Epidemiology*, Vol. 94, No. 2, 1971, pp. 105–111.
20 Bird, J., and L. Bird. *Sexual Loving*. New York, Avon, 1976.
21 Blackwell, B., I. B. Hanenson, S. Bloomfield, G. Magenheim, S. I. Nidich, and P. Gartside. "Effects of Transcendental Meditation on Blood Pressure: A Controlled Pilot Experiment." *Psychosomatic Medicine*, Vol. 37, No. 1, 1975, p. 86.
22 Bloomfield, H. "Applications of the Transcendental Meditation Program to Psychiatry," *Modern Therapies*, B. Rimland, A. Binder, and V. Binder (eds.). Englewood Cliffs, N.J., Prentice-Hall, 1976.
23 Bloomfield, H. "Assertive Training in an Out-Patient Group of Chronic Schizophrenics: A Preliminary Report." *Behavior Therapy*, Vol. 4, No. 2, March 1973, pp. 277–281. Also in *Annual Review of Behavior Therapy: 1974 Edition*. New York, Brunner, Mazel Publishers, 1974.
24 Bloomfield, H. "Transcendental Meditation as an Aid in Medical Practice." *Practical Psychology*, Vol. 2, No. 8, August 1975, pp. 30–39.
25 Bloomfield, H. "The Transcendental Meditation Program: Rediscovery of the Body's Hidden Potential," *Rediscovery of the Body*, C. A. Garfield and J. Garfield (eds.). New York, Dell, 1977.
26 Bloomfield, H., and R. Kory. *HAPPINESS: The TM Program, Psychiatry, and Enlightenment*. New York, Simon and Schuster, 1976.
27 Bloomfield, H., M. Cain, D. Jaffe, and R. Kory. *TM: Discovering Inner Energy and Overcoming Stress*. New York, Delacorte, 1975.
28 Boudreau, T. "Future Directions in Health Care," *Proceedings of the Conference on Future Directions in Health Care: The Dimensions of Medicine*. New York, December 10–11, 1975, pp. 129–141.
29 Boudreau, L. "Transcendental Meditation and Yoga as Reciprocal In-

hibitors." *Journal of Behavioral Therapy and Experimental Psychiatry*, Vol. 3, 1972, pp. 97–98.

30 Bowers, P., M. Banquer, and H. Bloomfield. "Utilization of Non-Verbal Exercises in the Group Therapy of Out-Patient Chronic Schizophrenics." *International Journal of Group Psychotherapy*, Vol. XXIV, No. 1, 1973, pp. 13–24.

31 Breslow, L. "A Quantitative Approach to the World Health Organization Definition of Health: Physical, Mental, and Social Well-Being." *International Journal of Epidemiology*, Vol. l, No. 4, 1972, pp. 347–355.

32 Brook, R. "Limits of Medicine," *Proceedings of the Conference on Future Directions in Health Care: The Dimensions of Medicine.* New York, 1975, pp. 38–49.

33 Brosse, T. "A Psychophysiological Study of Yoga." *Main Currents in Modern Thought*, July 1946, pp. 77–84.

34 Brown, B. S. "The Life of Psychiatry." *The American Journal of Psychiatry*, 133:5, May 1976, pp. 489–495.

35 Bujatti, M., and P. Riederer. "Biogenic Transmitter Metabolites in Transcendental Meditation." Proceedings of the Fifth International Congress of Endocrinology, Hamburg, West Germany, 1976.

36 Carkhuff, R., and B. Berenson. *Beyond Counseling and Therapy.* New York, Holt, Rinehart, and Winston, 1967.

37 Carlson, R. "Holistic Approaches to Health Care, Specific Applications," *Proceedings of the Conference on Future Directions in Health Care: The Dimensions of Medicine.* New York, December 10–11, 1975, pp. 110–120.

38 Carlson, R. "Holistic Approaches to Health Care, the Concept," *Proceedings of the Conference on Future Directions in Health Care: The Dimensions of Medicine.* New York, 1975, pp. 59–62.

39 Carlson, R. *The End of Medicine.* New York, Wiley Interscience, 1975.

40 Carrington, P., and H. Ephron. "Meditation as an Adjunct to Psychotherapy," *New Dimensions in Psychiatry: A World View*, S. Arieti (ed.). New York, John Wiley and Sons, 1975.

41 Carrington, P., and H. Ephron. "Meditation and Psychoanalysis." *Journal of the American Academy of Psychoanalysis*, Vol. 3, No. 1, 1975, pp. 43–57.

42 Cassell, E. *The Healer's Art: A New Approach to the Doctor-Patient Relationship.* Philadelphia, J. B. Lippincott Company, 1976.

43 Comfort, A. *The Joy of Sex.* New York, Crown, 1972.

44 Datey, N., S. Deshmunh, C. Dalvi, and S. Vinenar. "Shavasan: A Yogic Exercise in the Management of Hypertension." *Angiology*, Vol. 20, 1969, pp. 325–333.

45 Deikman, A. J. "De-Automization and the Mystical Experience," *Altered States of Consciousness*, T. Tart (ed.). New York, John Wiley and Sons, 1969, pp. 23–44.

46 Deikman, A. J. "Experimental Meditation," *Altered States of Consciousness*, T. Tart (ed.). New York, John Wiley and Sons, 1969, pp. 199–218.

47 Deikman, A. J. "Implications of Experimentally Induced Contemplative Meditation." *Journal of Nervous and Mental Disease*, Vol. 142, 1966, pp. 101–116.

48 Doyle, J. T., et al. "Relationship of Cigarette Smoking to Coronary Heart Disease: The Second Report of the Combined Experience of the Albany, New York, and Framingham, Massachusetts, Studies." *Jama,* Vol. 190, 1964, pp. 886–890.

49 Duhl, L. J. "The Health Planner: Planning and Dreaming for Health and Wellness." *American Journal of Health Planning,* Vol. No. 2, October 1976, pp. 7–14.

50 Eckhart, M., quoted in *The Perennial Philosophy* by Aldous Huxley. New York, Harper Colophon Books, 1970.

51 Egan, G. *Encounter: Group Processes for Interpersonal Growth.* Belmont, Calif., Brooks-Cole Publishing Company, 1970.

52 Erikson, E. H. *Childhood and Society,* 2nd ed. New York, W. W. Norton and Company, 1963.

53 Eysenck, H. J. "The Effects of Psychotherapy: An Evaluation." *Journal of Consulting Psychology,* Vol. 16, 1952, pp. 319–324.

54 Eysenck, H. J. *The Effects of Psychotherapy.* New York, International Science Press, 1966.

55 Farrow, J. T. "Physiological Changes Associated with Transcendental Consciousness, the State of Least Excitation of Consciousness," *Scientific Research on the Transcendental Meditation Program: Collected Papers,* Vol. 1, D. W. Orme-Johnson and J. T. Farrow (eds.). West Germany, MERU Press, 1976, pp. 108–133.

56 Fensterheim, H., and J. Baer. *Don't Say Yes When You Want to Say No.* New York, David McKay Company, 1975.

57 Ferenezi, S. "Silence Is Golden," *Further Contributions to the Theory and Technique of Psychoanalysis.* London, Hogarth Press, 1950.

58 Ferguson, P., and J. C. Gowan. "TM—Some Preliminary Psychological Findings." *Journal of Humanistic Psychology,* Vol. 16, No. 3, 1976.

59 Fort, J. *Alcohol: Our Biggest Drug Problem.* New York, McGraw-Hill Book Company, 1973.

60 Frank, J. "Holistic Approaches to Health Care, the Concept," *Proceedings of the Conference on Future Directions in Health Care: The Dimensions of Medicine.* New York, December 10–11, 1975, pp. 62–77.

61 Frank, J. D. *Persuasion and Healing.* Baltimore, Johns Hopkins Press, 1961.

62 French, A. P., A. P. Schmid, and E. Ingalls. "Transcendental Meditation, Altered Reality Testing and Behavior Change: A Case Report." *The Journal of Nervous and Mental Disease,* Vol. 161, No. 1, July 1975, pp. 54–58.

63 Freud, S. *A General Introduction to Psychoanalysis.* New York, Permabooks, 1953.

64 Freud, S. "Analysis Terminable and Interminable." *The International Journal of Psychoanalysis,* Vol. 18, 1937, pp. 373–405.

65 Freud, S. *Civilization and Its Discontents,* trans. J. Strachey. New York, W. W. Norton and Company, 1962.

66 Freud, S. *New Introductory Lectures on Psychoanalysis,* trans. J. Strachey. New York, W. W. Norton and Company, 1965.

67 Freud, S. *The Problem of Anxiety,* trans. H. Bunker. New York, W. W. Norton and Company, 1936.

68 Frew, D. "Transcendental Meditation and Productivity." *Academy of Management Journal,* Vol. 17, No. 2, 1974, pp. 362–368.

69　Friedman, M. *The Pathogenesis of Coronary Artery Disease.* New York, McGraw-Hill Book Company, 1969.

70　Friedman, M., and R. H. Rosenman. *Type A Behavior and Your Heart.* New York, Knopf, 1974.

71　Fromm, E. *Zen Buddhism and Psychoanalysis.* New York, Harper and Row, 1970.

72　Gazzaniga, M. S. "The Split Brain in Man." *Scientific American,* Vol. 22, 1967, pp. 24–29.

73　Gellhorn, E., and W. F. Kiely. "Autonomic Nervous System in Psychiatric Disorder," *Biological Psychiatry,* J. Mendels (ed.). New York, John Wiley and Sons, 1973, Chapter 11, pp. 235–263.

74　Ghiselin, B. *The Creative Process.* New York, Mentor, 1952.

75　Gibb, J. "The Effects of Human Relations Training," *Handbook of Psychotherapy and Behavior Change,* A. E. Bergin and S. L. Garfield (eds.). New York, John Wiley and Sons, 1971, pp. 839–862.

76　Glasser, R. *The Body Is the Hero.* New York, Random House, 1976.

77　Glasser, W. *Positive Addiction.* New York, Harper and Row, 1976.

78　Glasser, W. *Reality Therapy: A New Approach to Psychiatry.* New York, Harper Colophon Books, 1975.

79　Glueck, B. C. "Current Research on Transcendental Meditation." Rensselaer Polytechnic Institute Symposium on The Science of Creative Intelligence and Management Science, Hartford, Conn., March 13, 1973.

80　Glueck, B., and C. F. Stroebel. "Biofeedback and Meditation in the Treatment of Psychiatric Illnesses." *Comprehensive Psychiatry,* Vol. 16, 1975, pp. 303–321.

81　Goldstein, K. *The Organism.* New York, American Book Company, 1939.

82　Gomez, J. *How Not to Die Young.* New York, Pocket Books, 1973.

83　Green, E., A. Green, and E. D. Walters. "Voluntary Control of Internal States: Psychological and Physiological." *Journal of Transpersonal Psychology,* Vol. 2, No. 1, 1970, pp. 1–26.

84　Grinker, R. R. "Psychiatry Rides Madly in All Directions." *Archives of General Psychiatry,* Vol. 10, 1964, pp. 228–237.

85　Hall, E. *The Hidden Dimension.* New York, Doubleday, 1966.

86　Hammond, E. C. "Life Expectancy of American Men in Relation to Their Smoking Habits." *Journal of the National Cancer Institute,* Vol. 43, 1962, pp. 951–962.

87　Hammond, E. C. "Smoking in Relation to the Death Rates of One Million Men and Women," *Epidemiological Approaches to the Study of Cancer and Other Diseases,* W. Haenzel (ed.). National Cancer Institute Monograph No. 19, 1966, pp. 127–204.

88　Harris, T. A. *I'm OK—You're OK.* New York, Avon Books, 1973.

89　Hay, D. R. "Smokers—A Gloomy Prospect for the Neglected Addicts." *Modern Medicine,* November 15, 1976, pp. 52–59.

90　Hjelle, L. A. "Transcendental Meditation and Psychological Health." *Perceptual and Motor Skills,* Vol. 39, 1974, pp. 623–628.

91　Honsberger, R. W., and A. F. Wilson. "The Effect of Transcendental Meditation upon Bronchial Asthma." *Clinical Research,* Vol. 21, 1973, p. 278.

92 Honsberger, R. W., and A. F. Wilson. "Transcendental Meditation in Treating Asthma." *Respiratory Therapy: The Journal of Inhalation Technology,* Vol. 3, 1973, pp. 79–80.
93 Howard, J. *Please Touch: A Guided Tour of the Human Potential Movement.* New York, McGraw-Hill Book Company, 1970.
94 Hume, R. (trans. from Sanskrit). *Thirteen Principal Upanishads,* rev. 2nd ed., reproduction of 1931 ed. London, Oxford University Press. 1971.
95 Huxley, A. *The Perennial Philosophy.* New York, Harper and Row, 1970.
96 Illich, I. *Medical Nemesis.* New York, Pantheon, 1976.
97 Illich, I. "Medicine Is a Major Threat to Health." Interview with Sam Keen in *Psychology Today,* May 1976, pp. 66–77.
98 International Medical News Service. "Well-Being Aids Sex-Therapy Outcome." *Clinical Psychiatry News,* Vol. 4, No. 5, May 1976.
99 Jacobson, E. *You Must Relax.* New York, McGraw-Hill Book Company, 1957.
100 Janov, A. *The Primal Scream.* New York, Dell, 1970.
101 Jarvik, L. F. "Thoughts on the Psychobiology of Aging." *American Psychologist,* 1975.
102 Jevning, R., et al. "Plasma Prolactin and Cortisol During Transcendental Meditation," *The Proceedings of the Endocrine Society 57th Annual Meeting.* New York City, June 18–20, 1975.
103 Journal of Holistic Health, L. Pellettiri (ed.). San Diego, Calif., 1975–1976.
104 Jung, C. G. *Aion: Researches into the Phenomenology of the Self,* trans. R. C. F. Hull, Vol. 9, collected works, Bollingen XX. Princeton, N.J., Princeton University Press, 1959.
105 Jung, C. G. *Analytical Psychology: Its Theory and Practice.* New York, Vintage Books, 1970.
106 Jung, C. G. *Modern Man in Search of a Soul.* New York, Harcourt Brace, 1933.
107 Jung, C. G. *The Structure and Dynamics of the Psyche,* trans. R. C. F. Hull, Vol. 8, collected works, Bollingen XX. Princeton, N.J., Princeton University Press, 1959.
108 Jung, C. G. *Two Essays in Analytical Psychology,* trans. R. C. F. Hull, Vol. 7, collected works, Bollingen XX. Princeton, N.J., Princeton University Press, 1959.
109 Kambe, T., and K. Sato. "Medical and Psychological Studies on Zen; Electroencephalogram and Electromyogram During Zen Practice." *Proceedings of the 26th Convention of JPA,* No. 289, 1962.
110 Kaplan, H. *The Illustrated Manual of Sex Therapy.* New York, A & W Visual Library, 1975.
111 Kasamatsu, A., and T. Hirai. "Science of Zazen." *Psychologia,* Vol. 6, 1963, pp. 86–91.
112 Khan, M. M. R. "The Concept of Cumulative Trauma." *Psychoanalytic Study of the Child,* Vol. 18, 1963.
113 Kleitman, N. *Sleep and Wakefulness,* rev. and enlarged ed. Chicago, University of Chicago Press, 1963.
114 Kline, N. S. *From Sad to Glad.* New York, Ballantine Books, 1975.
115 Knowles, J. H. "Future Directions in Health Care," *Proceedings of the*

Conference on Future Directions in Health Care: The Dimensions of Medicine. New York, December 10–11, 1975, pp. 148–154.

116 Kory, R. "Toward a Theory of Consciousness: A Return to the *Veda* by Way of Psychoanalysis." Department of Philosophy, Yale University, July 10, 1972.

117 Kory, R. *The Transcendental Meditation Program for Business People.* New York, AMACOM, 1976.

118 Kovel, J. *A Complete Guide to Therapy.* New York, Pantheon, 1976.

119 Kris, E. "On Some Vicissitudes of Insight in Psychoanalysis." *International Journal of Psychoanalysis,* Vol. 37, 1956, pp. 445–455.

120 Kris, E. *Psychoanalytic Explorations in Art.* New York, Schocken Books, 1964.

121 Kuhn, T. *The Structure of Scientific Revolutions.* Chicago, University of Chicago Press, 1962.

122 Lazarus, A. A. *Behavior Therapy and Beyond.* New York, McGraw-Hill Book Company, 1971.

123 Lazarus, A. A. "Behavior Therapy in Groups," *Basic Approaches to Group Psychotherapy and Group Counseling,* G. M. Gazda (ed.). Springfield, Charles C. Thomas, 1968, pp. 149–175.

124 Lazarus, A. A. "Multimodal Behavior Therapy: Treating the Basic Id." *Journal of Nervous and Mental Disease,* Vol. 156, No. 6, 1973, pp. 404–411.

125 Lazarus, A. A. "Notes on Behavior Therapy: The Problem of Relapse and Some Tentative Solutions." *Psychotherapy: Theory, Research, and Practice,* Vol. 8, 1971, pp. 192–194.

126 Lazarus, A. A. "Psychiatric Problems Precipitated by Transcendental Meditation." *Psychological Reports,* Vol. 39, 1976, pp. 601–602.

127 Lazarus, A., and A. Fay. *I Can If I Want To.* New York, William Morrow, 1975.

128 Lemon, F. R., and J. W. Kuzma. "Biologic Cost of Smoking: Decreased Life Expectancy." *Archives of Environmental Health,* Vol. 18, 1969, pp. 950–955.

129 Leonard, G. "The Holistic Health Revolution." *New West,* May 10, 1976, pp. 40–49.

130 Leonard, Jon N., J. L. Hofer, and N. Pritikin. *Live Longer Now: The First One Hundred Years of Your Life.* New York, Grosset and Dunlap, 1976.

131 Lesh, T. V. "Zen Meditation and the Development of Empathy in Counselors." *Journal of Humanistic Psychology,* Vol. 10, No. 1, 1970, pp. 39–83.

132 Levine, P. "The Coherence Spectral Array (COSPAR) and Its Application to the Study of Spatial Ordering in the EEG," Proceedings of the San Diego Biomedical Symposium, 1975.

133 Lifton, R. J. *The Life of the Self: Toward a New Psychology.* New York, Touchstone/Simon and Schuster, 1976.

134 Loewenstein, R. M. "The Silent Patient." *Journal of the American Psychoanalytic Association,* Vol. 9, 1961, pp. 2–6.

135 Loomie, L. S. "Some Ego Considerations in the Silent Patient." *Journal of the American Psychoanalytic Association,* Vol. 9, 1961, pp. 56–78.

136 Lowen, A. *Physical Dynamics of Character Structure.* New York, Grune and Stratton, 1958.

137 MacNutt, F. *Healing.* New York, Bantam, 1977.

138 Maharishi Mahesh Yogi. *On the Bhagavad-Gita: A New Translation and Commentary,* Chapters 1–6. Baltimore, Penguin Books, 1969.

139 Maharishi Mahesh Yogi. *The Science of Being and the Art of Living.* Stuttgart, Germany, Spiritual Regeneration Movement Publications, 1966.

140 Maharishi Mahesh Yogi. Videotaped course on The Science of Creative Intelligence. Tapes available through International Film and Tape Library (IFTL), Academy for SCI, Livingston Manor, N.Y.

141 Mandell, A. J. Proceedings of the annual convention of the Society of Biological Psychiatry, San Francisco, 1976.

142 Martin, W. C. "Report on the Health of the Nation." *Natural Food and Farming,* March 1956.

143 Maslow, A. H. "A Theory of Meta-Motivation: The Biological Rooting of Value-Life," *Readings in Humanistic Psychology,* A. J. Sutich and M. A. Vich (eds.). New York, Free Press, 1969.

144 Maslow, A. H. *Motivation and Personality.* New York, Harper, 1954.

145 Maslow, A. H. "New Introduction: Religious Values in Peak Experiences." *Journal of Transpersonal Psychology,* No. II, 1970.

146 Maslow, A. H. "Psychological Data and Value Theory," *New Knowledge in Human Values,* A. Maslow (ed.). New York, Harper, 1959.

147 Maslow, A. H. *Religions, Values, and Peak Experiences.* New York, The Viking Press, 1970.

148 Maslow, A. H. *The Farther Reaches of Human Nature.* New York, The Viking Press, 1971.

149 Maslow, A. H. *The Psychology of Science.* Chicago, The Henry Regnery Company, Gateway Edition, 1969.

150 Maslow, A. H. "Theory Z." *Journal of Transpersonal Psychology,* Fall 1969, pp. 31–47.

151 Maslow, A. H. *Toward a Psychology of Being.* New York, D. Van Nostrand Company, 1968.

152 Masters, W. H., and V. E. Johnson. *Human Sexual Inadequacy.* Boston, Little, Brown, 1970.

153 Masters, W. H., and V. E. Johnson. *Human Sexual Response.* Boston, Little, Brown, 1966.

154 Masters, W. H., and V. E. Johnson. "Principles of the New Sex Therapy." *American Journal of Psychiatry,* Vol. 133, No. 5, 1976, pp. 548–554.

155 McKeown, T. "Limits of Medicine," *Proceedings of the Conference on Future Directions in Health Care: The Dimensions of Medicine.* New York, December 10–11, 1975, pp. 24–38.

156 McNerney, W. "The Crisis in Health Care," *Proceedings of the Conference on Future Directions in Health Care: The Dimensions of Medicine.* New York, December 10–11, 1975, pp. 4–8.

157 McQuade, W., and A. Aikman. *Stress.* New York, E. P. Dutton, 1974.

158 Miskiman, D. E. "Long-Term Effects of the Transcendental Meditation Program in the Treatment of Insomnia," *Scientific Research on the Transcendental Meditation Program: Collected Papers,* Vol. 1, D. W.

Orme-Johnson and J. T. Farrow (eds.). West Germany, MERU Press, 1976, p. 299.

159 Miskiman, D. E. "The Treatment of Insomnia by the Transcendental Meditation Program," *Scientific Research on the Transcendental Meditation Program: Collected Papers*, Vol. 1, D. W. Orme-Johnson and J. T. Farrow (eds.). West Germany, MERU Press, 1976, pp. 296–298.

160 Morehouse, L. E., and L. Gross. *Maximum Performance*. New York, Simon and Schuster, 1977.

161 Morehouse, L. E., and L. Gross. *Total Fitness*. New York, Simon and Schuster, 1975.

162 Moustakas, C. E. (ed.). *The Self: Explorations in Personal Growth*. New York, Harper Colophon Edition, 1974.

163 Nacht, S. "Silence as an Integrative Factor." *International Journal of Psycho-Analysis*, Vol. 45, 1964, pp. 299–303.

164 Naranjo, C., and R. E. Ornstein. *On the Psychology of Meditation*. New York, The Viking Press, 1971.

165 *New York Times*. Summary of a U.S. Health Report, January 8, 1965.

166 Nidich, S., W. Seeman, and T. Dreskin. "Influence of Transcendental Meditation: A Replication." *Journal of Counseling Psychology*, Vol. 20, 1973, pp. 565–566.

167 Orme-Johnson, D. W. "Autonomic Stability and Transcendental Meditation." *Psychosomatic Medicine*, Vol. 35, 1973, pp. 341–349.

168 Orme-Johnson, D. W., and J. T. Farrow (eds.). *Scientific Research on the Transcendental Meditation Program: Collected Papers*, Vol. I. West Germany, MERU Press, 1976.

169 Ornstein, R. E. *The Psychology of Consciousness*. San Francisco, W. H. Freeman and Company, 1972.

170 Otis, L. S. "If Well-Integrated but Anxious, Try TM." *Psychology Today*, Vol. 7, No. 11, April 1974, pp. 45–46.

171 Overweight, Its Prevention and Significance. Metropolitan Life Insurance Company, 1960.

172 Parloff, M. B. "Shopping for the Right Therapy." *Saturday Review*, February 2, 1976, pp. 14–20.

173 Pelletier, K. "Influence of Transcendental Meditation on Autokinetic Perception." *Perceptual and Motor Skills*, Vol. 39, 1974, pp. 1031–1034.

174 Pelletier, K. R. *Mind as Healer, Mind as Slayer*. New York, Delta Books, 1977.

175 Perls, F. S. *Gestalt Therapy Verbatim*. Lafayette, Calif., Real People Press, 1969.

176 Perls, F. S., R. F. Hefferline, and P. Goodman. *Gestalt Therapy*. New York, Delta Publishing Company, 1951.

177 Purdue Opinion Panel, *Report of Poll 86: Current Views of High School Students Toward the Use of Tobacco, Alcohol, and Drugs or Narcotics*. Purdue University Measurement and Research Center, Lafayette, Indiana, 1969.

178 Reich, W. *Character Analysis*. London, Vision Press, 1948.

179 Reik, T. "The Psychological Meaning of Silence." *Psychoanalytic Review*, Vol. 55, 1968, pp. 172–186.

180 Rogers, C. R. *Client-Centered Therapy*. Cambridge, Mass., Riverside Press, 1957.

294 • The Holistic Way to Health and Happiness

181 Rogers, C. R. "Toward a Theory of Creativity," *Creativity and Its Cultivation*, H. H. Anderson (ed.). New York, Harper and Row, 1959.
182 Rosenfeld, A. "The Psychotherapy Jungle: A Guide for the Perplexed." *Saturday Review*, February 2, 1976, pp. 12–13.
183 Routt, T. J. "Low Normal Heart and Respiration Rates in Individuals Practicing the Transcendental Meditation Technique." *Scientific Research on the Transcendental Meditation Program: Collected Papers*, Vol. 1, D. W. Orme-Johnson and J. T. Farrow (eds.). West Germany, MERU Press, 1976, pp. 256–260.
184 Samuels, M., and H. Bennett. *Be Well*. New York, Random House, 1975.
185 Samuels, M., and H. Bennett. *The WELL Body Book*. New York, Random House, 1973.
186 Schmidt, W., and J. De Lint. "Mortality Experience of Male and Female Alcoholic Patients." *Quarterly Journal for the Study of Alcoholism*, Vol. 30, 1969, pp. 112–118.
187 Seeman, W., S. Nidich, and T. Banta. "The Influence of Transcendental Meditation of Self-Actualization." *Journal of Counseling Psychology*, Vol. 19, 1972, pp. 184–187.
188 Seltzer, C. C. "An Evaluation of the Effect of Smoking in Coronary Heart Disease. 1. Epidemiological Evidence." *JAMA*, Vol. 224, 1973, pp. 1005–1007.
189 Selye, H. *The Stress of Life*. New York, McGraw-Hill Book Company, 1956.
190 Shafii, M. "Adaptive and Therapeutic Aspects of Meditation." *International Journal of Psychoanalytic Psychotherapy*, Vol. II, No. 3, 1973, pp. 364–382.
191 Shafii, M. "Affective States of Integration in Sufu Meditation." Unpublished paper.
192 Shafii, M. "Silence in the Service of Ego: Psychoanalytic Study of Meditation." *The International Journal of Psycho-Analysis*, Vol. 54, Part 4, 1973, pp. 431–443.
193 Shafii, M. "Smoking Following Meditation." Department of Psychiatry, University of Michigan Medical Center, Ann Arbor, Michigan, 1973.
194 Shafii, M., R. Lavely, and R. Jaffe. "Meditation and Marijuana." *American Journal of Psychiatry*, Vol. 131, 1967, pp. 60–63.
195 Shafii, M., R. Lavely, and R. Jaffe. "Meditation and the Prevention of Alcohol Abuse." *American Journal of Psychiatry*, Vol. 139, 1975, pp. 942–945.
196 Shapiro, A. K. "The Placebo Effect in the History of Medical Treatment: Implications for Psychiatry." *American Journal of Psychiatry*, Vol. 116, 1959, pp. 298–304.
197 Shapiro, J. "The Relationship of the Transcendental Meditation Program to Self-Actualization and Negative Personality Characteristics," *Scientific Research on the Transcendental Meditation Program: Collected Papers*, Vol. 1, D. W. Orme-Johnson and J. T. Farrow (eds.). West Germany, MERU Press, 1976, pp. 462–467.
198 Shapiro, J. G., and T. Voog. "Effect of the Inherently Helpful Person on Student Academic Achievement." *Journal of Counseling Psychology*, Vol. 16, No. 6, 1969, pp. 505–509.

198a Shecter, H. "The Transcendental Meditation Program in the Class-room: A Psychological Evaluation." *Scientific Research on the Transcendental Meditation Program: Collected Papers*, Vol. 1, D. W. Orme-Johnson and J. T. Farrow (eds.). West Germany, MERU Press, 1976, pp. 403–410.

199 Sheehy, G. *Passages: Predictable Crises of Adult Life*. New York, Dutton Publishers, 1976.

200 Simon, D., S. Oparil, and C. Kimball. "The Transcendental Meditation Program and Essential Hypertension," *Scientific Research on the Transcendental Meditation Program: Collected Papers*, Vol. 1, D. W. Orme-Johnson and J. T. Farrow (eds.). West Germany, MERU Press, 1976, pp. 268–269.

201 Sinnott, E. *The Biology of the Spirit*. Los Angeles, Science of the Mind, 1973.

202 Smith, M. J. *When I Say No, I Feel Guilty: How to Cope—Using the Skills of Systematic Assertive Therapy*. New York, The Dial Press, 1975.

203 Sobel, D. *Ways of Health: Holistic Approaches in Ancient and Contemporary Medicine*. New York, Grossman/Viking, 1976.

204 Sperry, R. W. "The Great Cerebral Commissure." *Scientific American*, Vol. 117, 1964, pp. 42–52.

205 Stek, R., and B. Bass. "Personal Adjustment and Perceived Locus of Control Among Students Interested in Meditation." *Psychology Reports*, Vol. 32, 1973, pp. 1019–1022.

206 Sugi, Y., and K. Akutsu. "On the Respiration and Respiratory Change in Zen Practice." *Japanese Journal of Physiology*, Vol. 26, 1964, pp. 72–73.

207 Suzuni, T. "Electroencephalographic Study During Zen Practice." *Proceedings of the 15th Convention of JPA*, 1963, p. 346.

208 Szent-Györgyi, A. Quoted in *Brain-Mind Bulletin*, Vol. 1, No. 13, May 17, 1976, p. 3.

209 Szent-Györgyi, A. Address before the Conference on Interdisciplinary Science Education, Washington, D.C., January 23, 1969.

210 *Tao Te Ching*, trans. A. Waley. New York, Grove Press, 1958, p. 188.

211 Tart, C. T., (ed.). *Altered States of Consciousness*. New York, John Wiley and Sons, 1969.

212 Tart, C. T. "A Psychologist's Experience with Transcendental Meditation." *Journal of Transpersonal Psychology*, Vol. 3, No. 2, 1971, pp. 135–140.

213 Tart, C. T. "States of Consciousness and State-Specific Sciences." *Science*, Vol. 176, June 16, 1972, pp. 1203–1210.

214 Tart, C. T., (ed.). *Transpersonal Psychologies*. New York, Harper, 1976.

215 Terhune, W. *The Safe Way to Drink*. New York, William Morrow, 1968.

216 Torrey, E. F. Quoted in "Psychiatry: Dying or Dead?" Baltimore *Sunday Sun*, January 25, 1976, Section C, p. 1.

217 Toynbee, A. J. *A Study of History*, rev. and abridged ed. Oxford, England, Oxford University Press, 1972.

218 Travis, J. *Wellness Inventory*. Mill Valley, Wellness Resource Center, 1975.

219   Travis, J. *Wellness Workbook*. Mill Valley, Wellness Resource Center, 1977.

220   Truax, C. B., and R. Carkhuff. *Toward Effective Counseling and Psychotherapy*. Chicago, Aldine Publishing Company, 1967.

221   Truax, C. B., and K. Mitchell. "Research on Certain Therapist Interpersonal Skills in Relation to Process and Outcome," *Handbook of Psychotherapy and Behavior Change*, A. E. Bergin and S. L. Garfield (eds.). New York, John Wiley and Sons, 1971, pp. 299–344.

222   Ubell, E. *How to Save Your Life*. New York, Penguin Books, 1976.

223   United States Bureau of the Census. *Statistical Abstract of the United States: 1972*. Washington, D.C., U.S. Government Printing Office, 1972.

224   United States Department of Health, Education, and Welfare. *National Institute of Mental Health: First Special Report to the U.S. Congress on Alcohol and Health*. Washington, D.C., U.S. Government Printing Office, 1971.

225   United States Public Health Service. *The Health Consequences of Smoking*. U.S. Department of Health, Education, and Welfare, 1975.

226   Van den Berg, W. P., and B. Mulder. "Psychological Research on the Effects of the Transcendental Meditation Program on a Number of Personality Variables." *Heymans Bulletins*, Psychologische Instituten R.U., Groningern, NR: HB-74-147 Ex.

227   Van der Heide, C. "Blank Silence and the Dream Screen." *Journal of the American Psychoanalytic Association*, Vol. 9, 1961, pp. 85–90.

228   Walker, A. R. P. "Can Expectation of Life in Western Populations Be Increased by Changes in Diet and Manner of Life?" *South African Medical Journal*, Vol. 42, 1968, pp. 144–150.

229   Wallace, R. K. "Physiological Effects of Transcendental Meditation." *Science*, Vol. 167, 1970, pp. 1751–1754.

230   Wallace, R. K., and H. Benson. "The Physiology of Meditation." *Scientific American*, Vol. 226, 1972, pp. 84–90.

231   Wallace, R. K., H. Benson, and A. F. Wilson. "A Wakeful Hypometabolic Physiologic State." *American Journal of Physiology*, Vol. 221, 1971, pp. 795–799.

232   Watts, A. *Psychotherapy East and West*. New York, Ballantine Books, 1961.

233   Weir, J. M., and J. E. Dunn, Jr. "Smoking and Mortality, a Prospective Study." *Cancer*, Vol. 25, 1970, pp. 105–112.

234   Weldon, J. T., and A. Aron. "The Transcendental Meditation Program and Normalization of Weight," *Scientific Research on the Transcendental Meditation Program: Collected Papers*, Vol. 1, D. W. Orme-Johnson and J. T. Farrow (eds.). West Germany, MERU Press, 1976, pp. 301–306.

235   Wenger, M. A., and B. Bagchi. "Studies of Autonomic Functions in a Practitioner of Yoga in India." *Behavioral Science*, Vol. 6, 1961, pp. 312–323.

236   Wenger, M. A., B. Bagchi, and B. Anand. "Experiments in India on 'Voluntary Control' of the Heart and Pulse." *Circulation*, Vol. 24, 1961, pp. 131–132.

237   Wenger, M. A., T. Clemens, and T. Cullens. "Autonomic Functions in

Patients with Gastrointestinal and Dermatological Disorders." *Psychosomatic Medicine*, Vol. 24, 1962, pp. 267–273.

238 Wilson, A. F., R. Honsberger, J. Chiu, and H. Novey. "Transcendental Meditation and Asthma." *Respiration*, Vol. 32, 1975, pp. 74–80.

239 Wolpe, J., and A. Lazarus. *Behavior Therapy Techniques*. New York, Pergamon Press, 1966.

240 World Health Organization. "Smoking and Its Effects on Health." Technical Report Series 568, 1957.

241 Wynder, E. L. "Limits of Medicine," *Proceedings of the Conference on Future Directions in Health Care: The Dimensions in Medicine*. New York, December 10–11, 1975, pp. 49–58.

242 Yalom, I. D. *The Theory and Practice of Group Psychotherapy*. New York, Basic Books, 1975.

243 Zamarra, J., I. Besseghini, and S. Wittenberg. "The Effects of the Transcendental Meditation Program on the Exercise Performances of Patients with Angina Pectoris," *Scientific Research on the Transcendental Meditation Program: Collected Papers*, Vol. 1, D. W. Orme-Johnson and J. T. Farrow (eds.). West Germany, MERU Press, 1976, pp. 270–278.

244 Zeligs, M. A. "The Psychology of Silence." *Journal of the American Psychoanalytic Association*, Vol. 9, 1961, pp. 7–43.

245 Zingle, H. W., R. Dyck, and S. Truch. "Does an In-Depth Transcendental Meditation Course Effect Change in the Personalities of the Participants?" *Western Psychologist*, Vol. 4, 1974, pp. 104–111.

Index

ACTH (adrenocorticotrophic hormone), 71
Acupressure, 49
Acupuncture, 49, 55–56
Adler, Alfred, 59
Adrenaline, in stress response, 71
Adrenocorticotrophic hormone, 71
Age of Enlightenment Center for Holistic Health, 275
Aging
  anxiety about, 248
  stress and, 68–69
Airola, Paavo, 113 n.
Air pollution, emphysema and, 54
Akutsu, K., 63
Alameda County (Calif.) health survey, 14–26
Alcohol
  antihistamines and, 223
  anxiety and, 226
  depression and, 196, 232
  disease and, 223
  drinking problem and, 229–31
  "easing off" from, 227–28
  exercise as substitute for, 227
  healing silence and, 225–27
  physical effects of, 223
  need for, 225–27
  per capita consumption of, 224
  see also Drinking
Alcohol addiction, recurrence of, 231
  see also Alcoholism

Alcohol-dependent person, symptoms in, 229–30
Alcoholic, defined, 229–30
Alcoholics Anonymous, 84 n., 231–232
Alcoholism, 221–32
  anxiety and, 40, 226
  hospitalization in, 232
  liver disease and, 35
  psychotherapy and, 232
  in spiritual crisis, 248
  teen-age, 226–27
  treatment of, 231–32
American Cancer Society, 51
American Group Psychotherapy Association, 236
American Heart Association, 51
American Psychiatric Association, 203
Anand, B. K., 62
Anger, 271
Angina pectoris, 23
Annual checkup, 35
Antidepressant drugs, 187, 189
Anxiety, 24
  alcohol and, 40, 226
  in emotional distress, 169–75
  healing silence and, 171–73
  in holistic health program, 91
  physical effects of, 37
  as physiological condition, 170–71
  psychosomatic illness and, 54